The
Church
Comes
Home

The Church Comes Home

ROBERT & JULIA BANKS

HENDRICKSON
PUBLISHERS

ISBN 1–56563–179–X

First Printing—January 1998

The Church Comes Home: Building Community and Mission through Home Churches is a revised edition of *The Home Church: Regrouping the People of God for Community and Mission,* published in 1986 simultaneously by Albatross Books, P. O. Box 320, Sutherland, NSW 2232, Australia, and Lion Publishing, Icknield Way, Tring, Herts HP23 4LE, England.

Library of Congress Cataloging-in-Publication Data

Banks, Robert J.
    The church comes home: building community and mission through home churches / Robert and Julia Banks.
        Rev. ed. of: The home church.   1986.
        Includes bibliographical references.
        ISBN 1–56563–179–X (pbk.)
        1. House churches.   I. Banks, Julia, 1940–   .   II. Banks, Robert J.
    Home church.   III. Title.
    BV601.85.B36   1997
    250—dc21   97–16954
                                                                          CIP

Unless otherwise indicated, all Scripture quotations have been taken from the NIV.

The cover art is a detail of Joyce Kozloff's *New England Decorative Arts,* 1985, "Primitive" Landscape Mural for Harvard Square Subway Station. Hand-painted ceramic tile. Photo by Eeva-Inkeri.

TABLE OF CONTENTS

PREFACE vii

Chapter 1 THE INSIDE STORY
Word Pictures of New Styles of Church. 1

Chapter 2 IN THE BEGINNING
The Upside-Down Church of the Early Christians. 24

Chapter 3 A GREAT CLOUD OF WITNESSES
Participatory Forms of Church Life through the Centuries. . 49

Chapter 4 SMALL IS BEAUTIFUL
Testimonies and Hindrances to the Home-Church
  Experience 74

Chapter 5 FIRST STEPS
How Home Churches Come into Being 99

Chapter 6 EXPERIMENTS IN PROGRESS
Current Models of Home Churches and
  Home-Church-Based Congregations 126

Chapter 7 GATHERING TOGETHER
A Conversation about the Art and Craft of Home-Church
    Meetings 157

Chapter 8 GROWING PAINS IN THE FAMILY
Tensions in Home-Church Life 184

Chapter 9 THE IMPORTANCE OF INREACH
Ministering to Children and Adults 204

Chapter 10 AGENTS OF TRANSFORMATION
Reaching Out to the Community at Large 228

APPENDIX
Some Questions about Home Churches 249

SUGGESTED READING LIST 259

PREFACE

This book has grown out of our more than twenty-five years of involvement in church renewal and reform. It draws primarily on our own experience in Australia and in the United States. It reflects independent and denominational church life throughout North America and is indebted to conversations with people in other parts of the world.

Two terms turn up frequently throughout this book, namely, *home church* and *home-church-based congregation*. While both of these are defined in the book itself, it may be helpful to explain briefly what we mean by these terms. The first term, "home church"—for which other expressions such as "basic Christian community," "ecclesial," or "small faith community" are sometimes used—does not refer to the church in which people were brought up or to a Bible study or support group meeting in a home. Rather, it connotes a kind of extended Christian family that involves singles, marrieds, and their children. It meets regularly to develop communally a shared Christian life, to relate each member's faith to everyday life, and to deepen each member's relationship with God. They may meet in a house, a condominium, or an apartment—wherever "home" is for members of the group and wherever they feel most "at home." What they do is very much a "homemade" affair, rather than something that is run by a single leader or depends upon some kind of professional expertise.

The second term, "home-church-based congregation"—for which other expressions such as "home-church cluster" or "combined meeting" may be used—does not refer (as with the so-called house church movement in England) to something that begins in homes and develops into larger meetings in rented or owned buildings. Rather, "home-church-based congregation" refers to either a group or cluster of independent house churches that meet together regularly and have some common objectives or to a local church (whether denominational or nondenominational) that is made up mostly of home churches rather than the more usual types of small groups and church programs. Such a meeting may take place in a large space in a house, a community meeting hall, a park, or a building especially reserved for the congregation—whatever is conducive to the gathering's operating in a participatory way. The centrality of these terms indicates our belief that Christians need both kinds of meetings, that is, the smaller gathering of "the church in the home," and the larger gathering of "the whole church" (to use the language found in Paul's letters) if they are to have the full experience of church.

Writing and revising this book has been a complex but rewarding effort. Although we take responsibility for this work, we must note that it contains contributions from many groups and individuals. We also must note that we do not claim to speak for all who are involved in home churches or in home-church-based congregations. Within the growing movement of those who are heading in these directions there are several different strands. We do not, in any formal sense, represent even those who are closer to our way of being a church. Many who share our perspective would express certain things differently.

We wish to express our gratitude to all those who participated in the shaping of this book. There are too many to name, but our collaborators will no doubt recognize their contributions and will have fun trying to identify those of others. In particular, we wish to express our thanks to Ron and Eolene Boyd-Macmillan, who read through most of the manuscript and commented upon it in detail, and to Shirley Decker-Lucke, who (as with the companion to this, *Paul's Idea of Community*) proved herself to be the kind of editor writers dream about but only rarely encounter.

Robert and Julia Banks

1

THE INSIDE STORY

*Word Pictures of New
Styles of Church*

Something new is stirring in the church. A significant movement of its energy, shape, and spirit is under way. This shift is
not only breathing new life into the church but is also altering
its center of gravity. It is realigning both its membership and its
structures. It is "turning the church upside down," not as an
attempt to cause confusion within it, but to put it properly on
its feet.

So far this is happening mainly on the margins. But key figures in the mainstream are already beginning to call for a
change at the center. Disappointed at the meager results that
have come out of long-term efforts to bring new vision and life
into mainline churches, many are calling for nothing less than
the reinvention of the congregation. To envision the church of
the future we must recall the church at its beginning: we are
looking for "the once and future church" in order to develop
the new paradigm we so desperately need.[1]

THE QUIET REVOLUTION

This revolution in the church has two sides to it. First, all
over the world the church has started to come home to smaller,

face-to-face gatherings of Christians. Through the centuries Christians have occasionally returned to the humble quarters from which the church began; now people of God in many countries are deciding it is time to do so once again. Christians are gathering in their houses and apartments to sing and pray together, to provide mutual support, to eat a common meal, and to learn from one another.

Some have turned in this direction because they were bearing too heavy an organizational church load or because they had considerable personal need. Others have done so because they felt lost in an impersonal institution or disenchanted by its preoccupation with self-preservation. Some have stepped out on this journey because they came across signposts in Scripture or in the traditions of their own denomination. Some sensed there must be more to church than what they were experiencing. Others were feeling hurt and rejected by institutional Christianity. Some were searching for a deeper experience of community or for a more effective base for mission. Others were struggling with the loss of a place to call home or were looking for an alternative to a dysfunctional family. In some places political conditions were so intolerable, or the physical and social needs so great, that there was nowhere else to go. Whatever their starting point, whether driven by a biblical vision, personal desperation, or both, all these people are moving in the same direction: home—where the church began and where, at one level of its operation, it was always intended to be.

The gradual but universal homecoming of the church is one of the most significant social, as well as religious, movements of our time. Unlike the movements of refugees or emigrants, it is a journeying toward home rather than a flight from it, although it does involve both bidding farewell to familiar ways of doing things and some measure of physical relocation. Home churching does not necessarily require that people leave their church or denomination, but it does involve their letting go of many securities and comforts that have marked church life. Those who join this movement are able to do so because they are troubled by a divine disquiet. But they are also embarking on a new adventure: a journey of discovery in which the prize is a closer involvement with others, a deeper relationship with God, and a greater expression of their faith in their lives and ministry.

The second side to this revolution is that all over the world the church has started to become more interactive. In the past, church services were almost always a "one-man show" or small team effort. Going to church seemed mostly a spectator or performance-oriented affair in which most members looked, listened, and only occasionally took part.

But in many instances things are changing on Sunday mornings. Church is opening up, encouraging those who meet to act less as spectators and more as participants, engaging their hearts and spirits as well as their heads, inviting them to share their gifts and stories as well as interests and finances. People are finding it easier to laugh and cry in church, to clap and dance, to embrace each other and receive laying on of hands.

This is happening in some places more than others. Often the force of tradition, the size of the congregation, the kind of building, and the arrangement of the furniture restricts this. Sometimes this opening up is happening in ways that are fairly ritualized, individualistic, or programmed. Nonetheless, this more dynamic interaction demonstrates that people desire to be part of the action in church, not just part of the audience. There has been a breakthrough in understanding what a congregation is all about, both outside and inside its gatherings.

These trends are most noticeable in various parts of the third world. There the issues are sharper, the problems more severe, the stakes higher. In Latin America, for example, there are now tens of thousands of basic Christian communities, many based in homes or small community buildings. This is despite the fact that many of the denominational leaders who initially supported this move now feel threatened by it. In many communist countries Christians survived only because the church took on a house church form; tens of millions of Christians now gather this way.

In the West, far fewer Christians are moving their home-based meetings in the direction of church and opening up their congregational gatherings for greater interaction. Tranquilized by the satisfaction of our basic physical and political needs and cushioned by economic security and social opportunity, we have prevented our deep need for community and participation from surfacing. But it is surfacing in some places. A front-page article in the *New York Times* described the growing incidence of lay-led home church and home synagogue meetings across the country.[2] This is part of a wider trend. Large institutions have shown themselves less and less able to meet the needs or foster the capacities of those whom they serve; neither can they halt the deepening crisis in personal identity, family relationships, and friendships. The heart is going out of modern society, and all the desperate attempts to regain it through psychological techniques, mystical exercises, and discussion groups will not be enough.

Christians in the West are beginning to feel more keenly their deprivation in the areas of personal identity, family relationships, and friendships. There is a new quest among baby boomers for the church to be a place where they can belong and participate, a place where they can connect with others and help shape what happens. Among baby busters there is a new stress on personal relationships and group involvement. Charismatic services, seeker services, small groups, and recovery groups have developed to meet the needs of these groups. Yet none of these will be adequate to meet the needs: the former are too centered on individual expression or public performance to develop a genuinely interactive form of congregational gathering; the latter are too interest- or therapy-oriented to develop a truly communal life. None of these lead to the kind of personal transformation or corporate witness that our world needs.

This is why the heart beats weakly in some parts of the church, providing too little to fully sustain those who are within, and too little to attract those who are without. Recent experiments with small groups, house fellowships, cell churches, and the like have pointed in the right direction, but they are not wholehearted enough to take the church as far as it needs to go. Initiatives in developing body life, charismatic worship, and open church have also registered real gains, but they engage only part of the person and some of the people. All of these efforts fall short of providing a full sense of belonging and involvement. God is searching for those who will take these advances further and is willing to conduct them to their destination.

Only when the church comes home in the fullest way and interacts with the complete measure of what God has granted it is there a chance of its becoming the *home* of a heartless world and of its *interacting* with the world in a transforming way. To a large extent, the future of the world—the quality of its lifestyle, relationships, and structures—lies within the genuinely communal groups and broader interactive gatherings that are emerging in the church. While these types of Christian community are considered by many to be marginal, it is on the margins that the future always lies.

SOME EYEWITNESS ACCOUNTS

It is the nature of home churches and of congregations based on or built around home churches that they are better experienced than explained. People often mistakenly equate a home church with a cell or a house group. They read their own meaning into terms like "informal," "commitment," "relationships," "learning," "concern," "love," "sharing," and "fellowship," even after hearing a prolonged explanation. A home-church congregation is generally equated with contemporary or charismatic worship. But the user-friendly and more relevant character of the first and the greater participation in singing, extemporaneous prayer, and one-on-one ministry of the second only describe part of the home-church experience.

Those who do not understand the difference between home churches and small groups often find it hard to relate the word "church" to anything but a building and what happens inside it, thereby seeing a church in the home only as a small-scale version of a service in a church building. A number of years ago, our home church received an invitation to appear in a television series. After several weeks of discussing whether this would work effectively, we agreed to go ahead. As it happened, the television crew did not act as a restraint upon our meeting; if anything, we were less inhibited than usual. The editing and presentation of the sequence were handled with considerable care; the producer obviously desired to do justice to our gathering. But because he understood "church" largely in traditional terms, he focused on those elements that had the greatest affinity with a typical church service. This meant that such features as the depth of relating among the members, the infectious joy present in the gathering, and the recognition of the presence of God in even the most ordinary things (for example, washing up together) were not emphasized in his portrayal of our group. The same would no doubt have happened if the producer had been filming one of our larger meetings, when a number of home-based groups regularly congregate. The following description of a home church may prove helpful:

> Home-churching involves face-to-face meeting of adults and children who are committed to developing a common life in Christ. They meet weekly in a house, apartment, or other convivial space. More important than the setting is their mutual care for and accountability to one another. As an extended Christian family they desire to sing, pray, learn, share, love, play, and have a meal (which is also their Lord's Supper) *together*. Through their mutual ministry to one another they learn to identify and use the gifts God has given them, and they are therefore more confident in engaging in mission through various individual ministries in their homes, neighborhoods, workplaces, and wider communities. While they view themselves as church, they also recognize the importance of congregating regularly with a larger group of God's people.[3]

A home-church-based congregation—a gathering of member home churches that is still small enough for everyone to know each other in some degree, or a traditional congregation that has transformed its small groups and organizations into home churches—may be described as

> a wider gathering of people who also meet in vital small ecclesial groups. Though this is large enough to possess a full range of gifts and maturity, it is small enough for each person to know everyone, including the children, by name. Under the authority of Christ and the guidance of the Spirit, these gatherings meet together regularly but not necessarily weekly, in a convivial space where they can look at, sing to, learn from, and pray for one another. Such a space could be a large home, community building, or public park. More important than the place of meetings is the possibility of each smaller group making a contribution to the building up of the whole congregation, and the opportunity for individuals to seek each other's welfare over a common sacramental meal.

The best way to fully appreciate the difference between either of these gatherings and the typical small group meeting or worship service is to participate several times. How then can this book convey something of what it is like to belong to one of these groups? Only by using word pictures: firsthand accounts that visualize what happens and convey something of its spirit. There is some repetition in what follows; this is deliberate, for it is important to "see" a home church more than once and from more than one angle.

Laura: A Typical Meeting?

It was almost six o'clock on a balmy Friday evening. As I was putting the finishing touches to the dining room table, I heard one car door slam, then another, followed by two others being closed more discreetly. "Mom," called fourteen-year-old Jamie as he hurried down the hall to open the front door, "the Warrens are here." The next minute two energetic boys raced into the kitchen to show me their new Reeboks. "Where's Dan?" Timmy squeaked excitedly. "In his room," I replied.

The boys were followed by their parents and then by others, and within fifteen minutes our living room was a buzz of conversation as our home-church family gathered for its weekly celebration. Four couples, three singles, two teenagers, and five children under nine years of age were present. (I should explain that one of our "singles" isn't really. Mavis is a married woman in her late fifties whose husband doesn't attend church.)

It's not always easy to persuade the group to stop talking and to get on with things, and tonight was no exception. Wes had to suggest several times that we get out the hymn books before enough of us heard him and complied. Timmy and Stephen handed out the musical instruments and nearly came to blows over whose turn it was to have the tambourine with the red trim. We had planned to look at the "I am the Good Shepherd" passage, and Jim had chosen some hymns and songs with that in mind. Mavis was reminded of a song she had learned in Sunday School many years ago and sang it for us. "That's a great song," said twelve-year-old Dan enthusiastically, "perhaps you could teach it to us!" "Maybe next week," replied Mavis bashfully.

Jamie played the guitar while we sang three or four songs, including "Baa, Baa, Black Sheep" for our three-year-old. Anna began her introduction to the meal by reading from Isaiah 51, "We all, like sheep, have gone astray . . ."

As usual the meal was delicious: a hot beef stew with rice, salad, home-baked herb bread, followed by a couple of Sara Lee desserts. As we ate, we heard about everyone's past week: the visit of Jamie and Stephen's grandparents, shopping for the new Reeboks, a conversation that Anna had with a fellow passenger on the bus, the changing health of a mutual friend, the latest political scandal, and lots more besides.

While their parents put the two younger children to bed, the rest of us gathered together for a reading of the Good Shepherd story from the a children's Bible. That was followed by a time of prayer with the children, and then Howard, who is single, led Dan, Timmy, and Stephen to another room to do some craftwork and to play.

"I couldn't believe it when Anna read that passage from Isaiah," declared Wes as we seated ourselves comfortably in the living room. "Listen," he exhorted as he pushed the button on the CD player. "All we like sheep . . ." sang the choir of St. Martin in the Field. "The Messiah," explained Wes. Listening to the music helped us all transition from the busy time with the children to our study time together.

Catherine had volunteered to open up the discussion of John 10. After we asked the Holy Spirit's help and I reread the passage, Catherine asked us to describe our first reactions to the passage. Then we discussed what we had not understood or what had puzzled us. We talked about links we had made between this and other biblical passages, the passage's relevance for us today, and how the Holy Spirit may have spoken to us as we read the passage, either in preparation for our discussion or on a previous occasion. The time passed quickly, and it wasn't until Stephen returned to the room, rubbing his eyes and complaining that he was tired, that we realized we had been talking for almost an hour.

We called the others to join us, and, while Stephen cuddled up beside his father, we spent time praying together about some points that had emerged from our study, issues that had come up in our discussions over dinner, and a few additional concerns that people had raised. Wes reminded people that we would be gathering at the home of Anna and Jim at six o'clock the following Saturday evening. Since it was late, Mavis encouraged those with children to take them home while the rest of us set about clearing up and washing the dishes.

It was almost ten o'clock when the last car pulled out from the curb outside our home. As we turned back into the house, I asked Wes, "Why is it that I always get such a buzz out of being in church with these people?" "Always?" queried a more realistic Wes. I paused for a moment, remembering the difficult time he'd had a couple of months before when Mavis had been depressed and we'd all found her rather draining, or the occasion further back when Anna and Jim were so busy that their inability to arrive on time and their lack of preparedness was a source of frustration to the other members of the group. "Well, almost always," I replied with a grin.

Karlani: A Foot-Washing Meeting

A couple of months ago, as our church approached the Easter season, we considered the events that led up to Christ's death and resurrection. Eventually we got to the passages dealing with Jesus' act of washing the disciples' feet. During this discussion someone mentioned that certain churches have a sacrament of foot washing, and we decided unanimously that at our next gathering we would attempt something similar in a more informal home church setting.

I cannot remember exactly how many of us were present on that occasion—maybe eight or ten. I do remember that we were equally divided between men and women, ranging in age from people in their mid-twenties to those in their fifties. Our starting times are never really exact. We allow time for people to arrive and then quite naturally move into the meal introduction. This meal is also our Lord's Supper. Later, after the meal is over, we sing, reflect on Scripture, and pray.

This night we meditated on John's account of Jesus' relationship with his disciples during the last days of his life. Then we turned our attention to our own situation as a home church. How far had we come in these months? We were from various denominational traditions—Moravian, Catholic, Pentecostal, Episcopalian, and nondenominational. We also represented various cultures—Australian, Malaysian, Ecuadorian, English, and American. Yet we had much in common. Although some of us attended "denominational" church on Sundays, all of us were seeking something more. What that was varied from person to person, but it included a closer sense of belonging and a greater reflection of what we professed as Christians. Here we could be transparent with one another to the degree that we found comfortable. In a way, this foot-washing gave us an opportunity to get to a deeper level of intimacy.

As we took turns washing each other's feet, we spoke frankly about how we appreciated that person's presence in our home church. Feet were bathed lovingly, carefully, and some were given a thorough massage. It was a solemn time, a revealing time, and a quality fellowship time all rolled into one. There seemed to be a release to tell about deep things. This meeting was, for me, a milestone in the experience of home churching.

The significance of this time together can be gauged by the fact that one faithful but quiet member asked a few of us to stay behind afterward. Sara shared openly about the wounds and the struggles of her life. I think the Lord really helped us to open up to one another, pulled down some of the walls that separated us, and enabled us to give expression to things that otherwise may not have been shared.

Grace: Including the Children

Although most of the parents I know are only too happy to off-load their children during church services by sending them to the junior Sunday school, for me it is wonderful to have children in the group, even if these are only two preschoolers. I've never been in a home church without children, and I've always enjoyed their input. However, it has been a major adjustment for those who have never before experienced this. We've had some awkward moments, but we're all gradually learning how to include the little ones. I was thrilled to overhear one of our single women saying what a joy it was to have the children as part of the group, confessing that she hadn't anticipated that they would actually add something to our life together.

We're all amazed at the way Daniel has taken to Susan. She tends to be rather moody, and there are times when we all feel like we're walking on eggshells with her. However, Daniel seems oblivious to this and runs to greet her whenever she comes into the room. Perhaps he likes the bright clothes she wears. I think Susan is as amazed as the rest of us that he has taken to her, but she is trying to meet him at his own level. It's quite touching to see the effort she is making.

When the children first arrived in the group, I think we all wondered what had hit us. They tended to run wild, and it was almost impossible to get them to participate in what we were doing—except for the meal, of course. This is where it is advantageous to have someone in the group who is older and has experience. I was able to go to the parents privately and explain that it was important to help the children emulate adult participation in the group. To discipline the children to be quiet at times is a way of teaching them to be loving and considerate of others. Not to encourage them to behave appropriately is to teach them to be selfish, and that is not the message of the gospel. I don't think the parents are finding it easy, but they have been trying.

Having children in the group means that we've had to adjust our meetings to include them. We haven't found too many age-appropriate Christian songs to teach them, but we are content to add a couple of nursery rhymes, use percussion instruments, and even dance occasionally. We also have a story and share-prayer time with the preschoolers. While the grown-ups are discussing the weekly Bible passages, one of our members "entertains" the children by taking them for a walk, providing craft activities, playing games, and reading stories. Not everyone wants to volunteer for that, but most of us are happy to take our turn. I think the willingness of our church members to care for the children creates the climate for their parents to be willing to discipline them.

Bill: A Story Shared and Its Aftermath

Bruce has been a part of our house church for a couple of years now. He is rather shy and self-effacing. We're the first church he has ever joined, not that we can claim any credit for his conversion. That apparently happened when he was at university, but he never felt comfortable attending conventional church. How he came to be part of our group is a story in itself. Let's just say he met a member of the group who invited him to "come and see."

Periodically in our church we encourage one of the members to tell their life story: the good news according to John

Doe, as it were. These stories are always fascinating. It never ceases to amaze me how differently God moves in each of our lives. Hearing the stories also helps us understand each other better. Last Sunday Bruce told his story. He even brought along photographs of himself and his family. It was a great time. Not only did we enjoy hearing "all" about Bruce, but obviously it meant a lot to him to share himself with us in this way.

While preparing to tell his story, Bruce had found himself reflecting on God's activity in his life. Like Shasta in C. S. Lewis's *The Horse and His Boy,* he had come to see that God had been walking beside him throughout his life even though he was only aware of God's presence at certain points. In preparing to tell his story, Bruce came to realize that he wanted to be baptized. He was delighted when he discovered that we could celebrate his baptism together.

For the last few weeks we've been making preparations for Bruce's baptism. He wants to do it outdoors, in a mountain stream, in mid-winter! Even our hints that the Browns' hot tub would be suitable can't dissuade him from his preference. There is much excitement in the air. It is going to be a special day for Bruce, but I've a feeling it's going to be an even more important day for our church.

Max: Developing Traditions

A question that has come up over the years from people who haven't experienced home churching, particularly those from a liturgical church background, concerns our apparent lack of tradition. I was questioned about this again recently. Sometimes it's hard not to feel defensive. The question is a good one, though, and I found myself thinking more about it when I had time to myself.

The most obvious tradition we have is celebrating the Lord's Supper as a meal. It's really hard to convey to people what a difference that makes. It's not only the personal dynamics that change around a meal table. It's also the manner in which the meal is introduced. The variety of ways that people come up with help us understand its significance from God's point of view and ours.

Another tradition is celebrating the birthdays of the various members of the group. In addition to having a cake and singing

"Happy Birthday," we take time to listen to the birthday person's reflections on the year gone and hopes for the year to come. Then we sit that person in the center of our circle, lay hands on him or her, and pray.

A related tradition is that each of us takes a turn to share our life story. We do this about every six weeks. When we have new members who haven't heard some of the stories, we start again. The stories are never the same because they are told from the person's current perspective. These are wonderful opportunities to get to know one another better and to celebrate the work of the Holy Spirit in each of our lives.

We also celebrate when one of our members gets a promotion, finds a new job, or passes an exam. This is something we do as part of our prayer time, though a lot of fuss is made when the person arrives and the good news is shared. We may even open a bottle of champagne! (There's no fear of drinking to excess; a bottle shared among twelve or fourteen people doesn't go far.)

When people leave our group, we celebrate the occasion. That sounds odd, doesn't it? Let me explain. Recently a woman left for a job in another town. For her last night with us we dressed up and had a special meal. We spent the night celebrating our life together—sharing memories, grieving our loss, and praying with laying on of hands for our sister as she ventured forth to a new stage of her life.

As well as developing a ritual for bidding farewell to an individual or family, we've begun to develop one for "multiplying" or "growing" a new group. Once we come to a decision about growing a new group, we set aside an evening to celebrate. We thank God for our time together, acknowledge the pain we feel at having to part, and ask God's blessing on both the members of the new group and those of us who remain. Each time we've done this we've found unique ways to mark the occasion appropriately.

We have other traditions that we share with the "cluster" or congregation of house churches to which we belong. For example, our Easter and Christmas celebrations are cherished occasions. The individual home churches all come together for a combined meeting, that is, they gather as a large congregation. The tradition is more that we get together, not so much what we do together. These celebrations can be very loosely structured or more organized (never highly organized), depending on which group has the responsibility for planning the event. We attempt to involve everyone or every group in what transpires, whether it's as part of a choir, singing a special song, doing a dramatic reading of the Scripture or a play, participating in a dance, preparing special food, or whatever.

Traditions are important. But it seems to me that they are only important when they are a true reflection of the life of the church. We need to discover fresh, meaningful traditions. I think I've learned it's also important for every celebration that's part of a tradition to be unique. Each birthday party needs to be appropriate to the one whom we are celebrating. Each "multiplication" needs to be done in a manner appropriate to that particular time, place, and group of people. There should be no fixed orders of service. Rather, we should seek to follow the imaginative, creative leading of the Holy Spirit. Such events are not just an expression of a common life, but are themselves life giving.

Sandra: When Things Go Wrong

It was a more chaotic meeting than usual, and I was feeling frustrated by the delays and interruptions. To begin with, due to schedules and commutes, several of the newer members had trouble arriving by the six-thirty dinner hour. We did not get into the study of the parable of the shrewd manager (Luke 16) until almost eight o'clock, giving us only an hour before we normally end our time together. The babysitter was playing with three of the six children (all of whom were three years old or younger), while the other three were in the midst of the adults. I was particularly frustrated since two of the children with us were pushing, pulling, and even biting each other, with all of the screams and cries that accompany such behavior.

First I felt angry. "Why did we hire a babysitter only to be distracted by the ones who wouldn't go into the next room to play?" Then I thought, "OK, it's a stage. They're attached to their moms and dads now, but soon they will be able to play happily with their friends in the kids' room." Such reasoning, however, did not make listening and interacting any easier for me in the present. As the mother of two young children, I was hungry to participate in the study and learn.

As the discussion progressed, I was amazed to see how involved the others were—listening to one another and adding their own contributions. I had almost given the evening up for lost, when a comment made by Kate caught my attention. She felt her husband, who had been homeless for several years before they married, had gained a biblical perspective on money and friends. I began to think, "It's easy for me to spend money on family and friends, but rarely do I spend money on people to make friends for God's kingdom." The parable's radical meaning was coming home to me once more.

I left the meeting repentant of my attitudes that children were a nuisance and that God could not speak to me through all the distractions. I was grateful that God spoke to me in the midst of the chaos and more confident of God's ability to meet me whatever the circumstances.

Karen: A Visit to an Untypical Meeting

I went to visit a house church tonight that consisted mainly of seminary students. It wasn't something I wanted to do; it was just an assignment to be gotten out of the way. I'd had a rough term. Life as a single parent who home schools and studies is never easy, but there had been further complications—a sick mother and the aftermath of an earthquake.

When I arrived at the campus, I discovered that this would be a different meeting than normal. The group was beginning their evening by listening to a sermon that Carol needed to tape for a job interview. I felt a tinge of irritation at not being able to experience a "normal" house church. As a group of about seven of us listened to the member's sermon, my attitude began to soften. I realized how rare it is that we truly take time for each other, even in seminary. The support for the "preacher" was apparent and touching.

After the sermon, the group had decided to take a hike in the mountains. Again, this was not something they normally did. I was a little apprehensive, since I didn't know exactly where we were going and dusk was approaching. The group piled into one large car and drove into the foothills. As we drove, there were questions and discussion that I realized were based on healthy Christian relationships. These folk were intimately involved in the day-to-day aspects of each other's lives. They were careful to include me in the conversation, and I felt quite at home.

Arriving at our destination, we took a short hike to a vista point in the foothills. Here we stood and watched the sun set. Mark asked if I had ever taken a hike at church. There was laughter and fellowship as Luis took pictures of the group. We kidded him about stepping too far backward and off the mountain. Soon Sherry began to sing worship songs, and we all joined in. At times we laughed as we stumbled through the words, which didn't always come readily to mind. Other songs were sweet and directed intimately to the Lord.

After the hike we drove to a house to share a meal. Each person brought a contribution for the meal: a casserole, rice, salad, drinks, a cheesecake, preparing it ahead or at the house. When it was time to eat, Mark, who had brought bread, presented a short devotional and passed the bread to the person on his right. Then each person passed it to the next with a word of blessing.

After finishing the meal, the group made plans for a get-together with another house church. Many decisions had to be made about the time and place and about who was willing to volunteer and in which capacity. I was impressed that each member desired to participate in some way. These folk truly seemed to want to use their gifts and to share together. Then the group continued to sing and to pray for one another. The praise was sweet and the care for one another during the expression of needs genuine. I was encouraged to participate. The evening ended on the note that we are all called to oneness in the body of Christ.

While I would like to visit a house church on a "normal" evening, I left realizing how much I'd needed exactly what had taken place. The care and sharing of Christ's love through his children and the peace he had imparted to me in the foothills was overwhelming. I left feeling more whole, aware that I could not continue in the frenzy of pressure I had been under, which relegated my Lord to last place. While intellectually I knew this, I needed to experience his love and peace in order to give away those pressures surrounding me. In his continuing grace he has allowed that to happen.

Elizabeth: A Welcome and an Argument

As David said to two guests after the meeting yesterday, "Now you've seen the agony and the ecstasy of home churching." The ecstasy was experienced in the first half of the meeting. We'd gathered with the express purpose of welcoming the second child of Stephen and Rose James into our church. Emma was just ten days old, and this was her first attendance at the group. Stephen had told us the previous week that when he and Rose brought her along—most of us had already seen her through the glass at the hospital—they would like us all to dedicate her to God. So they encouraged us through the week to think of some contribution we would like to make to the occasion.

When the Jameses arrived, they were the center of attention. Since the hospital forbids visitors under five years of age unless they are family, some of the younger members had not seen Emma. Sarah, the Jameses' other child, was obviously very pleased with her new sister and also protective of her. Stephen's chest was twice its normal size and Rose had a smile from ear to ear. Everyone made the usual noises about how small babies are, how much hair she had, what long eyelashes, and so on. Emma seemed to accept all the attention as if it were her due.

We were later than usual getting the singing and the meal under way. The children were just beginning to get restless when David suggested to them that he bring out Emma (who was now asleep after a good feed) and put her bassinet on the floor in the center of the room. David said a few words about why we had gathered—to welcome Emma into our church family and to dedicate her to God. He then invited the little ones to sing a song for Emma. Monica and Reg spent twenty minutes or so reading out all the promises they'd found in the Bible for parents with respect to their children. At the end of their reading they gave a copy in the form of a long scroll to Stephen and Rose so that from time to time they could remind themselves of the promises. Mary and Brian sang a song of welcome that they had composed especially for the occasion. Jane read a poem out of A. A. Milne's *Winnie the Pooh* and presented Rose (who is a great A. A. Milne fan) with a copy to read to Emma as she grew up.

At the suggestion of eight-year-old Ruth, we sang "Jesus Loves Me." I read another Bible passage ("Suffer the little children . . ."), and then we gathered in the center of the room around Stephen, Rose, Sarah, and Emma. We prayed prayers of thanksgiving for Emma's safe arrival, prayers for Stephen, Rose, and Sarah, prayers for Emma herself, and prayers for our own responsibility to Emma and her family. David gave a quiet, encouraging, and highly relevant prophecy for Stephen and Rose.

When we finished praying, Terry explained that Lyn wanted to do a dance of welcome—one she had choreographed herself to the tune of Brahms's "Lullaby." However, when leaving home to come to church, they hadn't been able to find the disk. So we were requested to hum the tune while Lyn danced. It was a very moving occasion. In the truly unselfconscious manner that only a nine-year-old can manage, Lyn danced daintily around the bassinet. It's a pity Emma was asleep and missed seeing how Lyn, with arms outstretched in welcome and a perfectly executed bow, concluded her dance. Silence reigned for some time. There were some tears too. With her final gesture Lyn had managed to capture the spirit of the whole occasion.

The little ones went to bed while the dishes were done, and we settled down over cups of coffee to make some practical decisions for the next few weeks. After we planned a picnic, I suggested a change to one of our usual ways of doing things. Before we realized what was happening, we were in the midst of the most heated debate we'd ever had. Debate—it was more like a fight! How on earth could we have gone from the sublime to the ridiculous in so short a space of time? We were all very sobered by the affair and, as tempers cooled, began to apologize to God and to each other. Some of the tension still remains, however, and we're all likely to feel rather vulnerable for a while. None of us seems to find it easy to cope with conflict.

Margaret: Our Meal

This week our home-church meeting took place over breakfast. It was such a lovely morning that we decided to meet outdoors. It worked very well. We had orange juice, cereal, muffins, and coffee. John suggested we start by singing

"Morning Has Broken." What a very appropriate choice it was! Not only were we able to sing about birds and dew on the grass, but we were actually able to see them around us.

It was the Johnsons's turn to introduce the meal. Peter read the passage where Jesus, after his resurrection, prepares breakfast for the disciples on the shore of Galilee. Robyn prayed a very moving prayer, thanking God for the empty tomb and the resurrection of Jesus, for the fact that Jesus was present with us as we gathered in his name, and for Jesus' example—that though he was Lord of Lords, yet he waited on his disciples. She prayed that, rather than desiring that others attend to our needs, we would seek to attend to each other's needs.

During breakfast Robyn read the children a story. I think the adults enjoyed it too. Then Don and I took the children off to the park. The adults, deciding that it was too hot to stay outdoors, returned to the living room to discuss Jacques Ellul's *The Politics of God and the Politics of Man.* In view of impending elections and the fact that a number of people in the group are involved in government administration, the topic is very relevant.

Chuck: The Lord's Supper

As we stood around the table tonight, Simon asked the children to name the food that was on it. There was bread and butter, orange juice, wine, lasagna, a chicken concoction, cold meat, a bowl of green salad, and coleslaw. We had to agree it was quite a mixture. But, as Simon reminded us, we knew that it would make a very tasty meal and that we wouldn't want to be standing around a table that contained only bread and butter, or only coleslaw. It was the variety that made the meal rather special.

Then he turned to four-year-old Alex and asked him if Kim was like Frank. *No!* Was Esther like Joy? *No!* And so on, until it was determined that we were all different. "Just like the food on the table," concluded Simon, "we are all different and we all have something special to contribute to our coming together as a family." Then he invited each one of us to say a short prayer of thanks to God. As I waited for my turn to heap my plate with goodies, I looked around at the various members of our church and was struck anew by the diversity that exists. In many ways we couldn't be more different. Yet in divine wisdom God has brought us together in order to make us one. Some of our differences are hard to take at times and create some tensions between us, but how much we would lose if there were only a gray uniformity or superficial harmony among us.

Stan and Laurel: A Home-Church-Based Congregational Meeting

It was a wet Good Friday and members of three home churches met to celebrate the source of all celebrations: the death and resurrection of Jesus our Lord. The meeting place was a converted double garage that belonged to one of the families. With carpets on the floor and comfortable seating, it made an ideal venue for this kind of gathering. People streamed out of the rain into the warmth, shedding wet weather gear at the door (excepting little Brett's new yellow gum boots, which he refused to take off, even for sleeping). Contributions for our breakfast were taken to the kitchen.

By nine o'clock all were assembled. There were approximately fifty people, all sizes and ages, including babies and toddlers. There was no compulsion to attend, but not one member was absent. We felt that God had drawn us together, and this sense of oneness continued through the meeting.

Members of one group had planned the outline of the service, had chosen some hymns, and had asked the other groups to be responsible for various sections of the meeting. No one really knew what the whole service would include.

When all were settled in chairs or on the floor, the first group started with prayer and readings on the Last Supper. Annette had baked some unleavened bread, which was passed around in a basket for all to share in silence. The toddlers were free to move about, but at this early stage they were all quiet. Peace settled on everyone as we thought about Jesus and the disciples in the upper room, and the events that were to follow.

Our thoughts moved to the crucifixion, with members of another group singing "When I Survey the Wondrous Cross" to a gentle guitar accompaniment. Alistair spoke on what Good Friday meant to him. "God is not an absentee landlord," he said, "but someone who chose to suffer as we do, to share our lot and be one of us." Awareness of this had meant a great deal to him at a formative stage in his Christian life. Another group helped us contemplate the resurrection by doing a dramatic reading. The story was about a caterpillar who discovered the purpose of his life when he became a butterfly. He had spent all his life battling to beat his fellows in the "climb to the top," had trodden on others in the process, and had decided to withdraw from competition to live with a little yellow lady caterpillar. When that failed to satisfy him, he went back to the competition. Finally he was led by the lady to his true future, which meant a kind of death before transformation. Parts of the story were shared between children and adults in the group, and there was no need to explain the parallel with what Christ made possible for us through his own death and resurrection. We prayed and sang in gratitude, and Arthur read to us what Jesus said to his disciples when he shared food and drink with them on that last night.

For breakfast we started with hot cross buns and various kinds of homemade bread, with butter and honey and preserves. We drank fruit juices, tea, and coffee, recalling other occasions in the past when we had shared bread and wine before the informal meal. One Easter Sunday someone had brought champagne—an inspired choice, we felt, for such a significant celebration—and we had joined in a simple Jewish dance to express our joy and delight at Christ's living presence among us.

Breakfast continued with hot tea and coffee, the sudden appearance (and disappearance) of bacon and scrambled eggs, and good conversation. Members exchanged news, offered help, played with one another's children, and finally carried away the breakfast things when there was no further need for them. Amelia produced a basket of chocolate Easter eggs in brilliant wrappings; these were passed round, first to the children, then to adults who considered themselves children. The meeting broke up at the end of the morning. We had a strong sense that God had been with us and that something stronger than mere friendship was at work, making these larger meetings as significant to us as the smaller, more intimate ones.

CONCLUSION

As these descriptions indicate, home churching and home-church-based congregational life are characterized by considerable variety. There is no such thing as one approach, one style of worship, or one way of gathering. As one person said, "Our order of procedure is not binding, and members are free to suggest changes in order and content when they feel it is appropriate. What makes this possible is that in the home-church setting there is a kind of 'structured informality'; in the home-church-based congregational setting there is an 'informal structure'."

This means that the way home churches and the congregations developed around them organize their gatherings will vary from week to week and may change over time. No two home churches are alike. Sometimes the differences are relatively small, sometimes quite considerable. There are stable elements in all these gatherings—singing, praying, learning, sharing, and participating in the meal—but the form these take and the way they are combined is flexible. Much depends on the background and the composition of the group, their gifts and maturity, the age range of the children, and the forms of Christianity that have influenced those who belong to them.

As the above descriptions indicate, home churches and their congregations also possess a common spirit and ethos. Jürgen Moltmann, one of today's leading Protestant theologians, gives a wonderful definition of what church is intended to be. Church should be a new kind of living together for human beings that affirms:

- that no one is alone with his or her problems,

- that no one has to conceal his or her disabilities,

- that there are not some who have the say and others who have nothing to say,

- that neither the old nor the little ones are isolated,

- that one bears the other even when it is unpleasant and there is no agreement, and

- that, finally, the one can also at times leave the other in peace when the other needs it.

Does this open congregation of acceptance exist? We would be in a terrible situation if it stood before us only as a biblically based demand. If we open our eyes, we can also experience it in the power of the Spirit in our very midst. Whoever seeks finds!

In many churches today where there is much preaching but little community there are arising groups which seek community even at the expense of privacy. To that end they even open their own homes. "Grass-roots" and integrated congregations are already in existence. One need make only a small effort to seek them out. There are remedies against the sickness of a private kind of Christianity-without-commitment. Such communities are quite visible, for whoever cannot be seen cannot be accepted either. They are open communities in which everyone may participate. In those communities many persons find healing for the suffering society has inflicted upon them. The healing of the sick is a ministry in their midst. They are communities that eat and drink before open doors so that everyone can eat and drink with them. They are voluntary communities that allow for individual initiatives so that individuals must not only listen but may also speak and expect to find a hearing.[4]

Our snapshots of home churching and home-church-based congregations illustrate precisely the type and quality of church life that Moltmann describes.

NOTES

1. See L. Mead, *The Once and Future Church: Reinventing the Congregation for a New Mission Frontier* (Washington: Alban Institute, 1991) 6.

2. "More People Are Staying at Home to Worship," *New York Times*, December 1, 1991.

3. This and all subsequent extracts given without citation have been furnished by our unnamed but deeply appreciated contributors. For a description similar to this, see L. Barrett, *Building the House Church* (Scottdale, Pa.: Herald, 1986) 18.

4. Jürgen Moltmann, *The Open Church: Invitation to a Messianic Lifestyle* (Philadelphia: Fortress, 1978) 33–34.

2

IN THE BEGINNING

The Upside-Down Church of
the Early Christians

We have looked at some descriptions of home church and home-church-based congregations. It would be a mistake, however, to view these as expressions of the latest approach to church renewal or church growth. They are not to be understood as new programs for helping congregations change and become more relevant; rather, they spring from a concern to do justice to what the Bible has to say about community and mission. It is not the re-creation of the first-century church that is the goal. The desire is to recapture the spirit and dynamics of early church life in ways that are appropriate to our own culture.

GOD CREATES COMMUNITY

Before focusing on the early Christians, we shall consider passages in the OT and the Gospels that provide a background to our discussion of community and mission. According to the OT, community is rooted in the nature of God. At the climax of the opening chapter of Genesis, God declares: "Let *us* make humankind in *our* image" (Gen 1:26, NRSV). These pronouns may simply be a royal plural, in which a singular God is using plural pronouns to emphasize God's royal status, or they may refer to the spiritual beings that surround God in heaven. But they could also suggest a communal dimension to God. There is a close connection between these pronouns and the creation of human beings as a twosome. For "it is not good . . . to be alone" (Gen 2:18). The first couple is charged to assist one another (Gen 2:20–21) and to become one (Gen 2:24). This is part of what it means to be made in the "image" of God. The biblical writings show that God came to be increasingly understood as Father, Son, and Spirit, that is, as a communal being. If this is true of God, it would be very strange if we, as God's creatures, viewed ourselves only as individuals relating to God independently, rather than as interdependent beings who should be in community with one another as well as God.

God's people worshiped together first in their households and in large gatherings. The household (Deut 8:10–18) provided the setting for circumcising all male children (Gen 17:10), instructing the young in the Jewish faith (Deut 4:5–14), and celebrating the Passover (Exod 12:11). The Sabbath was also spent in the company of one's extended family. Responsibility for ensuring that God was honored and obeyed fell firmly on the parents, who acted, so to speak, as "priests" of the household.

The second context for corporate worship was the tabernacle (Exod 26, 36, 40) and later the temple (2 Sam 7, 1 Kgs 6–8). It was in these larger gatherings that various other Jewish festivals were celebrated (Exod 23:14–19; Lev 23). Here fellowship occurred, sin and guilt offerings were presented (Lev 1–7), and sacrifices for the annual day of Atonement were made (Lev 16). The temple was also a center for teaching (Exod 21–22; Lev 16) and for purification by the priests (Lev 12–13).

As the Jews were dispersed throughout the ancient world, the synagogue became the major large gathering. Synagogues originally met in people's houses. When they moved to separate buildings these buildings resembled houses and included accommodation for visitors. When the temple was rebuilt (515 BC), only people in the city of Jerusalem met in it regularly. Those living elsewhere continued to attend synagogues.

Meanwhile the people awaited the fulfillment of prophecies about the coming of the Messiah, during whose reign the sharp distinction between those who teach God's ways and those who are taught would end. Every person, from the greatest to the least, would know God directly from the heart, not just indirectly through the law (Jer 31:31–34). In those days the Spirit would fall upon all—old and young, men and women, sons and daughters, male and female servants. They would experience dreams, visions, and prophecy (Joel 2:28–29).

GOD DEEPENS COMMUNITY

Jesus placed a new emphasis on the family-like nature of the bond between God and the people (he calls God *Abba,* "Father"), and between Jesus and his disciples (whom he describes as "kin"). While there are many passages in which he does this, three in particular stand out; one from the beginning, one from the middle, and one from the end of his ministry.

> Then Jesus' mother and brothers arrived. Standing outside, they sent someone in to call him. A crowd was sitting around him, and they told him, "Your mother and brothers are outside looking for you." "Who are my mother and my brothers?" he asked. Then he looked at those seated in a circle around him and said, "Here are my mother and my brothers! Whoever does God's will is my brother and sister and mother." (Mark 3:31–34)

> "I tell you the truth," Jesus replied, "no one who has left home or brothers or sisters or mother or father or children or fields for me and the gospel will fail to receive a hundred times as much in this present age (homes, brothers, sisters, mothers, children and fields—and with them, persecutions) and in the age to come, eternal life." (Mark 10:29–30)

> Near the cross of Jesus stood his mother, his mother's sister, Mary the wife of Clopas, and Mary Magdalene. When Jesus saw his mother there, and the disciple whom he loved standing nearby, he said to his mother, "Dear woman, here is your son," and to the disciple, "Here is your mother." From that time on, this disciple took her into his home. (John 19:25–27)

In these passages Jesus affirms the familial character of the disciple group and associates it with their mission. Thus, it comes as no surprise to find Jesus gathering his disciples in homes for instruction (Mark 3:20; 7:17; 9:28, 33; 10:10) and for meals (Mark 3:20; 14:12–21; cf. 2:19), as well as for preaching and healing (Mark 2:1–12). According to biblical scholar Ernest Best, this had a double meaning for the early Christians:

As Jesus, in Mark's presentation, once took his disciples aside into houses to teach them, so now his words as they are read and discussed continue to teach Christians in their house churches. . . . All this has an allied aspect. The church is not "house" in the sense that any or all of its members are the stones with which the house is built but in the sense of "household." . . . The disciple who has had the experience of Jesus in finding that he is scorned or rejected by his family (Mark 3:20f; 6:1–6) finds within the church a new family or household, many more brothers, sisters, mothers, fathers than he ever had before (Mark 10:28f). . . . Those who belong are his "kinsfolk" and "kinsfolk" of one another.[1]

GOD MULTIPLIES COMMUNITY

After Jesus' death and resurrection the Spirit was poured out upon the disciples as they regrouped in the upper room (Acts 1:12). Peter addressed the crowd, many were converted, and immediately all the believers gathered for the purpose of learning, fellowship, breaking of bread, and prayer (Acts 2:42). This assembling together took place at two levels:

Every day they continued to meet together in the temple courts. They broke bread in their homes and ate together with glad and sincere hearts, praising God and enjoying the favor of all the people. And the Lord added to their number daily those who were being saved. (Acts 2:46–47)

In the larger temple-based meeting there was teaching by the apostles and broader fellowship with other believers. In the smaller house- or apartment-based meeting they praised God and ate a common meal together.[2] There was a high level of enjoyment—in God, food, and one another—and a close connection between the quality of their common life and the inflow of new disciples.

This two-tiered approach to meeting became common among early Christians in other places. For example, the author of Hebrews confirms the highly participatory nature of those meetings with their emphasis on "fellowship" as well as on what some term "worship":

Let us hold unswervingly to the hope we profess, for he who promised is faithful. And let us consider how we may spur one another on toward love and good deeds. Let us not give up

meeting together, as some are in the habit of doing, but let us encourage one another—and all the more as you see the Day approaching. (Hebrews 10:23–25)

Paul's writings present us with the clearest and fullest understanding of community and its close link with mission.[3]
Though built on OT foundations, Jesus' teaching, and early
Christian practice, Paul's understanding of community was in-
formed by his encounter with Christ on the Damascus Road,
when Jesus identified himself with his suffering church (Acts
9:4), and by his experience of the Spirit and of healing, which
came to him through a fellow Christian, not directly from God
(Acts 9:17).

PAUL'S APPROACH TO CHURCH

Paul was the first to use the word "church" extensively.
What did he mean by it? Today the word has a variety of
meanings:

- the body of Christians in a particular locality,

- the building in which they meet,

- the denomination to which they belong,

- the totality of Christians in the world,

- the full number of believers, living and dead.

When Paul uses the word, he is using it with the first meaning,
to refer to the regular gatherings of Christians, or to the
Christians who regularly gather, whether in small, home-based
groups or in larger citywide congregations. He does not use
"church" of any building, of any network of churches, or of all
Christians scattered throughout the world. In his later writings
he does refer to the heavenly assembly around Christ in
which we all participate by virtue of our inclusion in him; local
churches are the expression of this in time and space (Col
1:18, 24; Eph 2:5–6; 3:10).

Mostly, the word "church" refers to individual congregations
(cf. Rom 16:4; 1 Cor 11:18; Gal 1:2; 1 Thess 1:1) or to the home
churches that comprise them (Rom 16:5; 1 Cor 16:19; Col 4:15;
Phlm 2). Each gathering stands in direct relationship with God

but should not operate independently of the other churches. Christians belonging to home churches within a given region should express their unity by coming together in the Lord's name, through exchange visits, and through financial giving in support of one another. Yet each home church or congregation has a divine responsibility to become as full an expression of the heavenly community around Christ as possible.

What happened in Paul's churches differed from what happens in ours. It requires a considerable act of imagination to divorce our minds from what customarily takes place on a Sunday in most congregations today and to visualize what happened in the first century.[4] Smaller and larger meetings of church generally took place in a house or apartment, rather than in a special building (Rom 16:5, 23; 1 Cor 16:19; Col 4:15; Phlm 2). Such groups were not very large. Considering the size of average first-century houses (which were owned by less than 20 percent of the population), there were probably twelve to fifteen persons meeting in "the church in the house" and no more than sixty to eighty as "the whole church." Meetings were informal, joyful, and social. As biblical scholar Eduard Schweizer points out:

> The togetherness of the church and its services is not that of a theatre audience, where one or several paid actors act on the stage while everybody else is looking on. Each one takes part with his special gift . . . the body of Christ is not a body of soldiers in which one sees at best the neck of the preceding person . . . it is a body consisting of members living in their mutual addressing, asking, challenging, comforting, sharing of Christ and his gifts.[5]

This was also true of larger meetings. In these Paul encouraged a high level of mutuality, a common meal that was also the Lord's Supper, and contributions from each of the members (1 Cor 11-14). Some of these contributions—prophecy, teaching, a word of wisdom or knowledge—were chiefly directed to members' minds and built up their Christian understanding. Others—helping, administering, discerning of spirits—were mainly directed to members' personal lives and relationships. A third group of gifts—giving, healing, miracles—were primarily directed to the physical and financial care of those who were in need. There were other gifts—for example, speaking in tongues and singing in the Spirit—that were directed to the subconscious level of people's experience. Thus everyone was involved in helping everyone else move toward full personal and corporate maturity in Christ.

Sometimes these larger meetings included a visiting apostle or member of an apostolic team. Luke's account of one such meeting is interesting. Although a distinguished visitor, Paul, was present, the meeting nevertheless included more general participation than occurs in pastor-led services today:

> On the first day of the week we came together to break bread. Paul spoke to the people [dialogued[6]] and, because he intended to leave the next day, kept on talking until midnight. There were many lamps in the upstairs room where we were meeting. Seated in a window was a young man named Eutychus, who was sinking into a deep sleep as Paul talked on and on. When he was sound asleep, he fell to the ground from the third story and was picked up dead. Paul went down, threw himself on the young man and put his arms around him. "Don't be alarmed," he said. "He's alive!" Then he went upstairs again and broke bread and ate. After talking until daylight, he left. (Acts 20:7–11)

We note here a mixture of structured and informal elements, and there is a strong social, as well as religious, dimension. Church is a place where it is all right to sit on a window sill, where unexpected happenings are not unexpected, and where church life can occur down in the street as well as up in the room. Having a meal and conversing together are central to church. Since time is not a primary issue, the gathering lasts as long as it needs to!

FOUR ASPECTS OF PAUL'S APPROACH TO CHURCH

Four particular aspects of Paul's approach to church stand out: its homelike ethos, its holistic appeal, its participatory style, and its outgoing nature.

The Church's Homelike Emphasis

Paul frequently spoke of the church as a family. Comparing the church to the human body stresses the interconnectedness of the members and the importance of allowing room for them to minister to one another. The family analogy emphasizes the quality of members' relationships and their care for one another. In congregations today family terms are used loosely. Members refer to their church as "a family" or "the family of God" when most have only a limited knowledge of one another—like those advertisements for various firms that project their mass market of customers as members of one large, happy family. In other congregations family terms are used in a purely spiritual sense. The bridge between members carries only religious traffic.

Paul not only used family language as his primary vehicle of expression regarding the church but he used it on a number of levels.

- NT churches—whether in smaller or larger gatherings—met primarily in people's homes (Acts 2:43; 16:40; 20:8; Rom 16:5; 1 Cor 16:19; Col 4:15; Phlm 2).

- Paul and other apostles founded their churches primarily on converted households (Acts 11:14; 16:15, 25–34; 18:18).

- The church in the home was the basic building block of the congregation (Rom 16:23; 1 Cor 11:18, 33).

- The bond between church members is similar to that between family members (Rom 16:2, 13; Gal 1:2; 4:19; Col 4:9; Phlm 10; etc.).

- Congregations are described directly as the household of God (Gal 6:10; 1 Tim 3:15; Eph 2:19; etc.).

- The central activities of these churches were familial in character (1 Thess 5:26; Rom 12:9–10; 1 Cor 11:33).

- Ministry—whether by resident members or visiting members—was basically modeled on a Christ-centered form of ministry exercised in the family (1 Cor 16:15; 1 Tim 3:4; 5:1–2).

So there are multiple ways in which the church is a home-based, homemade, homelike affair. It can be argued that these days it is not always helpful to draw an analogy between the church and the family; so many families are abusive or dysfunctional that often people do not know what a good family is. We should remember, however, that families in the first century were just as ambiguous, if in different ways, and that the early Christians transformed the model of family life so that they could make use of it. This meant that in the best instances members became ideal fathers and

mothers, sons and daughters, brothers and sisters to one another. Their authentic relationships developed out of their belonging to a common family, with all the resulting privileges,
responsibilities, and rewards. This heightened sense of family included physical, psychological, social, and material dimensions. Members were to greet one another as a family
with a holy kiss. They were to treat each other as a family by
expressing affection for one another. They were to eat together on a regular basis, as a family. They were to love and
care for one another, as a family should.

For some early Christians the church family replaced the
original family that they had lost upon conversion. For others
relationships in their churches restored or deepened the family
bonds that already existed. In either case Paul intended that believers maintained a real involvement in each others' lives that
was based on a serious commitment to one another.

What difference would it make today if members of a congregation, like the members of a family, committed themselves
seriously to loving one another "for better for worse, for richer
for poorer, in sickness and in health"? We may not live under
the same roof, but, according to Paul, when I join with you in a
church, I am to take care of you and you are to take care of me.
You become my responsibility and I become yours. Both of us
have, as Martin Luther put it, a responsibility "to become to
each other what Christ is to us."[7] As the well-known Quaker
thinker Elton Trueblood often stressed, the church is not a "limited liability company" whose members are only accountable
to one another in a restricted way, but it is an unlimited liability
"company of the committed" who should be fully accountable
to one another.[8]

Paul emphasized the diversity of this family. It was made up
of people who were very different from one another. It cut
across the lines that existed between men and women, between masters and slaves, and between members of different
races (1 Cor 12:12; Gal 3:28; Eph 2:14, 19). Thus gender, status,
and ethnic distinctions came under challenge. Paul saw the
various groups within these churches as continuing to offer distinctives, though no longer on any basis of superiority. Different
communities could have their own subgatherings within the
congregation; sometimes a church in the house was predominantly Jewish or Gentile. But all believers and subgroupings
were to welcome one another wherever they met and to ex-

press their unity in the common meal that was held when the "whole church," that is, all the local home churches, came together as a large congregation.

Paul also encouraged these early churches to take an interest in members of their broader Christian family by welcoming visitors from other places (Rom 16:1–2), exchanging greetings through letters (1 Cor 16:19–20), and giving financial aid when the need arose. Paul's gathering of funds from the Gentile churches for the poverty-stricken Jewish-Christians in Jerusalem is the prime example of this (Acts 24:17; Rom 15:24–29; 1 Cor 16:1–4). In all these ways the early Christians built up a genuinely "ecumenical" or wider familial (the term "ecumenical" is derived from the word for "house" or "home") relationship between churches in far distant places.

The Church's Holistic Appeal

We tend to think of church as an occasion when we focus on God rather than on others, even though we do church in the company of others, at times singing or responding as a whole. But for Paul, God is also present within and through the people who have come together. Paul did not encourage his readers to go to church to concentrate on God alone, as if all were straining their heads in one direction (somewhere above the far end of the sanctuary). Since God is present in a special way among those who belong to Christ, we must focus on each other as well as on God. All bear the gifts and fruit of the Spirit. God can come to us, in word and action, through everyone and anyone who is present.

This leads us to a crucial insight: we cannot divide church into worshiping God and fellowshiping with others as if these were two separate activities. In most cases we do *both,* even though at times one may be emphasized more than the other. Whenever I pray, sing, or share the Lord's Supper, I have you in mind as much as God, for I want you to enter into my prayer, to take heart from my song, to have fellowship with me as we eat the Lord's Meal. And whenever I teach, prophesy, or simply do you a good turn in church, God acknowledges it as much as if I were directing it solely to God. Unless we understand how much worshiping God and fellowshiping with others interpenetrates with and depends on one another, we will misunderstand the nature of our common meetings, both the larger and the smaller ones. This understanding of the church is one of the most radical features of early Christian understanding and experience. We tend to think that only parts of ourselves can participate in church. Yet it is clear from Paul's writings that the whole of ourselves should be involved. We do not come together only as souls engaging with souls or as minds engaging with minds; our imaginations, feelings, and bodies should also be involved. Did not Jesus say that we should love God with *all* of our minds, hearts, and strength? There is room in church for laughter and tears, introspection and intimacy, doubts and certainties. There is opportunity, even in the middle of a prayer, to enjoy a good joke and, even in the midst of laughter, to convey a word from God. There are occasions when a touch, an embrace, or a kiss is the only way to convey what God wishes us to say. We should also be able to unburden our fears and leave them in the safekeeping of others, or to allow our convictions to soar, carrying everyone else with them. There is room for the expected and the unexpected, for the sublime and the routine.

We tend to think of church as an occasion to withdraw from everyday life and concerns. Surveys show that this has become a characteristic attitude among churchgoers. Yet unless we can draw in, talk about, pray into, and work through our daily and wider public concerns, then church is less than it should be. Paul's letters are full of references to such "unspiritual" matters, including:

• how husband and wife ought to view sexual relations;

• whether to marry or to remain single;

• how to treat your fiancée;

• how to properly value your possessions;

• whether to fraternize with people of other faiths;

• whether to buy certain kinds of meat at a local market;

• whether or not to eat in an unbeliever's home;

• whether or not to take another Christian to trial (1 Cor 5–10).

Paul also discusses people's financial and material needs, employer-employee relations, and conversations between Christians and unbelievers. These issues were often central to the church; early Christians incorporated the stuff of everyday life into their meetings. Indeed, in some respects their meetings must have seemed very ordinary and down-to-earth. We also tend to think that, except in emergencies, in church we do not have a responsibility for each other's physical and financial needs. It is commonly thought that all members should attend to the physical and financial needs of themselves and their dependents. Paul, however, expected those in his communities who were better off to help those who did not have enough. One of the problems at Corinth stemmed from the failure of the rich to share the food they had brought for the common meal with those who came empty-handed. To take another example, in the case of "a real widow . . . left all alone" with no one to provide for her, the church is to step in and look after her needs (1 Tim 5:16). As James reminded the members of his churches, "Suppose a brother or sister is without clothes and daily food. If one of you says to him, 'Go, I wish you well; keep warm and well fed,' but does nothing about his physical needs, what good is it?" (Jas 2:15–16).

Those in our immediate Christian community who are single parents, out of work, or handicapped in some way should be of special concern to us. God may call on our abundance to remedy their lack. In this respect, too, church is a place where the whole of members' lives are of concern and where practical decisions have to be made. But we should also remember that we are all disadvantaged or challenged in some way, and we all stand in need of compassion and help from the others. It is not as though there are only two kinds of people in the church—givers of help and receivers of help—one's need for help is all a matter of degree or timing (2 Cor 8:14).

The Church's Participatory Style

Paul's approach to church also recognized its participatory style. All members had something to contribute to the church when it gathered, for all were given one or more gifts from the Spirit for the others' benefit. Church is typically a time when "everyone has a hymn, or a word of instruction, a revelation, a tongue or an interpretation . . . for the strengthening of the church" (1 Cor 14:26). It is also a time to "bear with each other and forgive whatever grievances you may have against one another . . . [and] let the word of Christ dwell in you richly, as you teach and admonish one another with all wisdom" (Col 3:13, 16).

All this aims to build up the "common good" (1 Cor 12:4–11) so that the entire body can be brought to a point of "unity of the faith," to "mature personhood," and to the "measure of the stature of the fullness of Christ" (Rom 12:4, 6; Eph 4:13). In this process there are no spectators; all are participants. No one is just a consumer; each one is also a producer. What happens when we become a church is not an outcome that was prearranged by one person or group. It is the design of all or, rather, of the Holy Spirit through all. Since church in part revolves around the gifts and fruit of the Spirit, unexpected things can take place within it, such as a novel word from God (cf. Acts 13:2) or a dramatic response to an entirely unforeseen event (cf. Acts 20:9–10). Although Paul insisted on an orderly meeting (not on a fixed order) he urged the members to be "open to the Lord's intervention whenever and wherever he is willing to interfere."[9] This may be compared to an orchestra in which all have a role to play, though some contribute more than others. There are times when only one person is contributing, times when several are doing so in a harmonious way, and times when all are joining in.

Layout of a Traditonal
Congregational Meeting

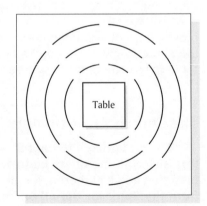

Layout of a Home-Church-Based
Congregational Meeting

The best arrangement for a congregation's meeting is not a rectangle containing rows of seats, all looking forward to what is happening in a space at the front. The best arrangement is a circle, in which each participant can look at the other, address the other, and hear from the other, preferably a circle around a table, so that all can also eat and drink together convivially in the Lord's name. In smaller home-based meetings the earliest Christians reclined on the couches surrounding the dining table, with room for children around them. In such a setting the Lord's Supper found its rightful, communal place. Even in the larger gatherings it was possible for many to contribute and for everyone to join in a full meal together. Though the dynamics of the two meetings were not identical, there was considerable overlap between them.

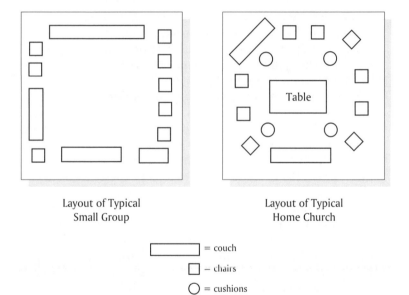

Layout of Typical
Small Group

Layout of Typical
Home Church

▭ = couch
☐ = chairs
◯ = cushions

For Paul, the church's participatory style also affected those first-century Christians who felt they had little to offer or were disadvantaged in some way. The church's attitude toward such people was a litmus test of its character. All had an obligation to attend to the situation of the "least important" members. Paul brings this out in a striking way when discussing the parallels between the church and a human body:

> Now the body is not made up of one part but of many. . . . God has arranged the parts in the body, every one of them, just as he wanted them to be. . . . But God has combined the members of the body and has given greater honor to the parts that lacked it, so that there should be no division in the body, but that its parts should have equal concern for each other. (1 Cor 12:14, 18, 24–25)

The participatory style of Paul's churches determined their leadership styles. If all church members are active, whenever they are contributing they are in effect giving the lead to the others and inviting them to follow. So to some extent everyone is involved in leadership. It is a corporate affair that involves the whole church, not just one person or elite group within it. But leadership qualities are not equally distributed among all; some have a greater capacity for it than others. Thus, there will be variety in the ways that different members exercise their leadership. When everyone takes responsibility for the content, form, and quality of what happens in church, it enhances what happens and benefits those who participate.

This corporate understanding of leadership relates to broader aspects of the church's life. Paul encouraged each house church and congregation to be able to look after its own affairs. He expected all members to be involved in this. His letters are addressed to "all the saints" not to a special group or a single leader. He constantly refers to the "brothers" and "sisters" as a whole. All were responsible for helping to discern the proper direction in which the church should move, the quality of its understanding and behavior, and the pastoral care and discipline of the members. Everyone should seek to admonish those who are not pulling their weight, to encourage those who feel inadequate, to assist those who need help, and generally to show patience toward all (1 Thess 5:14; Eph 4:4ff.). They could not simply delegate this responsibility to others. Even in notorious cases of misbehavior, it is the whole community that should take action (1 Cor 5:1–5; 1 Tim 5:19–20).

Yet Paul does not overlook the special role that some people played in the church. When there was a severe disagreement between prominent members (Phil 4:2–3) or the danger of a legal dispute (1 Cor 6:1–6), a third party in the congregation was instructed to help resolve the issue. When some members fell into error, more mature believers were told to gently help them to their feet again, exercising care lest they themselves make the same mistake (Gal 6:1). God endowed certain people with more pastoral ability and more personal maturity than others. Though these people did not possess a higher status than the rest of the congregation, they were to be held in special esteem and their contribution was to be appreciated. What set them apart was their greater devotion to serving others. Their role was not to reserve certain functions to themselves and expand their own ministry so much as to help others in the church develop their own gifts and maturity. Paul and his colleagues aimed to serve the congregations they founded and to help them stand increasingly on their own feet, not to render them perpetually dependent on outside ministry (cf. Eph 4:11ff.). Today's pastorally gifted people should follow in these aims.

The Church's Outgoing Nature

Finally, Paul's approach to church recognized its outgoing nature. The earliest Christians were not only interested in the quality of their common life but they also possessed a strong outward concern. These two go together. The best families are a good illustration of this. The members of a well-functioning family care about each other's welfare—they give time to each other, have meals together, talk with one another, and support each other. But they also open themselves up to outsiders, showing hospitality to singles, visitors, strangers, and the needy. They can do this because they have built up their own relationships sufficiently to have life and energy to give to others. These families have also learned among themselves the art of discerning another's longings and needs, and caring for them. Sometimes they include outsiders in their family meals and other social activities. Sometimes the whole family is involved in sharing its life with others; sometimes it is an individual or a subgroup within it. But whenever, wherever, and however this takes place, the outward giving further deepens, strengthens, and expands the family.

This provides a good analogy of the way the early churches engaged in mission. Their commitment to developing the quality of their own life was not at the expense of their commitment to sharing their lives with others. The two went hand-in-hand. Sometimes this was very evident. Paul gives two clear examples of the gospel striking home in the life of unbelievers as church was in progress, not through the preaching of a gospel sermon, but as a result of Christians speaking the word of God to one another (1 Cor 14:24–25) or sharing a meal in the Lord's name (1 Cor 11:26). In other words, *outreach* took place while they were focusing on *inreach!* Outreach could also take place when members were scattered. This was not so much an activity of the church as of an individual Christian or group of Christians in their homes, neighborhoods, or workplaces. Rather than an organized expression of the church, it was an indirect overflow of its life.

Michael Green gives an example of this in his book *Evangelism in the Early Church* when he summarizes the role of the home in the witness of the early Christians:

> One of the most important methods of spreading the gospel in antiquity was by the use of homes. It had positive advantages: the comparatively small numbers involved made real interchange of views and informed discussion among the participants possible; there was no artificial isolation of a preacher from his hearers; there was no temptation for either the speaker or the heckler to "play to the gallery" as there was in a public place or open-air meeting. The sheer informality and relaxed atmosphere of the home, not to mention the hospitality which must often have gone with it, all helped to make this form of evangelism successful.[10]

Green goes on to identify some of the homes that were used in this way, for example Jason's house at Thessalonica, Titius Justus's house, situated opposite the synagogue at Corinth, Philip's house at Caesarea, Lydia's and the jailer's houses at Philippi. All these were used as evangelistic centers.

There is a further interesting link between what happened in church and in mission. This had to do less with the home than with growing out of a dependency on others and growing into a source of benefit to others. In their meetings believers learned to seek each other's welfare (Phil 2:1ff.) and to do good to one another; they were not simply to take from others or to be dependent on others' good deeds. This more active attitude was to carry over into their attitude toward the people and the institutions of the cities in which they lived. This is the thrust of the repeated injunction in Paul and others to "do good" in general (e.g., Rom

13:3–4; 1 Thess 4:11–12; 2 Thess 3:6–13). Paul's command could be summed up: "become a benefactor to the people and place in which God has set you and so commend the generosity of the gospel visibly to outsiders."[11]

In addition to their houses or apartments, Christians sought to commend the faith in their workplaces (Eph 6:5–8), through their social contacts (Col 4:5–6), and in their accountability to others (1 Pet 3:15–16). Since, as already mentioned, the early Christians worked as well as worshiped in houses, the connection between church and marketplace was far closer than it generally is for us today. More socializing took place in homes than it does today (1 Cor 10:27ff.). This is not to say that outreach only took place in homes. The Acts of the Apostles identifies many other settings, for example, the marketplace, along streets, outside temples, by rivers. Early Christians did not operate on the assumption that outsiders had to be drawn into their activities for mission to take place. They took the gospel with them wherever they went. There was an opportunity to form a Christian congregation wherever people normally congregated.

LEARNING FROM THE EARLY CHURCH'S APPROACH

Church as a Corporate Picture of the Gospel

Paul's fourfold approach to church continues in relevance because it flows directly out of the gospel he preached.

The church's homelike emphasis: we are to become a genuine Christian family because God has made us an integral part of the divine family, sending "the Spirit of his Son into our hearts, the Spirit who calls out '*Abba*, Father' " (Gal 4:6). God calls us to enter into a real relationship with one another so that we love one another with brotherly and sisterly affection (Rom 12:10).

The church's holistic appeal: every part of us is to be involved in our church endeavor because every cell of our body has become the "temple" of the Spirit (1 Cor 6:19). Every aspect of our lives is to be involved because God has reconciled everything that has been created, including our bodies (Col 1:20).

The church's participatory style: since we will one day "judge angels" and "the world itself," we are quite able to deal with matters affecting our common welfare in church (1 Cor 6:2–3). This is just one evidence of the way God has taken those of little account and turned them into something quite resplendent (1 Cor 1:26–30).

The church's outgoing nature: we are to reflect in our own lives, corporately as well as personally, the love and faith that claimed us, so that those outside the church can feel its impact (1 Thess 1:4–8). When we are with them, the grace that we have experienced should fill our conversation and behavior (Col 4:6).

In other words, our life together as Christians is not some subordinate appendage to the gospel. Rather, it is the gospel itself expressed in corporate form. Christian community is the shape the gospel takes when translated into relational terms. Paul viewed the church as a prism through which the light of the gospel is variously refracted.

Church as a Creaturely Reflection of the Trinity

As theologian Colin Gunton says, "Church is . . . a temporal echo of the eternal community that God is."[12] Our life together should reflect the dynamics and interrelations of the Trinity. But it also reflects the shape of things to come. The community's meal not only remembers the darkness of Christ's death but anticipates the delights of the Messiah's table. Here amid sadness and laughter, reflection and conversation, deference and kindness, word and action, eating and sharing, we express the sacrificial love of Christ in our active concern for one another and experience the fellowship of the saints that will one day fill our lives. While primarily a meal for those who have welcomed God through Christ into their lives, this meal also proclaims Christ to others. It is a visible way of saying to any who wander in from off the streets: look, taste, consume! See, feel, and absorb what Christ has done for you.

In what respect should the way the earliest Christians went about being and doing church affect our own practice? In answering this, people often try to isolate Paul's so-called enduring statements of principle from his so-called culturally conditioned practice. And yet it is not just the principles that we should be looking for. We should also be concerned about the motives and dispositions Paul said people should have, the qualities of character they should possess, the model of behavior some people embodied, and the images of church life he put forward. For Paul, principle and practice, content and form, are too closely bound together to be separated.

The Danger of Idealizing the First Christians

In attempting to draw contemporary applications from Paul's churches, we should not idealize these early Christian communities; doing so only creates unrealistic expectations. The communities Paul addressed often failed to embody the vision he had for them. Too often we have romantic notions about church life in the first century. To guard against this we need to look at some of the problems that arose in Paul's churches, especially in connection with the four aspects of life together already mentioned.

Paul wanted the members of his churches to see themselves as part of a Christian family. But relationships within a family are not always warm and supportive. Families have their ups and downs, which include periodic problems and occasional crises. Because members of a family live together so intimately, there is the potential for extreme disharmony. Such tensions were present in Corinth. Some members had fallen out with each other and had resorted to the courts to settle their disputes (1 Cor 6:5-7). Others were quarreling about who was the best (1 Cor 1:11-13) or who was in the right (1 Cor 11:18-19) and were inclined to form exclusive subgroups in the community (1 Cor 11:20-22). Certain individuals were behaving without any regard for the effect their actions might have on more sensitive members (1 Cor 8:7-9). Others tended to show off, causing less gifted members to feel inferior (1 Cor 14:16-19). There was a general lack of accountability or discipline (1 Cor 14:23, 26-27), and too little attention was given to those who were older and more mature (1 Cor 16:15-18). Paul is able to see a positive element to this familial discord; it is only through disagreements and conflict that the truth, and those who hold to it, can be known (1 Cor 11:18-19).

Paul also encouraged people in his communities to open themselves up to the Holy Spirit. But in doing this Paul ran the risk that people would confuse the Holy Spirit with their subjective desires or with the spirit of the age. Some of the Corinthians adapted themselves too much to the prevailing ideas of their time (1 Cor 15:32–34) and the current moral standards (1 Cor 6:15–16). While one might look down on her fellow citizens in a judgmental way (1 Cor 5:12–13), another is surpassing the moral crudity of his pagan neighbors (1 Cor 5:1). Ironically enough, much of this behavior went hand-in-hand with a sense of superior spirituality.

In Paul's church, there was a high emphasis on each individual's participation, far higher than in any other religious group of his day. But this participation could lead to excesses, especially on the part of those who had not experienced such freedom before, and gatherings sometimes became unruly. Too many people were trying to speak at once (1 Cor 14:27) or were going on longer than they should (1 Cor 14:29–32). Too many kept interrupting with questions (1 Cor 14:35). Some were so preoccupied with their private religious experiences at the expense of intelligible public ones that others felt left out (1 Cor 14:23). Some gave too free a rein to their ecstatic impulses, excusing what appeared to be blasphemy in the process (1 Cor 12:3). These problems forced Paul to explain that freedom has its forms, spontaneity its rhythms, and participation its responsibilities.

In spite of the fact that abuses crept in, Paul never retracted his assertions on how the church should operate. He never moved away from his view of the church as an extended family or clanlike gathering, never suggested that the local church should limit itself to issues of personal spirituality and its common life, never retreated from his belief in mutual ministry and shared authority. It would have been easy for him to move in a more institutional direction and to insist that responsibility for order be vested in an official leadership. Yet even in Corinth, where the most extreme distortions of his teaching arose, Paul unceasingly continued to stress his fundamental principles. He looked beyond the Corinthians' failings to their fullest potential for being the church and for being God's presence in the world. Despite all his realism about the actual situation, for Paul the reality and power of Christ among the community was far greater.

The Danger of Inappropriately Copying the First Christians

There are at least three respects in which we cannot regard Paul's approach as applicable to us today. In each of these areas changes in social and cultural conditions, partly stemming from the influence of the gospel itself, have affected the way we give form to Paul's vision.

First, types of relationships within the church differ. In establishing his churches, Paul utilized the prevailing social structure of the household. Though some first-century families were not very different from modern nuclear families, others included slaves and their dependents, clients and friends, older kin and single relatives. Households also tended to act as a single unit, as the many "household baptisms" in Acts indicate. One result of this was a greater continuity between the social networks people belonged to before and after their conversion. The two may not have been very different, Jesus' words about the gospel often dividing families notwithstanding. When a church was formed within a converted household, there was little need for people to spend time getting to know one another. It is very different today. Communal groups in the church are made up mostly of people who have had little previous contact. The challenge to the early Christians was to redeem a network of existing relationships; our challenge is generally to create community where little has existed before.

In the first-century household patterns were also more stratified. There were status distinctions between masters and slaves, patrons and clients, benefactors and recipients. Social conventions governing relationships between husbands and wives and between parents and children were more formal than they are today (cf. 1 Pet 3:6). These social norms, however modified in Christ, would have given the dealings of Christians a flavor that has little parallel in our more egalitarian societies.

Second, lines of authority within the church differ. Authority within a first-century household generally centered on the husband/father/master. A particular household could also have authority over less socially advantaged families or individuals. When people converted, the household to which they belonged could become the fulcrum around which pastoral oversight in a new church revolved. Not that this took place automatically. Paul gave his commendation only to households that turned their positions of privilege into a base for service. Although men played the dominant role in ancient societies, Paul's approach to authority was flexible enough to allow women to share in the oversight of the churches in their homes (Rom 16:3-16; Phlm 1-2); a widow might even become the most prominent person within them (Col 4:15).

The abolition of slavery and the liberation of women, both prompted in part by Christian impulses, have altered the balance of authority in modern society. Education and employment are available to all, affording everyone the opportunity to take on responsible positions in the workplace and in voluntary organizations. This has lessened the social gap between men and women and between employers and employees. The separation of work from home life and the separation of the aged from their offspring has altered the authority previously possessed by parents. Though we have to reckon with the continuing existence of minor social, gender, and familial distinctions, these changes create the conditions for a more varied approach to authority within the local church than was possible in Paul's day.

Third, aspects of church meetings differ. For instance, in the first century bread and wine were people's basic food and drink. The breaking of the one and the drinking of the other customarily marked the beginning and conclusion of a meal. When the Lord's Supper commenced with the breaking of bread and ended with the drinking of wine, it was not a separate ritual but an ordinary meal given an extraordinary significance. While bread is still a basic element for us, even formal meals rarely begin by breaking and sharing it. And while wine is not unusual at evening meals, it is coffee that is commonly drunk at the conclusion of the meal. It would therefore be difficult for us to celebrate the Lord's Supper in exactly the same way as the early Christians.

This meal took place in an apartment or home. Since this was also the place where people worked and through which welfare was channeled, the context of church took place in a workplace and a social service agency as well as a domestic setting. These links with the wider world gave a more down-to-earth and world-related feel to the typical home church—or home-church-based congregational—gathering. We have to find other ways of connecting what happens in church to the stuff of everyday life.

The Danger of Sidelining the First Christians

Some have argued that what we find in Paul, especially in his first letter to the Corinthians, is so shaped by the particular concerns of this community that it is not useful for general application. But Paul's approach in this letter is not untypical of the practice in his other churches. As the biblical scholar James D. G. Dunn notes, what comes through in this letter is the distinctive character of early Christian meetings when compared to those of other first-century religious groups:

> It did not meet on consecrated or special premises; its context was the home of one of its members. It did not center round a sacred text or particular ritual acts; its raison d'être was rather the sharing of the shared grace *(charis)* of God in its particular expressions *(charismata)*. It was not characterized by an established pattern or liturgy nor did it depend on an official leadership to give it direction; rather it was to be expected that the Spirit would exercise sufficient control through the interplay of gifts and ministries ordered by him. Its aim was to bring about the mutual edification of all through a being together and through a doing for one another in word and action as the body of Christ in mutual interdependence on the Spirit.[13]

Dunn continues that, for all its unusual disorder, it would be a mistake to regard that church as a special case. The presence of parallels elsewhere (e.g., 1 Thess 5:9–22; Rom 12) indicate that Paul's response in Corinth was consonant with the general guidelines he gave his churches. In short, 1 Cor 14:26–40 can be taken as Paul's picture of how any local church should function when it meets for worship. As such, it remains a challenge and inspiration to any group that meets today as the body of Christ.

CONCLUSION

The above examination is not an effort to restore the NT church. As Gene Edwards says, studying the NT churches ". . . does not imply that we meet the way they met. Rather, that we discover in the same way they discovered how to meet."[14] We need to find the appropriate twentieth-century equivalent to the first-century church. This is true for the way we meet and engage in mission. Down through the centuries various groups have drawn deeply from these early Christian wells and have poured what they found into different channels to nurture their own lives and to bring life to others. We can learn from and be encouraged by these models. They demonstrate that the two-dimensional approach to church found in the NT was far from a historical or cultural curiosity.

NOTES

1. E. Best, *Following Jesus: Discipleship in Mark* (Edinburgh: T. & T. Clark, 1981) 227–28.

2. The high profile of this form of meeting prompted the Presbyterian writer William Arnot to entitle his reflections on the book of Acts *The Church in the House: A Series of Lessons from the Acts of the Apostles* (New York: Carter, 1893).

3. See further R. Banks, *Paul's Idea of Community: The Early House Churches in Their Cultural Setting* (rev. ed.; Peabody, Mass.: Hendrickson, 1994).

4. For an attempt at recreating the first-century church, see R. Banks, *Going to Church in the First Century: An Eyewitness Account* (Beaumont, Tex.: Christian, 1990).

5. E. Schweizer, "The Service of Worship," in *Neotestamentica* (Zurich: Zwingli, 1963) 335–36.

6. This is the meaning of the Greek original.

7. M. Luther, *The Liberty of a Christian* (London: Marshall, Morgan, & Scott, n.d.) 30.

8. E. Trueblood, *The Company of the Committed* (New York: Harper & Row, 1961) 100.

9. Schweizer, "Service of Worship," 338–39.

10. M. Green, *Evangelism in the Early Church* (London: Hodder & Stoughton, 1976) 207–8.

11. See further B. Winter, *Seek the Welfare of the City: Christians as Benefactors and Citizens* (Grand Rapids: Eerdmans, 1994).

12. C. Gunton, *On Being the Church: Essays on the Christian Community* (Edinburgh: T. & T. Clark, 1989) 69, 71, 78.

13. J. D. G. Dunn, "The Responsible Congregation, 1 Corinthians 14:26–40," in Charisma *und* Agape (ed. P. Benoit, et al.; Rome: Abbey of St. Paul before the Wall, 1983) 235–36.

14. G. Edwards, *How to Meet Under the Headship of Jesus Christ* (Beaumont, Tex.: Message Ministry, 1993) 37.

3

A GREAT CLOUD OF WITNESSES

*Participatory Forms of Church Life
through the Centuries*

Down through the centuries the idea of grouping church life around the home and developing interactive forms of congregational life has had many advocates. Some of these advocates—both individuals and movements—are not well known. The insights of those that are well known have been overlooked or downplayed. Today, in various parts of the world, supporters of this approach continue to appear. In this chapter we will do our best to identify the most significant past and present witnesses.

THE WITNESS OF CHURCH HISTORY

From the Early Church to the Middle Ages

Postapostolic Developments

For a long time after the NT period early Christians continued to meet in homes. This was the norm until well into the third, in some places even fourth, century AD. The Christianity that conquered the Roman Empire was essentially a home-centered movement. Early liturgies attest that there was also a stronger participatory element in various larger meetings, even though in time certain figures came to play more prominent roles and subsequently became a separate caste of clergy.[1] Though the story is a complex one, the great historian Adolf Harnack makes a strong case for the assertion that the practice of hospitality within Christian homes did more to forward the advance of Christianity than anything else.[2] This is one of the most extraordinary aspects of early Christian expansion, one that stands as a continuing challenge to those who claim that only large, highly organized institutions with powerful, publicly recognized representatives can make a real impact on the world around them.

The earliest clericalizing and formalizing of the church did not go uncriticized, especially in rural areas. Already in the second century groups reacted against this trend. Prompted by prophetic experiences and apocalyptic beliefs, small groups of close-knit believers banded together into churches, modeling themselves on the first Christian community in Jerusalem. This group, called the Montanists—who formed a morally rigorous, doctrinally inventive charismatic movement in the second and third centuries—encouraged spontaneous contributions in their gatherings, endorsed the role of women in leadership, and held each other accountable to live obediently under Christ. They believed that the Holy Spirit was as alive and well in their midst as it was among the earliest believers.

During the first few centuries after Christ other changes began to take place in the way Christians met. Homes and apartments were replaced by special buildings, and domestic meetings were transformed into public services. William Barclay describes what happened to the celebration of the Lord's Supper as a series of movements:

> 1. There is the movement from the house to the church. It is not in doubt that the Lord's Supper began as a family meal or a meal of friends in a private house. This was inevitable for the simple but sufficient reason that more than a century was to pass before there was such a thing as a church building . . . worship was therefore a thing of the house church and the small group and the home. It was there that the Lord's Supper was born in the church. It was like the Jewish Passover which is a family festival at which the father and the head of the household is the celebrant. . . . The Lord's Supper began in the house and moved to the church.

2. The Lord's Supper moved from being a real meal into being a symbolic meal. The very way in which in the early accounts excesses of eating and drinking are condemned shows that it is a real meal that is in question. . . . The Lord's Supper originated in a meal of hungry people, for the Jews who sat down to the Passover late in the evening had not eaten since at least midday. For many, for the slaves and the poor, the Lord's Supper must have been the one real meal of the week. The idea of a tiny piece of bread and sip of wine bears no relation at all to the Lord's Supper as it originally was. . . . The Lord's Supper was originally a family meal in a household of friends.

3. The Lord's Supper moved from bare simplicity to elaborate splendour. . . . That which had been a family occasion became a service at which the bishop dispensed the sacrament, surrounded by the presbyters detached from the congregation. It inevitably became something to be watched from a distance. . . . With the increasing idea of the conversion of the elements into the actual body and blood of the Lord, the sacrament became less and less the grateful memory of the death of Christ and more and more the awestricken encounter with the glorified King of heaven and earth. It was coming into the presence of the King, and all the trappings of the court began to be used. . . .

4. The celebration of the Lord's Supper moved from being a lay function to a priestly function. In the NT itself there is no indication that it was the special privilege or duty of anyone to lead the worshipping fellowship in the Lord's Supper. In the Didache again there is no mention of any special celebrant. In fact, the prophets are to be allowed to hold the eucharist as they will. In Irenaeus the celebration is not confined to any special person.[3]

This progression from the home to the church building, from a real to a symbolic meal, from simplicity to elaboration, from the concrete to the abstract, from the lay person to the priest has dramatically changed the nature of the Lord's Supper. This progression has also changed other aspects of early Christian meetings and organization, although space limitations prevent us from going into detail here. In the third and fourth century there was a noticeable drift toward church becoming a collective rather than communal affair; it catered to larger numbers of people and acquired a passive rather than an interactive character.

The Monastic Movements

From the fourth century onward protests against these formalizing tendencies arose in the form of monastic movements that developed a deeply communal life. These fraternities operated as extended Christian families in which everyone was valued as a channel of God's grace and in which each member had a distinctive contribution to make. Both men and women, in separate establishments, were attracted to the quality of members' personal holiness and common life and found a place in this movement. Even though set at a distance from urban centers and towns, monasteries increasingly developed a mission to them.

A different combination of community and mission arose in the orders that emerged in the Catholic Church from the twelfth century onward, beginning with the Franciscans and Dominicans. These were the vanguard of a second wave of monasticism throughout the ancient world. At their heart was a strong communal life, based on regular worship and genuine fellowship. These groups also focused on mission to the wider community and church and sometimes adopted an itinerant lifestyle. Dean Kelley suggests that these be viewed as intentional little churches within the wider church, "These movements typify the ecclesiolae in ecclesia . . . which have infused new vigor and resilience into the churches throughout the centuries."[4] It was one of these groups, called the Brethren of the Common Life, that influenced Luther's quest for a new understanding of divine grace and Christian lifestyle.

Other Groups

Prior to the Reformation certain anti-Catholic groups also reclaimed aspects of the communal and participatory nature of early church life. In France the persecuted Waldensians met at farms and houses throughout the countryside, supporting each other in strongly familial ways and encouraging the contribution of lay as well as ordained members. In England, partly as a result of Wycliffe's influence, groups of lay people called Lollards met informally in cities and towns to study Scripture, pray, and encourage one another.

The Period of the Reformation

Martin Luther

Although the mainline Reformers did not reintroduce the mixture of home church meetings and combined meetings of home churches described in the NT, Luther saw this as the goal to which his congregations should aspire. It was his profound depression over the general ecclesiastical situation that led him to this radical view of the "church." After riding the crest of the reforming wave for a time, the movement lost impetus. People attracted to it became more hesitant, and political circumstances became more complex. More importantly, churches that had responded to his teaching were lacking in spiritual vigor. Luther was also puzzled by the growth of the Anabaptists, in whose churches he saw a quality of life that he coveted for his own. This placed him in a difficult position, for he felt he had to warn his people against these "enthusiasts" while developing a model of church life similar to theirs.

Luther set out his intentions most fully in a little-known preface to his *German Liturgy,* which until recently was either bypassed or ignored by his latter-day successors. In this passage Luther identifies three kinds of worship. The first, he says, is the Latin Mass; the second is the "contemporary" service in the German language; the third is very much like a home church.

These [first] two kinds, then, we must let alone and allow it to happen that they are held publicly in the churches before all the people, among whom there are many who do not yet believe or are Christians. . . . For here there is not yet any ordered and certain assembly in which one could govern the Christians according to the gospel. . . . But the third kind which should have [the] true nature of evangelical order would not have to happen so publicly in the open among all kinds of people, but those who seriously want to be Christians and to confess the gospel in deed and word would have to register their names and gather themselves somewhere in a house alone. . . . Here one could also conduct baptism and communion in a brief and fine manner, and direct everything to the word, prayer and mutual love. . . . In brief, if one had the people who earnestly desired to be Christians, the order and manner could quickly be brought about. However, I cannot and do not wish yet to set up or to organize such a congregation, for I do not yet have the people for it. I do not see many who ask for such a thing. But if it comes that I must do it and am compelled, so that I cannot with good conscience leave it undone, then I shall gladly do my part in it and give the best help I can.[5]

Unfortunately, Luther was never able to act in accordance with his profound understanding of the church, partly because more radical Anabaptist groups struck out in apocalyptic directions that deeply troubled him. But he was not alone among the mainline Reformers in grasping the importance of smaller Christian communities within the parish church. In Strasbourg Martin Bucer advocated something very similar.[6] Like Luther, he was heavily influenced by his contact with the Anabaptist wing of the Reformation. In Scotland John Knox also encouraged "privy kirks," or home meetings for earnest believers.

The Anabaptists

The Anabaptists lived out what Luther envisioned. They formed what one writer has described as "covenanted and disciplined communities of those walking in the way of Jesus Christ. Where two or three such are gathered, willing also to be scattered in the work of the Lord, there is believing people."[7] These churches were founded on several important principles that generated a deeper level of community between their members and a greater degree of participation in their gatherings. This went hand in hand with a stronger involvement in evangelism and mission. The so-called marks of these churches included voluntary membership expressed in baptism; mutual edification, assistance, and discipline; an emphasis on the ministry of the laity rather than a special ministerial class; a functional approach to church order and structure; a stress on ministry in daily life; and an understanding of the church as a missionary community within the wider culture.

All this was based on a desire to restore essential elements of early church life and practice. The first recorded Anabaptist meeting took place in Zurich in 1525, when a dozen or so people trudged through the snow to meet in a home near the cathedral. A few years later an Anabaptist under interrogation by the authorities described what normally happened when such people came together:

They have no special gathering places . . . they send messages to one another by a boy or girl. When they have come together they teach one another the divine Word and one asks the other: how do you understand this saying? Thus there is among them a diligent living according to the divine word.[8]

The spirit of these gatherings is beautifully expressed in an early Anabaptist hymn:

What is this place where we are meeting?
Only a house, the earth its floor,
walls and a roof sheltering people,
windows for light, an open door.
Yet it becomes a body that lives
when we are gathered here,
and know our lord is near.
Words from afar, stars that are falling,
sparks that are sown in us like seed.
Names for our God, dreams, signs and wonders,
sent from the past are what we need.
We in this place remember and speak
again what we have heard:
God's free redeeming word.
And we accept bread at his table,
broken and shared, a living sign.
Here in this world, dying and living,
we are each other's bread and wine.
This is the place where we can receive
what we need to increase:
God's justice and God's peace.[9]

This vision of justice and peace extended to the whole society. As well as revitalizing the practice of evangelism among the people of God, Anabaptists developed a distinctive commitment to justice for those who were falsely persecuted by the civil or political authorities and to peacemaking in a time that was rife with discord and conflict. They pursued these goals communally, exemplifying in their life together the very characteristics they endeavored to bring to the world around them.

Though it was a century before comparable movements emerged in England, early Baptist meetings there possessed a similar character. Except where they were forced by persecution to gather in fields, lanes, and even caves, they initially met in private dwellings, barns, or rented rooms. A letter dating from 1608 describes a typical meeting. It included general prayer among those present, reading of Scripture and conversation about its meaning, extemporaneous teaching as several members were led by the Spirit, a concluding prayer and exhortation by the main speaker of the day, and a collection for the poor. There was also opportunity for members to engage in loving actions toward one another. The average length of such smaller meetings was around four hours.[10] Once a month several groups would come together in a combined gathering for corporate worship and mutual accountability, as well as to organize gifts for the needy in the wider community.

The Renewal Movements

During the following two centuries several major movements revitalized the life of the church. All of these affirmed the importance of smaller gatherings of believers, principally held in houses and farms, and of the accountability of every member for doing ministry inside or outside the congregation. In England the Quakers originally met as cells in homes while they continued to attend conventional places of worship. Only later did they separate from the established church. In their meetings they waited on the Spirit and shared as they were led. This practical embodiment of the priesthood of all believers extended to their ministry of evangelism and social action.

On the Continent the Pietist movement within German Lutheranism sought to bring the work of Reformation to its logical conclusion. Though this movement is generally viewed as being centered on renewing individual Christian experience, at its base it was a rethinking of the nature of the church. Instead of envisioning this in terms of clergy and laity, or public services and personal piety, leaders of the Pietist movement emphasized the priesthood of all believers, including women, and the place of what they termed *collegia pietatis* or spiritual gatherings within the church for Bible study, prayer, and mutual encouragement. A key leader of the movement saw this movement as reintroducing "the ancient and apostolic kind of church meetings."[11] In these meetings members performed the functions that pastors carried out in the larger meetings. Such participation produced elders who could help oversee the life of the congregation. Corporate worship could be conducted fully by lay people when necessary. Pietism also developed a range of organizations through which members of the church could address the physical, material, educational, and cultural needs of the wider society. Links between the *collegia* inside and outside Germany established a loose ecumenical network.

The Moravians

Nikolaus von Zinzendorf catalyzed and reorganized the exiled Moravians in Herrnhut, Germany. He developed what were essentially ecclesiolae, or little churches, within the broader ecclesia of the official Lutheran Church. These met mostly in homes and later in simple structures. Though these contained certain formal elements, such as appointed leaders, spontaneous reactions to the presence of the Spirit through sharing of the word, prayer, tears, and embraces were permitted. After a time Zinzendorf introduced smaller groups or "bands" within the congregation, consisting of only a handful of similarly aged or placed people who prayed, shared, and disciplined each other. Besides holding these and other common meetings, the Moravians placed a strong emphasis on every person's being accountable in ministry through their chosen work or itinerant mission. Indeed, they radically minimized the clergy/laity distinction by implementing the doctrine of the priesthood of all believers—both women and men—more fully than any Christian group up to that time.

Since the Moravians expressed their commitment to small church groups in communal settlements, in a sense they were a more everyday, family-centered, Protestant version of earlier Catholic monasteries, where personal, social, civic, and worship life formed a seamless web. In another sense they were heirs of the Catholic orders rather than the Free Church tradition. Zinzendorf viewed the Moravians as a renewal movement within the wider church rather than as a separate denomination within it. They sought to deepen and unify the life of all branches of the worldwide church. Again we find an intensive experience of community going hand in hand with an extensive commitment to mission.

Few have understood or explained the link between intensive experience of community and effective involvement in mission, especially evangelism, as well as Zinzendorf did. For him inreach and outreach were two sides of the same coin. For that reason, he said,

> we must establish the principle that the happy, fruitful, and almost irresistible calling in of many thousands of souls, supposes a little flock in the house, cleaving to our Savior with body and soul, . . . in such a manner that we may as it were point to such a people with the finger, when we are inviting others; that is an advantage, a blessing, a preaching of the gospel to purpose, if we can say: "Come, all things are ready, I can show you the persons, who are already there, but do come and see." . . . This is simply that thing called preaching the gospel.[12]

In addition to preaching the gospel, providing for the needs of the poor was integral to Zinzendorf's understanding of church. Proportionally, the missionary dimension of Moravian life exceeded that of any Christian group from the first century. Never has a single expression of the church had so many of its members involved in mission, traveled to so many places, reached out to so many different peoples, or influenced so many other churches to follow its example.

The Methodists

It was through a Moravian that John Wesley's heart was "strangely warmed" during a meeting in Aldersgate. But he learned more from the Moravians than the place of the affections in genuine religion; he adapted their structure to the needs of the new movement that grew up around his preaching. Howard Snyder has provided a detailed account of Wesley's approach, demonstrating how radical was his understanding and organizing of the church. Wesley encouraged his people to stay within their local Anglican churches, but it was the smaller "class" meetings within the larger Methodist "societies" that constituted the heart of the movement.

> The primary point of belonging was that this more intimate level of community and membership in a class was required before one could join the society. . . . The class meeting was the cornerstone of the whole edifice. The classes were in effect house churches (not classes for instruction, as the term class might suggest), meeting in the various neighborhoods where people lived. . . . They normally met one evening each week for an hour or so. Each person reported on his or her spiritual progress, or on particular needs or problems, and received the support and prayers

of the others. Advice or reproof was given as need required, quarrels were made up, misunderstandings removed. And after an hour or two spent in this labour of love, they concluded with prayer and thanksgivings.[13]

One of the first manuals for class leaders contains the following description:

It is clear as daylight that that kind of communion (experienced in class meetings) has the express warrant of holy Scripture; and that something more than church communion in the sacrament of the Lord's Supper was enjoyed by the primitive Christians. They had "fellowship" as well as "breaking of bread." How, for instance, could they exhort one another daily? How could they comfort and edify one another? How could they provoke one another to love and good works? How could they confess their faults to one another and pray for one another? How teach and admonish one another in psalms and hymns and spiritual songs? How bear one another's burdens? How weep with those who weep and rejoice with those who rejoice, if they never met together for the purpose of conversing on experimental religion and the state of each other's souls? Whatever persons may say to the contrary, those churches, the members of which do not observe or in which they have not the opportunity of observing the foregoing precepts which are enjoined in the New Testament scriptures, are not based on the model of the apostolic churches.[14]

In time Methodism deeply affected the official church in England. We the authors have a story in our own family history about a clergyman who encouraged and attended a home meeting in his parish in Kent in the 1820s. This was a meeting for church and supplemented the weekly morning service. He and the others were prosecuted and fined because all such meetings had been forbidden by law since the mid-seventeenth century. This prohibition partly explains why there was less of this kind of activity than we might expect.

Methodism had an even greater impact in the New World, in terms of not only the proportion of the population brought into the church but also the influence that its small-group structure exerted on other denominations. In the nineteenth century early forms of the Brethren movement in England and the Disciples of Christ in the United States also emphasized the mutual ministry of all believers, a more participatory form of congregational life, and a commitment to renewing the wider church rather than starting a new denomination.

THE WITNESS OF CONTEMPORARY CHRISTIANS

In our own century, particularly during the last three decades, the church has begun to turn upside down again. In the West since the 1960s Bible studies, prayer groups, and fellowship groups have become more relational in character, inclusive of "worship," and increasingly based in the home. Factors that have contributed to this development include a greater emphasis on the importance of relationships, the widespread influence of the charismatic movement, and the emergence of a more educated laity. Nowadays other groupings—cell groups, family clusters, pastoral circles, cross-generational classes, home dialogue meetings, and other types of informal gatherings—have appeared. Mostly these do not claim to be ecclesial or churchlike in nature, that is, equal in importance to gatherings of the whole congregation. We shall look more closely at the differences between these meetings and home churching later. Congregational gatherings have also become more participatory, as is indicated by the increase in experience of body life, the now common presence of ministry as well as worship during services, and the growing number of so-called open churches. But these meetings are not as expressive of mutual ministry as they might be.

Non-Western Voices

It is primarily outside the West that Christians have made more substantial moves in a home-church direction, especially in past or present communist countries and in Latin America. In Russia, prior to its recent halting steps toward democracy, many Christians met in homes as underground churches. Since it was forbidden for groups of a certain size to meet regularly, it was often necessary to camouflage meetings as celebrations. This meant that individual members might have six or seven birthdays a year, to which everyone received a formal invitation and brought a present! Through their authentic and costly Christian commitment and their quiet but persistent refusal to become an organ of the state these groups paved the way for the wider social changes that have now come about. Many of these groups continue to meet, although churches can now meet openly, freely, and without fear of reprisal. Others have moved toward a more traditional form of church life that centers on a building, a pastor, and public services.

Mainland China

More interactive forms of church life continue to flourish in mainland China and parts of the third world, where Christianity still faces political or social oppression. After the communist revolution in 1949 the buildings used for religious purposes were closed, forcing Christians to meet in smaller groups elsewhere. While some officially registered churches, such as the Three Self Movement, were able to retain a public presence, they did so at the risk of official supervision by the government and regular penetration by party workers. As a result the bulk of Christians chose to meet unofficially wherever they could. Sometimes they met in open fields and forests, especially when believers could all volunteer for work details or find some other excuse to gather. Mostly they met secretly in homes. Since pastors were more likely to come under scrutiny and face imprisonment, leadership of such groups increasingly fell into lay hands. Since men were more closely watched, women often played a vital part in evangelism and in planting churches.

In the 1960s the Cultural Revolution intensified the danger of meeting in this semiclandestine way, especially in larger cities. Despite the freer atmosphere of the post-Mao period and the gradual reopening of churches for public worship, only a portion of these groups have linked up with the Three Self Movement or have registered themselves officially with the government. Although estimates vary, there are probably more than fifty million believers in China today. The number attending official churches is at most only several million, which means that house churches are far and away the "mainstream" form of church life in mainland China.

While some of these house churches are about the size of a small congregation in the West, others are essentially extended Christian households. Some have a leader who wields considerable authority in the church, and others are still in the hands

of mature lay people. The key characteristics of these indigenous house churches are their family base and household setting, simplicity of corporate worship, lay ministry and
leadership, emphasis on prayer and healing, sharing of Scripture, and loving service to others in difficult times. As in the
early church, there are also some unbalanced emphases in
teaching and practice, as well as leadership struggles and conflicts. Indeed, there is a particular need now for greater instruction and consolidation (such as a movement toward forming
home-church-based congregations).

An account of one Chinese house church, written in the
seventies by a college professor who was ousted from his post
during the Cultural Revolution, is not untypical:

> Yes, we regard our meetings at home as a local church in spiritual
> fellowship with the worldwide Christian community. We began
> as a prayer group for Christian students at the University about
> 1952 when it had become untenable to have our meetings on
> campus ground. . . . So we met in my quarters in the professors'
> compound at four every Wednesday afternoon. We did the things
> we had always done in varsity fellowship— singing, Bible studies,
> intercession, fellowship, but with, I believed, more depth and
> more openness. . . .
>
> Between 1952 and 1964, the prayer group had its ups and downs.
> We never had more than thirty or so students. In 1962, there was
> only my wife and me. But the important thing was that God had
> left a Christian witness on campus. . . .
>
> Unknowingly, our group turned itself into a church. By 1964 our
> church had about thirty people worshipping on Wednesdays.
> Only seven were students or members of the faculty. Others
> came from the neighbourhood. We had a weekly communion
> service. . . .
>
> The years of the Cultural Revolution were a blank so far as our
> home meeting was concerned. We had no meeting. I was as-
> signed to work in a fruit-preserving factory. My wife went to live
> with her parents. There was not much to do. . . . Now I am back
> teaching physics and I have also got back my quarters. We have
> resumed our house worship, but of the twenty we had before the
> time of the Red Guards, only eight are still around. However more
> new people have joined us. . . .
>
> I am in two minds about our future. On the one hand I would love
> a pastor to come to us, have a small church near the University

and do good evangelism work. On the other hand, I can't help feeling that, given our peculiar situations, it might be best for us to continue to meet in homes, away from the limelight, quietly refracting the light of the Lord.[15]

Latin America

Since the late fifties a significant reorientation of church life has been taking place within the Catholic Church in Latin America. From Honduras to Chile, from the Atlantic to the Pacific, basic ecclesial, or base Christian, communities have appeared among the people. Most of these come from the poorer, though not necessarily the poorest, members of society. Many have grown up in shantytowns on the edges of large cities, which are often the product of social injustice, political oppression, and economic deprivation. Though accurate numbers are hard to come by, there are probably more than two hundred thousand such groups in various parts of Latin America.

In places where there is a desperate shortage of priests, these communities start from the vision and encouragement of an animator or facilitator who is sometimes a member of an order or a religious community. The people begin to take responsibility for organizing corporate worship, generally appointing several of their own number, including women, to lead the prayers, interpret the Scriptures, and celebrate the sacrament, interacting with the congregation in the process. Generally they meet in a house or community room. There are also smaller midweek groups that address members' everyday situations. These base communities network with one another and organize quarterly and annual meetings for young people and all their members. Priests and bishops are invited to these meetings as attendees rather than speakers, so that they can hear the concerns of the people and receive their insights. In this way the hierarchical character of the church is partly turned on its head, and it is not surprising that in many places relationships between these groups and the authorities are strained.

What are the key features of these communities? Since they reflect all the essential characteristics of the universal church, worship and sacrament are essential elements in their gatherings, love is foundational to their way of life, prayer and the word of God are central to their meetings, and mission to and prophetic advocacy for the needy is an integral part of their call.[16] Their extraordinary growth in Latin America is aided by their common Catholic heritage and the communal links that still exist in subcultures that have not yet suffered the full impact of the Industrial Revolution and the Enlightenment. They also appeal to popular religious piety. The emergence of similar groups among some Pentecostal churches will become increasingly significant as Latin America becomes increasingly more Protestant than Catholic.

In an eloquent passage the Brazilian theologian J. B. Libanio underscores the essentially ecclesial character of the basic Christian communities:

> They are not a movement, an association or a religious congregation. . . . They are not a method (or *the* only method) of building up the church: they are the church itself. . . . They are not an ideal: they are a sign of the kingdom, though they are not the kingdom. . . . They are not a natural community . . . identified with a race, language, people, family. . . . They are not special groups for special people. They are the church committed to the ordinary person, to the poor, to those who suffer injustice. . . . They are not closed: they are open to dialogue with all. They are not a reform of anything in pastoral work: they are a decisive pastoral option, made in order to construct a new image of the church.[17]

Other Places

Basic Christian communities have developed in the Philippines and in other parts of southeast Asia. Cell groups and house churches are growing among independent churches in Africa. In India, the planting of house churches in poverty-stricken states such as Kerala is proving a vital way forward.

Voices from the West

While it is mainly in non-Western countries that the most thoroughgoing experiments in regrouping the church around the home and in developing home-church-based meetings are taking place, there are voices in countries with long-standing Christian traditions that are calling for the same kind of change. These voices are not confined to any one denomination or form of Christianity. So far these voices have gone largely unheeded, but their arguments for the home church approach have become even more applicable in recent years. During the last decade their number has increased significantly. Endorsements of home churches, "base communities," "small faith communities," and the like have also begun to appear in the reports of ecclesiastical, interdenominational, and ecumenical bodies. The viewpoints that follow come from a broad range of denominational, nondenominational, and transdenominational contexts. They were formulated by people who have acted on, as well as reflected on, their convictions.

An Episcopalian Voice

In his book *On Being the Church in the World* Bishop John A. T. Robinson views the church as existing on three levels: as the individual home church, as the large congregation where home churches meet as a whole group, and as a third level of organization. He begins by insisting that the house church should not be regarded as a temporary expedient in a new area or as an evangelistic weapon for reaching outsiders. He argues that both of these conceptions are inadequate from the point of view of the NT. The church in the house is theologically necessary. This is the first level at which the church exists. The second level is the regular coming together of these house churches as a large group to worship and fellowship together. The third level involves the occasional gathering of all the congregations in a particular place, in a kind of cathedral-like (or stadium-like) setting. He views the third organizational aspect of a congregation's life as an optional extra, whereas recovering the small home-church basis is one of the most important theological and practical tasks for today's Christians. Out of his own experience of home churching Robinson identifies three elements of permanent significance for the church as a whole:

1. The first is a living experience of a *form* of the church different from that which most people in this country have ever actually known. And it is a form which compels those who find themselves within it to face questions which other levels of Christian living still allow them to evade. When there *is* no church to go to, one can only be the church. At this level, there is a new constraint both towards mission and towards deeper involvement with one's neighbour in Christ. One cannot ignore either the house next door (there is no real "next door" to the parish church) or the Christian next to one (the parlor is very different from the

pew). . . . At the same time there is being built up in the house church something much less vulnerable to disintegration from without. In the event of persecution, the church does not have to go underground; it *is* underground, even if the superstructure has to go.

2. The second thing that is being discovered is the meaning of holiness. By uniting the words "holy" and "common," hitherto defined as opposites, Christianity created something entirely new. . . . By taking the Holy Communion from the sanctuary . . . nothing of reverence is lost, but rather . . . henceforth the most common is sensed as holy.

3. The third question that is being thrown up is the nature and future of the ministry. . . . The significance of the house church is that it raises this question precisely in the right form and with immediate urgency. It shows a new type of ministry to be a necessary requirement of the normal (parochial) form of the church's mission and not merely of evangelistic adventures that might (very wrongly) be dismissed as side-lines or stunts. It shows the real need to be not mere assistants at the parish church (lay readers, permanent deacons, etc.), but the breakers of bread, priests of indigenous churches. . . .

The experiment is full of dangers and shortcomings, of which those are most conscious who are most deeply quickened. But I should like to put on record for what it is worth—and I measure my words carefully—that I believe this development of the church in the house to be the single most important new thing that is happening in the Anglican Church today.[18]

More recently, in several books David Prior has argued for a similar reshaping of Anglican church life.[19]

A Presbyterian Voice

A pioneer who brought the church into the house in the Church of Scotland was Tom Allen. His book *The Face of My Parish* recounts his experiences. For him the starting point was the divorce that existed between the church and the ordinary life of people. The cause of this divorce was that the church was only a pale reflection of authentic Christian community. He realized that to rectify this problem it was not enough to replace church organizations with vocational Christian groups, industrial chaplaincies, or lay resource centers. These groups play a significant role in training lay people for their various

ministries of daily life and in breaking down the barrier between the gospel and secular culture. But because they are
relatively homogeneous, gathering people around their work
or mission, they do not produce inclusive and holistic commu-
nities in the deepest Christian sense. Allen maintains that we can only begin to experience Christian community in the fullest way by developing "the church
within the church." This would take the form of

> live cells of Christian community springing up like oases within
> our parched churches. These intensive groups of Christian fel-
> lowship will prescribe for themselves ways of walking together
> that spring out of a concern for people in all their troubles and
> sorrows. . . . [T]he church can only fulfill its function, and pene-
> trate the secular world, when it is exhibiting the life of a genuine
> and dynamic Christian community—the koinonia of the New
> Testament.[20]

These groups were made up of people who were brought
together by their vision of the body of Christ, not organized by
pastoral planning or decision, and they depended chiefly on
the commitment and ministry of the people. Though they did
not set out as educational or evangelistic enterprises, they became training schools for discipleship and mission, as well as
seedbeds for building community within the congregation.

A Baptist Voice

In *A New Face for the Church* Lawrence O. Richards argues
that the "small group" meeting as church is the basic building
block of the congregation. We can only be the church if we
know each other well, because personal acquaintanceship is a
crucial avenue for the transformation of attitudes, values, and
personality. Such transformation is primarily accomplished in a
community in which the word of God is made flesh. This is why
we need the "church in the house." It will be difficult for the
church at large to rise to this challenge because decentralization is contrary to the structures that the church has developed
and, once in place, a centralized approach tends to change the
structure of congregations overall. Richards sees the following
pattern emerging:

> 1. The smallest churches . . . are neighbourhood gatherings, no
> larger than can comfortably fit in a home. In these meetings all

the functions of church take place, and this is the prime location for mutual ministry. . . . As gifts emerge and are recognized, church leaders are selected.

2. The church at times will assemble as a larger group for a variety of purposes, for the Sunday meeting, or to consider some problem facing it as a whole.

3. The leaders of the church meet together . . . one or more may be supported to free them for full-time ministry. . . . There is no one prominent person in the local fellowship: no single pastor to whom we all look![21]

Since Richards' chief interest is in Christian education, specifically children's ministry, he enlarges on the difference between their formation in such a setting and in the prevailing "schooling" model. Gone is the more formal atmosphere of the classroom. What is sought instead is a stronger impact of each person's life upon that of others, of faith being more than handed down from one generation to another but being vitally caught throughout the generations. This overcomes the segregation of children into narrow, graded groups and restores them to significant participation with adults in a nurturing environment. When children are part of the same support group as their parents, their lives are touched in broader and deeper ways than in other settings. Only through home churching can children fully experience the biblical model for Christian education.

A Catholic Voice

In their book *Dangerous Memories: House Churches and Our American Story,* Bernard Lee and Michael Cowan argue on theological, psychological, and cultural grounds for reshaping the increasingly middle-class Catholic Church in America around a Western-style version of basic Christian communities. These house churches are

small groups of persons who gather regularly. They pray, sing, and share their human stories. They bring their stories and The Story into serious dialogue. The members know one another personally. They offer support to one another. Together they often confront the injustices of their world. With other groups, they form a network of communities. For the most part, they are grass-roots groups. No one told them to gather: they bring themselves together. They are, therefore, non-hierarchical. But [this] does not mean that they are anti-institution. Rather they are choosing to take care of needs (e.g., a more deeply interpersonal community) and convictions of faith (e.g., that God's reign in history requires changing unjust structures) that the institution is not addressing adequately. They do not think of themselves as extra-ecclesial, but as genuine church, as basic ecclesial units.[22]

Basic Christian communities are as ancient as they are new. Indeed they call the Catholic Church back to its NT roots. All the basic elements of church—fellowship, worship, learning, and service—take place within them. We cannot reproduce the life of the early church, but home churching provides a metaphor that can transform our present congregations. That transformation is already starting to take place. In their present form these groups are a relatively recent movement, but they are already beginning to reconstruct the ecclesial life of Christians in the United States. As dynamic structures between ordinary people and their social world, and as countercultural communities, they are also beginning to challenge the individualism and materialism of the American way of life. For the sake of the church and the culture at large, both of which need to be renewed and reinvented, they must continue to do so. Lee and Cowan are not the only ones to assert that the basic Christian community is an idea and a way whose time has come. The work and writing of Arthur Branowski on "small faith communities" offers a similar path for revitalizing and reshaping Catholic church life and practice.[23]

A Transdenominational Voice

J. C. Hoekendijk was one of the first to speak for small groups within denominations that find themselves frustrated, isolated, and ignored. In his book *The Church Inside Out* he argues that for some only one road remains open: moving outside traditional church structures. Some people may choose to form groups that cross denominational boundaries. In these transdenominational groups they can more freely express their common convictions and develop deepening bonds as they worship together. Many involved in church-planting endeavors have also experienced this.

The traditional pattern of community life of the parish church will have to be tested as to its missionary usefulness as well. . . .

It emerged during the early Middle Ages and served the expansion of the church from the city into the surrounding area. . . . We have canonized the parish church; from an incidental pattern it became a normative model; from a historically conditioned phenomenon it became an unchangeable divine institution. . . . On this point a consensus is growing that can be summarized concisely as follows: the *parish church functions only in a stable society* for which it was originally intended. . . . In the modern world, in which the people are becoming "mobilities," a church that wants to enter into the missionary situation in an adequate fashion will have to structure itself as a mission church.[24]

It is precisely here, he says, that house churches come into view again as the most effective way of drawing people who have lost any sense of place and are constantly on the move. We will only meet this challenge if church is regarded as being essentially a lay enterprise rather than as being dominated by church officials. There is no need to wait for official permission to do missions. If people had waited in the past, very little mission work would have developed. Since lay people have a divine prerogative to take the initiative here, they ought to use it. Only in this way will these groups become effective agents of mission. There is also no reason why lay people should not celebrate the Lord's Supper in house churches. They should do so in a way that returns it to being a common rather than a cultic meal. Only so will it have its full power, and only so will these groups become full expressions of the church.

Many others have begun to write about the movement towards home church from a similar transdenominational stance. Mostly they write out of strong involvement in independent house churches that meet regularly as a larger group for highly participatory corporate worship.[25]

CONCLUSION

The voices heard above are not the only ones calling the church to develop small churches within the congregation, rather than just small groups or church organizations. Examples of other voices can be furnished, such as those of the Mennonites, who remind their members of the home church nature of their origins,[26] and those of the Lutherans, who testify to the invigorating power and the integrative effects of meeting as a home church.[27] According to several German theologians, including the Catholic Karl Rahner and the Protestant Jürgen Moltmann, we must move away from our individualistic or organizational understanding of congregation to one that embodies a new kind of living together.

For Moltmann the ideal congregation—as noted earlier—is one that affirms that

> no one is alone with his or her problems, no one has to conceal his or her disabilities, there are not some who have the say and others who have nothing to say, neither the old nor the little ones are isolated, one bears the other even when it is unpleasant and there is no agreement, and finally, the one can also at times leave the other in peace when the other needs it.[28]

This kind of congregation exists, he says, among communal groups within local churches meeting in homes. They are grassroots and inclusive in character and provide a warm welcome to the stranger, the handicapped, and the needy. At their gathering they eat and drink together, celebrate the Lord's Supper, and give everyone the opportunity to speak and to be heard. Only through the building up of such groups within our churches can the lack of human relationships within them be overcome.

This survey of past and present Christian practice has shown that home churches and home-church-based congregations are neither novel nor uncommon. These forms of church life appear and reappear as central to God's design from the first century through the twentieth, in different parts of the world and under various social and political conditions, across the spectrum of denominations and outside them. In our own day these forms of church life have begun to make their presence felt again. What John V. Taylor stated about "little congregations" (house churches) and Christian cells (home-church-based congregations) almost twenty-five years ago is still true:

> Their establishment as the normal unit of Christian community is still so patchy and experimental that it is easy to despair. The marvel is that the "little congregations" are already coming to be regarded as normative in so many places. The process is bound to go on as the mobility and fragmentation of human societies increases. These small units of Christian presence are emphatically

not a halfway house through which the uncommitted will eventually be drawn back into the local churches. Nor are they an interim structure which ought to grow into new local churches in due course. . . . Too many people in the church insist upon regarding any other form than the conventional congregation as subnormal and peripheral. They will not believe that such groups may have the fullness of Christ and should be allowed to possess all the resources and all the responsibilities of a local church. I believe that the parish structure will continue to minister to certain of the various areas of life . . . but it is the "little congregations" which must become normative if the church is to respond to the Spirit's movement in the life of the world.[29]

NOTES

1. See further the fascinating account by the Roman Catholic historian A. Faivre, *The Emergence of the Laity in the Early Church* (New York: Paulist, 1990).

2. See A. Harnack, *The Mission and Expansion of the Church in the First Three Centuries* (vol. 1; London: Williams & Norgate, 1905) 219ff.

3. W. Barclay, *The Lord's Supper* (London: SCM, 1967) 101–4.

4. D. Kelley, *Why Conservative Churches Are Growing* (New York: Harper & Row, 1972) 114.

5. See M. Luther, *Luther's Works* (ed. U. Leupold; Philadelphia: Fortress, 1965) 53–54. There is a discussion of this passage in E. Brunner, *The Christian Doctrine of the Church, Faith and the Consummation* (trans. D. Cairns; Philadelphia: Westminster, 1962) 175–76.

6. R. Peter, "Informal Groups in the Reformation: Rhenish Types," in *Informal Groups in the Church* (ed. R. Metz and J. Schlick; Pittsburgh: Pickwick, 1975) 231.

7. D. F. Durnbaugh, *The Believer's Church: The History and Character of Radical Protestantism* (New York: Macmillan, 1968) 33.

8. So Ambrosius Spitalmeier, quoted in W. Klassen, *Anabaptism in Outline* (Scottdale, Pa.: Herald, 1981) 124.

9. Originally published in Valerius's *Neder-landische gedenck-klanck* (Zürich: n.p., 1626). An early collection of Anabaptist hymns.

10. See further B. White, *The English Separatist Tradition: From the Marian Martyrs to the Pilgrim Fathers* (Oxford: Oxford University Press, 1971) 126–27.

11. P. Spener, *Pia Desideria* (trans. T. G. Tapper; Philadelphia: Fortress, 1964–67) 89.

12. N. von Zinzendorf, *Nine Public Discourses upon Important Subjects in Religion* (Iowa City: University of Iowa Press, 1973) 43. An accessible description of the Moravian vision and practice is provided by H. Snyder, *Signs of the Spirit: How God Reshapes the Church* (Grand Rapids: Zondervan, 1989) 123–82.

13. J. Wesley, quoted in H. Snyder, *The Radical Wesley: Patterns of Church Renewal* (Downers Grove, Ill.: InterVarsity, 1980) 53–54.

14. Ibid., 56.

15. R. Fung, *Households of God on China's Soil* (Geneva: World Council of Churches Publications, 1982) 24–28.

16. In general see J. O'Halloran, *Living Cells: Developing Small Christian Community* (rev. ed.; Maryknoll, N.Y.: Orbis, 1984) 29–33. The life of one such community is described in detail in P. Galdamez, *Faith of a People: The Life of a Basic Christian Community in El Salvador* (Maryknoll, N.Y.: Orbis, 1986).

17. J. B. Libanio, quoted in D. Prior, *The Church in the Home* (Basingstoke, U.K.: Marshall, Morgan, & Scott, 1983) 16–17. The fullest account of basic Christian communities from a Protestant perspective comes from G. Cook, *The Expectation of the Poor: Latin American Basic Ecclesial Communities in Protestant Perspective* (Maryknoll, N.Y.: Orbis, 1985).

18. J. A. T. Robinson, *On Being the Church in the World* (London: SCM, 1960) 84–85, 93–95.

19. D. Prior, *The Church in the Home; Creating Community: An Every-Member Approach to Ministry in the Local Church* (Colorado Springs, Colo.: NavPress, 1992).

20. T. Allen, *The Face of My Parish* (Glasgow: Loudoun, 1984) 63, 66.

21. L. Richards, *A New Face for the Church* (Grand Rapids: Zondervan, 1970) 129–30.

22. B. Lee and M. Cowan, *Dangerous Memories: House Churches and Our American Story* (Kansas City, Mo.: Sheed & Ward, 1986) 2.

23. A. Baranowski, *Creating Small Faith Communities: A Plan for Reconstructing and Renewing Catholic Life* (rev. ed.; Cincinnati: St. Anthony Messenger, 1993).

24. J. C. Hoekendijk, *The Church Inside Out* (London: SCM, 1967) 93–97, 102, 107.

25. Examples, as interesting for their differences as for their similarities, include C. Smith, *Going to the Root: Nine Proposals for Radical Church Renewal* (Scottdale, Pa.: Herald, 1992); N. Krupp, *God's Simple Plan for His Church—and Your Place in It* (Woodburn, Ore.: Solid Rock, 1993); and Edwards, *How to Meet*.

26. As does Barrett, *Building the House Church,* and D. Birkey, *The House Church* (Scottdale, Pa.: Herald, 1988).

27. See further O. Stenberg, *Do We Dare to Be the Church?* (Seattle: HMS, 1989); and W. Diehl, *Christianity and Real Life* (Philadelphia: Fortress, 1976).

28. Moltmann, *The Open Church,* 33.

29. J. Taylor, *The Go-Between God* (New York: Oxford University Press, 1979) 148–49.

4

SMALL IS BEAUTIFUL

Testimonies and Hindrances to the Home-Church Experience

In this chapter we will focus mostly on the home-church experience of a wide range of people. First, we will listen to some testimonies from a wide range of people who belong to home churches within nondenominational and denominational settings. Second, given the biblical warrant and historical precedent for home churching, we will consider why so little effort has been exerted making small home-church groups the basic unit of corporate Christian life.

TESTIMONIES TO THE VALUE OF HOME CHURCHING

What are the benefits of home churching? In this chapter a representative sample of people who belong to such gatherings speaks for itself. The following remarks have much in common, even though the home churches described meet in very diverse contexts. Some groups are independent of a denomination, although they regularly come together as a larger gathering. Several are part of a nondenominational or newer charismatic congregation. Others exist as subsets within a mainline or evangelical congregation. The following contributions come from people who have found a community where they belong; people who have experienced healing and felt empowered; people who have discovered "something more" in a home-church setting.

A Married Couple in their Late Forties

We have been members of a house church for thirteen years. From our previous experience with small groups we came to realize how much Christian growth can take place in such a setting. However, these groups were often frustrated in their purpose—through both inexperience and the lack of priority given to them in the congregation. In such groups we also often felt obliged to put people right and solve their problems for them. The house church to which we now belong is a top priority for its members, and this makes a considerable difference to the quality of our fellowship in it. We have also come to realize that it is more important to accept one another as we are than to try to set one another right. As Jean Vanier says, this allows us to "grow from where we are and not where we want to be, or where others want us to be."[1]

We have come to experience, in a way we had not known before, three important aspects of church life. First, we have discovered the importance of just being with others and valuing them for themselves, the worthwhileness of being committed to them as they are. This commitment to one another is seen in prayerful concern as well as practical help in time of need.

Second, we have investigated the truth of God's character, values, and perspective. As we have studied together God's nature, we have found that the Holy Spirit does act in people's lives to change long-established attitudes, opinions, and behavior patterns. A well-developed atmosphere of love and acceptance allows people the dignity of responding to God's Spirit in their own time, whether in the area of personal lifestyle, the call to social action, or special witness to the truth of the Christian gospel.

Third, we have learned afresh that each member is able to make a unique contribution to the whole. Since we meet for about four or five hours, there is room for participation by all members, including children, and for the full expression of the gifts of the Spirit. We have also gained great benefit from being able to recognize the meaning of the Lord's body, the church (1 Cor 11:29), through sharing in the fellowship of the Lord's Supper as an actual meal. In preparing and sharing the fellowship meal, we have come to appreciate and care about those aspects of one another's lives that would not otherwise be revealed.

A Woman in Her Mid-Thirties

For me, coming to the group was at first a tentative gesture of reaching out from a state of depression to companionship and a sense of belonging. Although at that stage unable to join in, I came away from the group with a sense of warmth and well-being that gave me the strength and incentive to carry on living. Now that I am a new person—having found Christ swiftly and unexpectedly—coming along to the group gives me a new meaning of growth, learning, and love. Christ is ever-present in the quiet, caring prayers, the sharing of weekly experiences, a smile, or a ready joke. To forgo the meeting for even one week would be a far greater starvation than forgoing daily food.

A Fifty-Three-Year-Old Pastor

For me, my house church in a Mennonite setting has been a brand-new experience. I had pastored a congregation of around two hundred people for nineteen years and resigned in order to deal with the burnout I was experiencing. I took a seminary sabbatical in order to renew myself spiritually. The house church has provided a place where it was OK for me to share the pain that I needed to work through in order to experience healing and new direction.

I am now committed to developing networks of groups where people can be the church, honestly sharing in body life together, in order to be the healing community Jesus our Lord exemplified. We need to become a close-knit body where pain is allowed to surface and where we regularly pray for each other and worship together. Since one weakness of house church is our tendency to become isolated in small communities, I would prefer to work at developing regular times of celebration where the larger body celebrates together weekly through music, testimony, and prayer.

A Divorced Woman in Her Late Forties

After moving to a new community, I was keen to find a church where I could belong, where I could build meaningful relationships and find a focus for my spiritual life. I settled into life in my denominational church, becoming part of a women's prayer group. After several months I began to feel spiritually fragmented. Then a friend introduced me to a house church that was not part of my congregation.

In the housechurch, we each participate by bringing our presence, our gifts, and our meal contribution to each other. I have been greatly blessed by one church member who shows her love and care for us by providing the most creative desserts I've ever eaten. I have been accepted as I am and allowed to participate as I feel able. This has been renewing for me after ten years of participating in two worship services and teaching Sunday school each week.

Please don't misunderstand. Because we're human, house church is not without the struggles and growing pains of any other church. But we do our best to work through these together and to support one another.

An Ex-Roman Catholic Priest

I was in the official priesthood twenty-five years and have now been married for twenty years. I find the dialogues and our liturgies especially nourishing, and our sharing of bread and wine in equality a true Christian experience. I believe our church reflects the character of the early Christian communities.

A Young Family

Home church has provided us with a support group in which caring, sharing, and praying play major roles. We have developed some meaningful friendships with other Christians, and the group has become like an extended family. The structure of home church requires participation as opposed to just sitting back and observing. This has resulted in a strengthening of our faith. We look forward to continuing to grow through our church family.

A Married Woman in Her Early Fifties

There's much I could say about the manner in which I feel I've grown as a Christian since being in a house church, but as I was ruminating on this in bed this morning, I found myself thinking more about the etceteras of our life together. In fact, the more I thought about them the more I began to realize that these things are really not etceteras at all, but essentials. What am I talking about?

First, I'm grateful for the fact that in our group we have a couple of keen gardeners. Without any of us being aware of it, those gardens have become a central part of our common life. In those gardens we relax, play games with the children, and every so often hold our meetings. The Joneses have a large backyard, and because they don't have a lot of money they have taken to growing their own vegetables and fruit. Their pleasure and sense of accomplishment have drawn us all into their garden to admire progress and ask questions. A few of us have even begun to plant some lettuce, tomatoes, Swiss chard, and radishes in our own gardens. One woman who lives in an apartment has a tiny vegetable and herb garden in pots on her balcony. The vegetables from the Joneses' garden have often formed the basis of their contribution to the meal, and the children (and adults) love being able to pick the loganberries and raspberries that we eat with ice cream for dessert. The Joneses have shared their surplus with the group as well. The Smiths keep ducks for eggs, and as a result the Joneses and another family in the church now keep ducks too. They really have a mini-farm developing on their block!

Which leads me to the second aspect of our church's life that I'm grateful for—the animals. How much richer our lives are for the part played by our pets as well as the ducks. I can't help but think of Abby, the welcoming cat. She seems to know when visitors are expected and positions herself on the doorstep to wait. As we draw up in our cars, she bounces down from her perch and prances across the yard as if to say, "There you are. I've been waiting for you!" After we pet her, she walks with us into the house, only to disappear at the sound of another car arriving. Because they are part of the lives of the group members, the pets become a part of ours too. It doesn't matter whether it's a dog, rabbit, hamster, parrot, or cat. How we all grieved when Sally, the dear old English collie that belonged to the Browns, was killed by a car outside their home!

The third thing I've appreciated about the group is the talents members share with one another. Take our musicians for example. Beyond helping us to sing God's praises, sometimes they prepare a special item for our enjoyment. Every time we visit one bachelor's pad he plays whatever new classical piece he's been practicing on his grand piano. Another time we had in our group two women in their twenties who loved to do an occasional Indigo Girls tune for us. Then there are the children who are cajoled into playing their latest piece on the guitar or recorder for us. The group's talents aren't limited to music. We have one woman in the group who is an excellent cook and loves to prepare "different" dishes for us. At another stage we had someone who made the most yummy desserts.

Even as I write, I can think of a fourth thing that I've appreciated: the way we've gradually begun to share tools, lawnmowers, ladders, preserving pans, mixers, and even, on occasion, cars. Those of us with teenaged children have certainly appreciated that our children have been able to borrow CDs from others rather than always "needing" to acquire the latest hit for themselves. Doing all this requires a certain amount of trust that we will treat each others' goods carefully. It also asks a degree of patience and forgiveness when something borrowed gets damaged or broken, as it periodically does.

I guess these things will seem like etceteras to some, but to me they are a real part of our common spirituality. Our life together as an extended Christian family under God would be so much poorer without them.

A Seventeen-Year-Old Girl

One of the aspects of house church I appreciate most is the opportunity to really get to know persons younger and older than myself. I feel I have learned much more from relating to people of different ages than I ever could have in a larger church youth group.

A Single Mother

As a divorced single mother of three, I have found it very healing to be a part of a church community where I am not invisible and can contribute to the life of the group. My previous experience in traditional churches was that people were not able to see beyond the "scarlet D" to see the person (gifts and strengths as well as brokenness and weakness). In my house church I am seen and accepted for who I am. No masks. No games. I am given opportunity to walk in the gifts that God has given me and am even held accountable in them. I am not passed over (or disregarded) because I am divorced, single, and a woman. I do not feel judged. I have also benefited from our group's emphasis on spiritual direction and spiritual friendships. As a single parent, I find support in the house church that I did not experience in the traditional church. My children have benefited from our mentors program.

A Single Woman in Her Mid-Twenties

What does being part of a home church mean? It is an environment of faith in which I am being opened, nurtured, challenged, supported. It is an occasion from which I go out to be more effective during the week as a result of the focus that the group offers. Home church is a place where I belong, where people are concerned for each other, and where I can be who I am without any façade. Home church is a forum where we can receive and consider new ideas and challenges, where we can worship in the context of shared lives. So home church offers the chance to experiment with old and new ways of worship that reflect the interests and personalities of the individuals involved—be it praise, prayer, meditation, or learning.

However, the commitment and responsibility of home church is not always easy. Home church is also the place where my busyness and tiredness prevent me from participating as I should, where my narrow-mindedness, which prevents me from being open, makes me judgmental and resentful, and where my contribution is yet another burden at the end of a week of demands. But in this conflict between the opportunity for and the burden of both giving and receiving, we find real growth. At the moment we are struggling with the difficulty of being open to a diversity among group members while maintaining some cohesion. We are fearful of a sterility that springs from our middle-class outlook and were unable to meet the needs of a few people who did not share our interest in the intellectual pursuit of our faith.

A Married Woman in Her Fifties

When we started as a small group, we all felt that something was missing from our lives, something our structured church services couldn't provide. Beginning with no firm ideas of what format our gatherings would take, we have now "put together" a meeting that is worshipful, joyful, and vital. We are always seeking new ways of getting to know Jesus Christ better and, through him, each other.

I have grown personally because I have learned in the group to accept the almost unbelievable fact that God loves me just as I am. Our prayer has been an enriching and rewarding experience. Prayers for healing, spiritual strengthening, and guidance have been answered.

The group has also grown together. We not only sustain each other in our worship, but give—and receive—positive help in many areas. It's a real joy to share thought-provoking, sad, and even mundane experiences with friends. The meeting has become for me a weekly happening that I don't ever want to miss.

A Person with a Gay Background

The loving and supportive fellowship that I find in my house church is providing the healing I need. Just like the early church, it celebrates a new way of life that brings peace and joy, even in the midst of guilt and shame. Although I have participated in the gay lifestyle, I have found acceptance. I stand a much better chance of finding true Christian love and support from this body of Christian believers than from another type of church. The house church I am a part of has a calling on my life where deep friendship is called forth in a radically different way; it draws the lowly, the poor, those who are failures in the eyes of the world, the sexually immoral, and the homosexual offenders. We have "been there" and know what it feels like to have wounded ourselves and others around us. We have known defeat, but now we know victory. We were losers, but we are in the process of

becoming overcomers. I am amazed at the growth and healing that is occurring in my life in my home church.

A Married Woman in Her Late Twenties

I have gained from our house church a new vision for
church growth, a new sense of direction, and the development of a personal ministry. I have a group of friends that I
call and relate to as a family. This is important to me because
my own family lives in another city. Now that I've resigned
from work, the studies have become extra valuable as they
provide mental stimulation and teaching about practical ways
of Christian living.

A Man in His Thirties with No Church
Background

I was a Christian. Well, at least I thought I was. I wasn't
really sure sometimes. I'd led a fairly secular life (in fact, I still
do), but then someone introduced me to some theology. I mar-
veled at the Bible—its completeness from the beginning of history to the end. This had credibility; it made sense, and so did
Christ. Anyway, it just felt like it had to be right, even though
many things I'd learned told me that it was all fairy tales.

So I was a Christian. But, wait, if I'm a Christian, how come I
hardly ever set foot inside a church? Well, I felt awkward and
self-conscious, asking myself, "Do I really belong here?" My
secular conditioning got the better of me. But it wasn't just that.
There was that organ music, which made everything quiet as I
walked somewhat cringingly toward a pew. Then there was the
sermon, usually too simplistic and lacking impact. But things
were a bit better in Sunday school: there was more participation. So, I didn't seem to really like church, but that was my fault
too; I didn't try hard enough. It was too easy to succumb to the
awkwardness I felt, to sleep in and give it a miss. Also, I didn't
have enough humility (and I still don't). So I thought, I don't
really know any Christians, I don't go to church, so maybe I'm
not really a Christian, I'm just kidding myself. For a very long
time, that's the way it was.

Then came along a different kind of church—house
church. What was the difference? Well, in a standard church, I

and everyone else stared at the front, all in one direction. In the house church we looked at each other. This was because there were fewer of us, with no one leader. We came as we were, and we were in a hospitable setting. There was no set protocol, we decided what we would do, as a body familiar with and accommodating to its parts. We connected spiritually in an intimate Christian setting. But that was scary too. Suddenly, it was real, and was I real enough to keep it up?

Well, I wasn't sure. But this time, I felt accountable, something like a team member, and team members aren't supposed to "sleep in" or give themselves excuses and let their teammates down. Besides, I had to bring the vegetables or the drinks, or I had to cook a meal. So now, with time, the secular conditioning is breaking down, the awkward unfamiliar is becoming the comfortable familiar, and I realize that real Christians aren't in essence any different from me after all (although there are certainly better ones than I!). I thank God for house church. I am a Christian, and I want to be baptized.

HINDRANCES TO THE DEVELOPMENT OF HOME CHURCHES

There are eight main reasons why mainline evangelical and nondenominational churchgoers have done little to incorporate or develop home churches within their common life.

Lack of Awareness

The majority of churchgoers continue to view Sunday church attendance as fulfilling their responsibility to "gather together" with God and one another. While a significant number of churchgoers are involved in relational small groups, many of them regard their small group as optional. In any case, as we shall see, taking part in a small group within the congregation still falls short of the full home-church experience.

An added problem is that in large services the emphasis is on the formal worship of God directed by the few; fellowship between groups in the church is only a secondary element. In the activities of a large church, for example, the communion of its members is only symbolized in its services and ritual, since true communion can be realized only in the direct fellowship of the persons who constitute its membership.[2] As a result, most people come to church to receive rather than to give, as individuals rather than as members of vital subgroups within the congregation. In these cases the lack of awareness is due to lack of proper biblical teaching. Biblical dimensions of church life are overlooked, sidelined, or weakened, and thus most people's view of church is narrow.

What is generally missing in both small and large meetings is the long-term commitment to a specific group of people with whom we are in close relationship and for whom we take practical responsibility. But only as we do this can we actually fulfill injunctions to "love one another earnestly from the heart" (1 Pet 1:22), "care for one another" (1 Cor 12:25), and "bear one another's burdens" (Gal 6:2). These words must become flesh; they cannot remain abstract. God asks us to incarnate them and to live them out among a particular group of people. Otherwise they remain comfortably general in scope and have only occasional application.

Home churching enables us to come to know, love, and serve a manageable group of people who will come to know, love, and serve us as well. In such a group we can gradually let down the masks we wear in public and begin to share our weaknesses, doubts, and fears as well as our strengths, certainties, and abilities. Thus we start to overcome the ironic situation of being less open and less honest in church than we are elsewhere. In small home-church groups we learn to give and receive, to teach and understand, to carry others' burdens and receive help with our own, to love and be loved. In such a group we can become more like Christ and assist others to become more like Christ too. In doing so we develop a common Christlike attitude, character, and way of operating. We become integrated into Christ more closely and more firmly.

What is generally missing in larger meetings is any contribution from various small groups within the congregation or among the cluster of house churches. Most members—except for a choir, drama group, or band—do not come to contribute as a group or on behalf of a group or in a way that consciously combines the resources of people from different groups.

As the editor of a denominational magazine observed, it is not just our own lives that are the poorer for the lack of community, but our mission as well.

Is it any wonder that we are feeling so alone? That we feel so frightened to become involved in evangelism or mission? That we feel so challenged by those who are taking seriously God's call to rediscover community?

I guess the encouragement from this issue . . . is to push the boundaries of fear and the unknown and make the discovery that we are not alone. That God has given us not only his Spirit, but each other to walk the journey of discipleship and life with.[3]

Risk of Commitment

Regarding commitment, Gordon Cosby, the well-known pastor of the Church of the Savior in Washington, D.C., asserts,

It says to a specific group of people that I am willing to be with you. I am willing to belong to you, I am willing to be the people of God with you. This is never a tentative commitment that I can withdraw from. It is a commitment to a group of miserable, faltering sinners who make with me a covenant to live in depth until we see in each other the mystery of Christ himself and until in these relationships we come to know ourselves as belonging to the Body of Christ.[4]

Such an involvement is too much for many people. At a meeting to arrange a day conference on the subject of community one of the organizers was overheard to say, "The more I hear about the contents of this conference, the less sure I am that I can afford to come along." She had already begun to feel the challenge of a call to greater commitment to others and had started to ask herself whether she was really prepared for it.

This small incident shows what contradictory creatures we are. We are capable of wanting and not wanting to commit ourselves at the same time.[5] There is nothing surprising about this. When some of us first heard the gospel clearly, we were drawn to it but also hesitant about it, knowing that it was demanding something from us as well as granting something to us. Similarly, some Christians feel both tantalized and threatened by the prospect of becoming involved in a small home-church group or interacting more fully in larger meetings.

This uncertainty about commitment is growing for other reasons. Many people have suffered because someone (possibly a parent, a friend, or a group) betrayed a commitment, and they are hesitant to risk themselves again. This is part of the reason why the younger generation, which desires commitment and is in principle open to it, finds it so hard to actually take the first step. They have seen too much abuse or lack of commitment. They, in particular, need to see its value clearly modeled and need to be wooed rather than pressured into a committed church family.

In a sense we all do well to hesitate before we move in this direction, just as we do well to count the cost before we accept the gospel. Community does not come cheap. But we should not hold back out of a fear that we will become too exposed or that we will lose our individuality. As Art Gish reminds us, genuine community does not involve "a loss of individuality and personal freedom." It is "a living relationship which gives us the freedom and power to be who God wants us to be. . . . It does not mean we are destroyed, but transformed into something new and better. . . . It is not so much the end of the old as the beginning of a new life."[6]

We do not really need to be told this. Many of us have had experiences at a retreat, parish conference, or church camp where we began to open up more of ourselves to others and to God, only to discover that we found more of ourselves and God in the process. It is a sad comment on the quality of our church life that we have to arrange such events in order to deepen the bonds between members. Church ought to be a sort of retreat each week, and that is exactly what home churching involves when it is operating properly, and what a meeting of the whole church can become if loosened from some of its traditional moorings.

Shortage of Time

Much is said and little is done about creating real community because people lack time. We live in a busy world. Few people have much time at their disposal. Those who are most interested in developing a greater experience of community— young marrieds, couples with growing families, and single people—tend to be overcommitted already. In addition to the demands of establishing a home, raising small children, and meeting responsibilities at work, such people often are the very people most involved in wider church activities and other causes and organizations.

Studies indicate that the average American has about thirteen fewer hours each week to spare than a decade and a half ago. Who has time to give to a home-church group or energy to participate in home-church-based gatherings? Over the last few years church marketing consultants have discovered that an increasing number of people in congregations—particularly baby boomers—want more community but are less willing to give time to it. They long for a group in the church to which they can more fully belong, but look for it to happen in the shortest possible time. Unfortunately, community is not built that way.

Even where people make a determined effort to join a home church or to participate more fully in congregational gatherings, they do not have the time or the energy to make it a priority, and it tends to receive their second-best attention. But second-best attention means second-best results. This is one reason why many home churches never really get off the ground. They are not anyone's top priority and therefore never develop their real potential. Even people who do make room for them may give only a couple of hours to them, may skip eating and drinking together, may not always attend, or may meet only monthly or every second week. Having shorter meetings less often may be the only way to begin a home church, but unless there is the possibility of meeting longer and more often, little will come out of it.

The cult of busyness and activism that infects Christians today is one of the greatest barriers to the church becoming what it should be. If Christians were willing to be more with each other and God, they would find that though they do less they achieve more. This is open to us all. It is simply a matter of working out what is important and giving it the priority it deserves.[7]

Increase in Mobility

Another factor that makes it difficult for people to develop a community of committed relationships is our increasing mobility. This affects us in two ways. First, people often work some distance from where they live and commuting time adds to the length of the work day. Commuting increases our tiredness and leaves us less time and energy to spend with family, friends, and church. Second, people frequently relocate in order to take advantage of job opportunities. This is a bigger problem in some areas than others, but it's one that, to some extent, we all have to deal with. In the United States people uproot on average every five years. Three-quarters of the population moves over a ten-year period. Young marrieds in large cities relocate every two years, while singles in hi-tech areas move at least once a year. Even the average stay of someone in pastoral ministry is only two to three years.

This mobility is a major contributor to the breakdown of community. What is the point of building in-depth relationships if you will only be in a place for a short period of time? It takes a major effort of the will to convince yourself that it is worth the necessary time and energy. But what alternative is there? Not to make that commitment leads to life lived with others at a very superficial level or to life lived largely in isolation in the middle of the crowd. Not a very satisfying existence! And that's all it is—an existence. It is not a life. No Christian should be happy with this because it falls short of the whole spirit of the gospel.

Difficult though it is to be part of a community in this mobile world, it is that very mobility that makes belonging to a community all the more necessary. We need to find a home where we can belong in this faceless, impersonal world. For it is in the home church that we can be loved and accepted for who we are. In the cut and thrust of personal relationships we grow to become the people God intended us to be. And we can draw help and encouragement from being with a group of others who are committed to finding, with God's help, creative ways of dealing with the pressures of our modern world.

Focus on Self

Unfortunately, the pressures of time and mobility feed into a cult that is all too prevalent in our society, the cult of individualism. This view of life sees *me* as the one around whom the rest of the world revolves. It is a worldview that is reinforced in a multitude of ways by the mass media. Repeated lies lead us to believe, "I am the most important person in the world." The church has been infected with this disease too. We Christians tend to judge church by what we can get out of it and how well it meets our needs, not by whether it is a group of people with whom we can be mutually committed (whatever that means).

The usual church service tends to encourage this attitude by having us sit in rows facing the front, which does not facilitate relationships. We "worship" God in the presence of others rather than as a group. So, for example, instead of singing songs and hymns to one another, as the NT urges us to do, we sing hymns to the back of the heads in front. A recent trend of people closing their eyes while singing hymns further isolates the individual from the body of Christ.

Even the communion service, which is meant to be the *family* meal of the people of God, is experienced individually, as a collective rather than a corporate activity. Participants move to the front of the church in lines to receive the elements or sit in the pews to receive their wafers and individual glasses of juice or wine. Any smile or communication during this period is seen as a desecration of the sacred moment. We are locked into our own space with God.

Many small groups also foster the cult of individualism, since they tend to develop around felt needs. You attend to receive help with a particular problem or life stage. It is very easy for an attitude to develop that thinks in terms of "the group for me" rather than "me for the group." This is particularly so if the group is, or is perceived as, therapeutic in nature. When the group no longer meets your needs or expectations, you leave.

Christians who are used to thinking in individualistic terms have to undergo a whole reeducation process to be able to function in an appropriate manner within a church in the home. They have to learn to think about what is the most appropriate way of contributing to the church so that the group as a whole and the individuals within it will mature in Christ.

Difficulty in Drawing on Emotion and Imagination

Most people in the West, female as well as male, suffer from imaginative and emotional deprivation. This means that when we meet together in small groups or home churches, our minds are more active than our imaginations and feelings. Yet we cannot understand or help one another properly unless we are emotionally sensitive and capable of getting behind surface conversation. We have to read emotional signals, for these are generally stronger clues to what people are thinking than what they are actually saying. We also need to be able to place ourselves in others' shoes in order to appreciate why they come at things in different ways.

This requires us to use our imaginations; otherwise we will tend to misunderstand what others are trying to communicate. In the West we are so often asked to use our practical reasoning abilities—at school, at work, sometimes even at play—that we have partly lost the capacity to be attuned to others. Women tend to be more sensitive to others than men are, but as their role in the world is transformed, women are losing this capacity. The Bible, on the other hand, reveals to us a God who is passionate and creative. From beginning to end the Bible is full of both emotional appeals and warnings, as well as imaginative symbols, parables, metaphors, and similes. We can only know God and the Bible (and achieve a better understanding of each other) if we are willing to open up our emotions and imaginations and let the Spirit make them soar. Yet too many groups and churches concentrate almost exclusively on our cognitive capacities. That is why critical-thinking Bible studies and sermons dominate so many meetings. They exclude those who are less academic, those who think with the help of images and associations rather than deduction and inference, and those who want to share valid imaginative and emotive experiences (e.g., parables and stories, intuitions and visions). Where emotion and imagination are given little place in a group, there will be only minimal communication and, therefore, minimal community with one another and with God.

A Program Orientation

Much of church life today is program- and performance-driven, so the temptation to apply techniques to small church life is very strong. Even when planning is very loose, it is easy for what is planned to take precedence over what actually needs to happen. The program is more important than the people who make up the group.

The mere act of including children in a home-church group means that nothing will work out quite as it is supposed to. There will be interruptions to the smooth functioning of the group simply because children do not act like grown-ups. They need more time and assistance doing certain things. They are more energetic, make more noise, are less predictable, and therefore (especially to those not used to being around children) more draining. Nothing can ever be guaranteed to run according to plan once children have been included in the group. Yet children's needs are not the only reason to set aside a program. There will be other occasions when, if we are really listening to each other and to the Holy Spirit, we need to set aside what is organized in favor of something else. It may be that a burning issue or need arises that must be addressed immediately. Or it may be that our wonderful ideas about what should happen on any given occasion are subverted by people arriving late, a mishap, an unexpected visitor, or various members of the group wanting to sing or pray longer than usual. For people who are program-oriented, these interruptions can be very frustrating. It is hard to see that the Holy Spirit can work through these events as easily as through planned activities. Part of the solution is coming to understand that it is the Holy Spirit who is in control, not us.

The problem of strict devotion to the program is aggravated by many people's notion of leadership. When most people come to a home church for the first time, they are expecting the leader to ensure that everything happens as it should, that is, that the program will be adhered to. But leadership in a home church is a corporate affair. It is something that emerges as all seek the building up of the body of Christ gathered in that place. This is countercultural thinking. Those used to being dependent on a leader must undergo a major change of perspective in order to realize that what happens in church is as dependent on them as on anyone else. This can be very scary for some people. It means personal risk. No longer can others be blamed for what happens.

Being program-oriented creates difficulties in another respect too. Not only must the program be followed through, but it must be done with a certain amount of finesse. People who are used to judging what happens in church by the quality of presentation are in for a shock in a home church. What is most important in a home church is that all contribute to the best of their ability, not that some "ideal" standard is met. In fact, it may well be that it is precisely when it seems as if everything is falling apart that the Holy Spirit is busy growing people. Ultimately home churching is about developing people, not programs.

Issues of Control

The major structures of a local church often hinder the establishment of home churches within it. Most congregations revolve around the pastor, so if he or she is resistant to the idea of home churches it is very difficult for them to emerge. This is why so many home churches and home-church-based congregations appear independently, unattached to a local church. As David Prior, a pastor who has initiated home groups, says:

> For many pastors and ministers, including bishops and archbishops, such home church life is very threatening. The reasons for this fear are profound and manifold. Clergy have not been trained to operate in this way. Orthodoxy in doctrine is usually seen to be of prime importance, and such home churches look like potential seedbeds of heresy. The human need to control situations for which we are held responsible becomes very urgent. There is, moreover, a crisis of identity and role amongst most clergy today. For many, uncomfortable experience of small groups in the past obstructs openness to the Spirit now. Even when scope is given for this pattern of church life, it is very tempting to keep tight control even while decentralising and delegating. To many clergy, delegation looks and feels like abdication, especially when the actual teething troubles begin.[8]

Yet pastors and other pastoral staff have an enormous amount to gain from the contribution of home churches, especially when they are prepared to belong to such a group themselves. In addition to what they receive in personal support and spiritual vitality, they gain insight into people's needs and longings, as well as with the pressures, dilemmas, and challenges they face. They also become more relaxed with other people and more real, less actors playing a role. A home church will help them discover their actual gifts as opposed to those others expect them to have.

In a congregation with home churches the mutual care that goes on reduces the pastoral work of ministers enormously. Pastors whom we know suggest that their workload decreases by up to 80 or 90 percent! As such groups take hold, they can also replace some congregational organizations, thus reducing the amount of time pastors and their overworked helpers must spend on planning and in committees. Individual home churches are also able to take responsibility for specific aspects of the congregation's life, such as arranging and leading corporate worship, interviewing those seeking baptism or marriage, and visiting the sick and bereaved. There is an additional way in which the issue of control can create difficulty for home churches. Some denominations do not as yet permit the decentralization of certain aspects of public worship into a home setting. The most frequent casualties are the sacraments. In some denominations, baptism and the Lord's Supper cannot be celebrated unless the pastor is present. Given the importance of sacraments for the life of a Christian community, this limits the extent to which such groups can become fully effective.

But even under these restrictions people can begin to meet together, include an agape meal regularly in their gatherings, and welcome children into their life and activities. This enables them to go a long way toward becoming a home church in the fullest sense of the term. Some other creative ways of dealing with denominational restrictions are discussed in chapter 8.

SOME FURTHER OBSERVATIONS

Several of the personal testimonies to the value of home churches spoke of the difficulties involved in this way of meeting, and the hindrances to developing home churches that we have just discussed suggest ongoing problems that might arise. Scott Peck speaks for us when he takes issue with those who argue

> that life in community is easier or more comfortable than ordinary existence. It is not. But it is certainly more lively, more intense. The agony is actually greater, but so is the joy. The experience of joy in community, however, is hardly automatic. During times of struggle the majority of members of a true community will not experience joy. Instead, the prevailing mood may be one of anxiety, frustration, or fatigue. Even when the dominant mood is one of joy, a few members, because of individual worries or conflicts, may still be unable to feel a part of the community spirit. Yet the most common emotional response to the spirit of community is the feeling of joy.[9]

So far we have let others speak or talk in a general way about the wider scene. We would like to close this section on an autobiographical note with some specific remarks about the relevance of home churches to changes that are taking place in our society.

A Personal Confession

Why do we belong to a home church ourselves? Despite the risk of repeating some points, we feel that we, the authors, should answer this question. Our answer involves our most basic reasons for writing this book.

We belong to a home church because we find that God is there in a fuller, more real, and more intimate way. This has something to do with the fact that we meet in an ordinary home—or occasionally outdoors. In the familiarity of a home or in the beauty of creation we come to experience God in a closer and more vivid way. It also has something to do with the fact that when we come together we see, feel, and overhear God in the others who are there. As everyone relates to God and to each other—as they talk and sing, laugh and cry, give and receive—God relates to us, shares with us, and gives life to us through them.

Our time together keeps us in touch with the different personal struggles, family responsibilities, work situations, social concerns, cultural pursuits, and specific types of ministry that we're involved in outside the group. These are taken up in conversation and in prayer and scrutinized in the light of biblical teaching, prophetic insight, and Christian experience. In this way many of our strengths and weaknesses, dreams and doubts, encouragements and hurts, hopes and fears are acknowledged, shared, and sifted.

As a result of our meetings, we have gained a clearer insight into what is happening to people and society around us and a stronger desire and ability to do something about this. Other people directly benefit as God works through us outside the group, sometimes in expected ways, sometimes in quite surprising ways. We find there is a definite overflow from our sharing in the group to our sharing with others in need whom we meet from day to day. We don't feel embarrassed to ask some of those we meet to come and join our group because we hope that they too can enter into what we ourselves experience.

We find church by turns provoking and stimulating, disturbing and comforting, demanding and heartening. It's full of variety, as people come with differing backgrounds and beliefs. It's full of change. Every time a new person joins our little community or some new problem and opportunity is worked through, its character alters. It's full of surprises, too, as we discover our own unconscious needs and desires and hear God's unpredictable response to us, either directly through an individual or gradually through the group.

It's the family character of our church that means so much to us. We have gained sisters and brothers, nephews and nieces, grandmothers and grandfathers whom neither of us had in our natural families. As an extended family, we try to be with one another beyond our regular meetings. Because we don't always live close to one another, this isn't always easy. But we do make an effort.

We have our high points and low points, agreements and conflicts, ups and downs. Doesn't any family? Sometimes we disappoint or fail one another. But we Christians often do that to ourselves anyway. The main thing is that we are committed to working through our difficulties with one another, not running away from them. This is just as well, for tensions come out more in our kind of group than in a normal group or congregation, and we are forced to come to terms with our own and others' limitations. Although there is always some pain involved during these growing times, what comes out in the end is always worthwhile. These often turn out to be the growing points in our personal life and church life.

As we grow closer, we are discovering that we can open up to one another our feelings, as well as our ideas. We can give each other a hug or kiss, as well as say we care. We have also discovered that, in the supportive environment our church provides, several of us have been able to take risks for God that otherwise might have daunted us. Or we have been better able to cope with what might have been an overwhelming crisis. We have come to see that the quality of our common life is affecting and changing us more than anything else.

Last, but by no means least, church is generally the social and humorous highlight of the week, especially as we eat and drink together in the Lord's name, delighting in a simple but superb meal, good company, and the presence of God. There we catch a glimpse of what it will be like when we sit down together with Christ in his kingdom. If what we experience week to week is a little foretaste of heaven, then we can hardly wait to get there!

Thus, belonging to a home church is an indispensable part of our Christian life. It is the most vital means of the Spirit's working in our lives. We cannot conceive of living and growing in Christ without belonging to one. This is why we plead so strongly for the development of home churches within existing congregational and denominational frameworks, as well as among unchurched or dechurched people. This is why we urge that home churches become the basic unit of church life. While larger gatherings are also important—and today benefit from an increasingly homelike atmosphere and stronger lay participation—they are still secondary to the fundamental building blocks of corporate Christian life: the home church.

A Cultural Comment

In our discussion we say "home churches" deliberately, not "small groups." The latter have their place but do not encompass all aspects of corporate Christian life and are rarely fundamental to a congregation's life. Establishing home churches is the most effective way of creating a far-reaching family bond between the members, of grounding their gatherings in the realities of everyday life, and of enabling them to exercise their gifts and fulfill their responsibilities.

How realistic is it to insist on home churches as the best type of church? Does it make sense in the light of contemporary social conditions and cultural changes? There can be little doubt that it does. The weakening of family ties, due to increased mobility and marital breakdown, has imposed a great burden on the traditional nuclear family and on single-parent families. In some cases this burden is giving rise to a longing for extended family networks and, for singles especially, semi-communal and cooperative living arrangements. This longing can be seen in many segments of our community.

For instance, the extraordinary growth of twelve-step or recovery groups over the last decade or two—estimates now suggest there are around five hundred thousand in the United States—indicates people's desire to open up about their difficult problems with others who will understand them. The nonprofessional character and leadership of these groups shows that it is possible for ordinary people to support and strengthen each other effectively without expert help.

People in midlife are often rethinking the importance of family as compared with work. This rethinking is sometimes accompanied by a willingness to give church a second chance. These people, members of the so-called baby boomer genera- tion, are looking for a place to belong in the church, for an ex- perience of community, and for the opportunity to participate in a significant way, even if the time they have to give is limited.

The younger generation, the so-called baby busters or gen- eration X, places a high value on friendships, especially on just "hanging out" with their peers over a meal. They are looking for new ways of doing things and are willing to test out new possi- bilities. They are looking for a shared approach to leadership rather than a top-down model.

Surveys by the chief pollster in North America, George Gal- lup Jr., show that ordinary people are increasingly looking for contexts in which they can share their life journeys, including the spiritual dimension. They are also interested in shaping the character and direction of church so that there is more of a team approach to running it.[10]

CONCLUSION

There are many Christians who are longing for what can be found in a home church. There are growing numbers of people within today's churches looking for more than is currently available. Some manage to hold on at the edges of congrega- tional life. Some find a temporary resting place in parachurch activities of one kind or another. Some are too disenchanted with standard church life to stay within it and depend on infor- mal meetings with fellow Christians. What these people have in common is a deep sense of desperation. They ache to be- long to a genuinely compassionate and relevant community. For them this is no vague longing for a desirable option. It is a life-and-death matter, a case of spiritual integrity and survival. These are people who have passed, or are just about to pass, the point of no return in their church life. Those who have reached this point include pastors and other church leaders.

For the sake of the vitality of the church as a whole, for the sake of those who are feeling marginal in it, and with a view to those most open to the gospel, we need to rediscover that *small is beautiful* and then restructure congregational life accordingly. The conditions are ripe for rejuvenating the church through home churches. It's time we rose to the opportunity.

NOTES

1. J. Vanier, *Community and Growth* (New York: Paulist, 1979) 18.
2. J. MacMurray, *Conditions of Freedom* (London: Faber, 1968) 50.
3. D. Nash, *Downstream* (December 1993) 6.
4. G. Cosby, quoted in E. O'Connor, *Journey Inward, Journey Outward* (New York: Harper & Row, 1968) 24.
5. On this phenomenon see further E. Dayton, *Whatever Happened to Commitment?* (Grand Rapids: Zondervan, 1984) esp. 177–218.
6. A. Gish, *Living in Christian Community* (Scottdale, Pa.: Herald, 1979) 52.
7. For a fuller discussion of this theme see R. Banks, *The Tyranny of Time* (Downers Grove: InterVarsity, 1984).
8. Prior, *The Church in the Home*, 25.
9. M. S. Peck, *The Different Drum: Community Making and Peace* (New York: Simon & Schuster, 1987) 105.
10. See the Gallup Poll Index, *Survey of the Unchurched American* (Princeton: AIPO, 1978, updated in 1988).

5

FIRST STEPS

How Home Churches Come into Being

How can home churches *come into being?* Notice that we have not asked, How can we *start* a home church? The second formulation places the emphasis on us and what we can do, not on the role of the Spirit. Yet any church—small or large—should spring primarily from God's initiative, not ours. Unless God wills it, we should not start it. So the basic question anyone must ask is, Does God want a home church to happen? It is not enough that people need it. It is not enough that people are asking for it. Is there a core group with a common vision? Are there the gifts to sustain it? Is now the time to begin? Praying, having wisdom, and listening for God's response are crucial prerequisites to answering these questions.

DIFFERENT TYPES OF SMALL GROUPS COMPARED TO A HOME CHURCH

A home church and the variety of small groups that are currently a part of many traditional churches are not the same thing. Granted, it is not unusual for home churches to grow out of small groups, and there can be some overlap in what the home church and a particular small group do. For many people, small groups are the closest thing to a home church that they have ever experienced, which may explain some of the confusion about the distinctiveness of the home church. Nonetheless, there remains a substantial difference between a home church and the various types of small groups. These differences will be examined in the following discussion.

Small groups came into churches in a big way in the sixties. Before that subgroups within the congregation mainly met in Sunday school classes. Other Bible studies, prayer meetings, and mission groups—like larger youth, women's and men's groups—also met on church premises. Small groups that met in homes were suspected of being inwardly centered, cliquish, and prone to going off the rails. Beginning in the sixties, local churches decentralized many of their meetings into people's houses or apartments. Home Bible studies and home fellowship groups multiplied. New kinds of groups also appeared, for example, support groups, cell groups, charismatic groups, discipleship groups, renewal groups, and care groups, as well as family clusters and task forces. Most recently, even in denominations that have a particular attachment to the Sunday school concept, more people are now preferring small groups. These small groups are of many kinds: some focus on prayer and praise (kinship groups), some on enriching members' lives through meditation and testimony (renovaré groups), some on people holding each other accountable for their obedience to God (covenant groups), and some for helping each other deal with various addictions (recovery groups).

Small groups have altered the landscape of churches in the West. In North America more than 20 percent of the population belongs to a small group attached to a church and almost 15 percent attend a community small group such as Alcoholics Anonymous, Weightwatchers, a single parent group, or a group for people dealing with domestic violence. These groups are lay led and highly participatory. They have brought new life and vitality to churches and individuals. An interesting survey of vital churches in Australia found that, while reasons for this vitality varied from place to place, the only common denominator was an effective small group life. The well-known sociologist Robert Wuthnow conducted another survey, the most exhaustive investigation of church-based small groups so far, that describes the strengths of these groups and the "quiet revolution" they have effected. Their strengths include providing a place to belong, developing a closer relationship with God, establishing a stronger link between and care for members, offering greater opportunity for participation, sustaining more engaged study of the Bible, and administering more effective services to needy groups.[1]

Small groups are valuable and certainly have their place. But they are not the same as home churches. The clearest way to explain the differences between them is through diagrams. Small groups fall mainly into three categories. We may describe them as "interest groups," "action groups," and "support groups." In a fourth category, "accountability groups" combine certain elements of these three groups and fall between them and a home church or basic Christian community. A fifth group, cell groups forming part of a "cell group church," comes closest to what we are presenting, but differs from it in various ways. It is in our discussion of the sixth group, "home churches," that we describe the optimum arrangement.

Interest Groups

The first kind of group draws people together around a common interest that they wish to engage in for their own benefit. It can be represented in the following way:

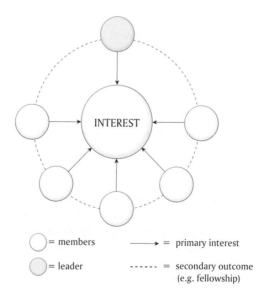

Members of a group gather primarily to concentrate on a particular interest with God's help. In North American churches this is most often a Bible study, but people could also come together to discuss some other book, to work through the pastor's materials, to follow some discipleship format, to sing hymns together, or to engage in meditative exercises. While they do build some community, they do not meet primarily for this purpose. Most groups are composed of adults who are about the same age or who are in similar circumstances, for example, marrieds, singles, young people. Generally they have an appointed leader who has the main responsibility for organizing what happens. These groups are seen as secondary to corporate worship. They do not have a sacramental dimension and are usually regarded as an optional extra.

Action Groups

The second type of group brings people together around a common activity that they wish to pursue for the benefit of others. It can be represented in the following way:

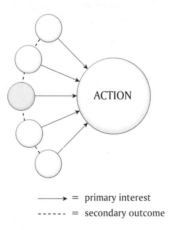

⟶ = primary interest
------ = secondary outcome

The various members of this group gather primarily to concentrate on undertaking some activity for God's sake that will benefit others, either inside or outside the church. The group's activities may include pastoral care, evangelism, social action, music ministry, or compassionate assistance. While those who take part often build up some measure of community, this is not the group's main purpose. Such groups generally exclude children, although children could make up a group of their own. These groups also have a leader or small group of leaders. They are a consequence of corporate worship and are highly important, but they are secondary to the corporate worship of the congregation.

Support Groups

In the third type of group people gather out of a common desire to help each other in various ways. It can be represented in the following way:

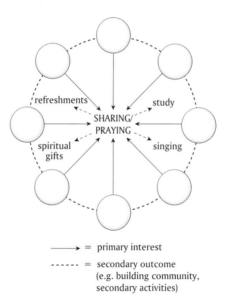

The group members come together primarily to concentrate on fellowshiping with each other in God's presence. Individuals take an interest in each other and share and pray about what is happening in their lives. Sometimes these groups focus on a particular need such as marital breakdown, parenting, abusive relationships, addiction, or vocational issues. More than in the interest and action groups, the interaction in support groups builds up a real community between the members. Development of community is sometimes aided by the lack of a definite leader or by the rotation of leadership among group members.

These groups differ from home churches in that the main focus of the group is meeting needs rather than creating a small, continuing community of God's people that seeks to discern and live out God's kingdom values in all areas of members' lives. In a recovery or support group a person who reaches a certain point of growth may feel free to leave it. A person whose needs are not being met will often go in search of a different group. Some members may regard a support group as more helpful than corporate worship, and the group may have the Lord's Supper together occasionally, but group members do not regard what they do as being on the same level as corporate worship. As with the other kinds of small groups, children are not usually in evidence, except perhaps playing in the background.

Accountability Groups

A fourth kind of group brings people into a strong but limited commitment in God's name to each other. It can be represented in the following way:

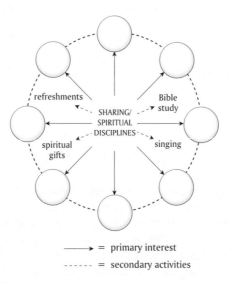

refreshments

Bible study

SHARING/
SPIRITUAL
DISCIPLINES

spiritual gifts

singing

⟶ = primary interest

----- = secondary activities

The members of this small group go beyond being generally supportive of one another to making themselves accountable for and responsible to each other. This commitment may have a distinct focus, for example, discussing the way they lived out their discipleship during the preceding week, engaging in certain spiritual exercises, or helping each other discern their vocation. These groups include study of Scripture, prayer and meditation, and sometimes singing and communal worship. Members would see their time together as complementing what they do in church rather than as having the nature of church. They do not share the Lord's Supper as a group. Children are absent.

Cell Churches

A fifth group differs from the others in defining itself partly as a small church. It can be represented in the following way:

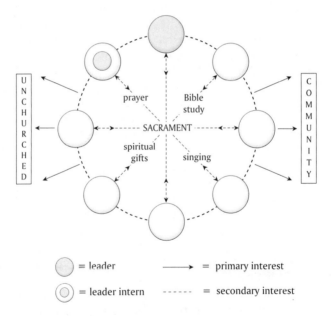

Influenced by the practice of the early Christians, cell group churches organize members into home cells and stress the role of every believer in these meetings. These groups encourage members to build up one another's faith and love, and often share a common meal in the Lord's name. In all these respects they are similar to home churches.

But there are significant differences between this model and the one we are advocating.[2] First, the cell-church model interprets the structure of the early church too much in terms of an organizational grid that reflects a twentieth-century managerial mind-set. Although leadership is described as nonspecialist and nonhierarchical, each group has a specified leader, every cluster of five home churches has a higher leader, and a congregation of twenty-five groups or more has a still higher leader or pastor. Though the language of servant leadership is used, all positions of responsibility are described as "offices." In contrast to the "program based design" of most congregations, which is built up in yet another managerial fashion, around a hierarchy of specialists, committees, and organizations, the cell group church describes itself as a "people based design."

While to some extent we all tend to read our own ideas and frameworks into the biblical accounts, the precise numbers and organizational grid attached to this reconstruction does this in an observable, somewhat managerial, way. The model moves away from a hierarchical view of leadership, but the focus on the leader and leader intern in the individual cells and on zone leaders who look after a cluster of house churches (plus zone pastors over them, and district pastors over the zone pastors) suggests a vertical chain of authority that is different in character from the early Christian approach, with its emphasis upon more fluid and less status-conscious approaches to leadership. Congregational meetings are too large to operate in a sufficiently interactive way.

Second, there are a number of important functional differences between cell groups and home churches. The former normally meet for around an hour and a half, not three or more hours, and appear more task oriented. Cell churches aim to grow new groups every four months, so they change rapidly and allow little time for deep relationships to build. When there are a sufficient number of cell groups to form a congregational network, people are often redistributed into new groups, further weakening the communal bonds they need to develop. Children and teenagers in cell groups are regarded more as witnesses to what takes place than full participants; in some cases, they may have separate cell groups altogether. Indeed, cell groups can be relatively homogeneous rather than being a microcosm of the whole church. Thus, while there are some similarities between the cell group church and interactive congregations based on home churches, there are also some notable differences.

Home Churches

All these groups have some similarities with a home church. Like members of the first three kinds of groups described above, members of a home church come together to pursue interests, tasks, and needs. Like the accountability groups and cell churches, home churches meet to encourage accountability and outreach. But there are also fundamental differences between these groups and home churches. In a home church there is a much stronger emphasis on becoming a Christian family by building a common life with God and one another over a long period. The home church may be represented in the following way:

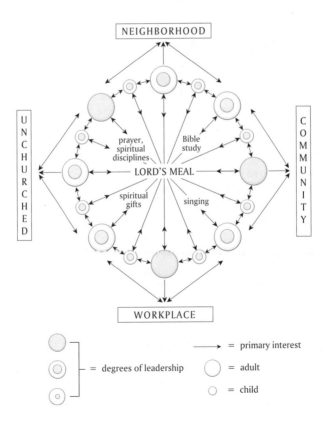

In a home church, the various members gather primarily to concentrate on God and each other, in addition to growing into personal maturity, witnessing more effectively, and supporting and caring for one another. To achieve this they study the Bible, pray, sing hymns, discuss books, and meditate together as an interest group might do. They occasionally plan and undertake some corporate action of witness in the larger congregation or in the wider community, and they certainly help all their members discover and fulfill their particular ministry inside and outside the church. In these ways home churches overlap with action groups. Home church members share personal, familial, and vocational problems or opportunities and extend general support and accountability to one another, just as members of support groups and accountability groups do. But the primary goal of a home church is to develop a quality of common life under God, one in which the attitudes, values, priorities, and commitments of the kingdom of God become communally visible. Children are a vital part of the group and are regarded as full members. Home church members share the sacraments and view them as an indispensable way of building up their common life in God. What they do is as much church as the meeting of the large (home-church-based) congregation and is of equal importance with it. In fact, generally the home church meetings occur more frequently than the large group meetings, even in some denominational churches that contain home churches within them.

In identifying the differences between other kinds of small groups and home churches, we do not wish to give the impression that we regard the former as lacking value. Each type of group makes its own contribution. At times we should meet around a common interest or action, gather with others to provide support or create accountability, or, when engaged in a larger exercise in mission, be in a cell-group structure. But belonging to a home church provides the greatest possible experience of community on an intimate level.

PREREQUISITES FOR BEGINNING A HOME CHURCH

How can we be confident that starting a home church has God's blessing? There are several crucial prerequisites.

A Solid Foundation

Over the years too many home churches have failed, because they were not built on a proper foundation. Any individual who decides to start a home church simply on his or her own initiative has taken a risky step. First, there should be conferences with other interested people to confirm God's leading. While God may encourage an individual to initiate discussion and prayer about this matter, it is not until others have corroborated God's initial leading that anything definite should get under way.

Let us give an example out of our own experience. On returning to a particular city after a time away, we wondered whether God was leading us to join an existing home church or to begin a new one. After talking over the matter between ourselves for some time, we were fairly confident that we should begin a new group. Although we had come to this conclusion jointly, we knew that we ought to test it on other interested people, primarily by sharing our hopes for the group and seeing if we could come to a common mind under God.

Several weeks passed before all the people involved decided that it seemed good to us and to the Holy Spirit to form a church. You might say that we were initially involved in a kind of "dating" exercise, trying to discern whether God was supporting our developing relationship enough that we should declare our intentions and start a new Christian family.

Sometimes it takes longer than a few weeks to do this; once when we helped another group—many of whom were strangers to one another—to discover whether God was calling them to begin a home church, the inquiry took about four months. Three of the original number decided that they were not ready to commit themselves to the enterprise. If this group had regarded itself as a church from the beginning, the departure of those three could have disrupted the venture seriously.

If uncertainties about starting a home church linger, other meeting options remain open. For example, if there are insufficient people and gifts to commence a home church, a few may agree to meet regularly for mutual support until God adds to their number and provides a wider range of gifts. Sometimes when people discuss more fully what they are seeking, they discover that they are really looking for a more relational Bible study or a Christian therapy group.

Even the quest for deeper fellowship is not sufficient reason for beginning a home church. Such a quest can still bring people together to meet a particular need but not to develop a communal Christian *life*. People coming to find fellowship are looking at the group as a means to an end—experiencing fellowship—rather than as an end in itself—becoming a Christian family that is based on commitment to one another and to God. If people are seeking primarily fellowship but fail to find it, they may leave the group in search of better fellowship elsewhere. It's not their Christian brothers and sisters they are primarily interested in, but fellowship for themselves.

This is not to say that home churches cannot begin their life as a particular interest group. In fact, this is not an unusual development. Those who came together may have done so originally to study the Bible, to pray together, or to support one another. But over a period of time their involvement with one another deepens, and they realize that they wish to go beyond study and actually "church together." With much prayer and discussion the group evolves into a home church.

A Basic Commitment

Not all current and future members of the group must have this depth of commitment; the home church is able to include, even invite, others who may come to it initially to fulfill a certain interest or to meet a particular need.

But there does need to be a core group that maintains a commitment to developing a common life. Scott Peck recognizes this commitment as an indispensable or "an across-the-board rule of community."[3] This core group may consist of only three or four people who make such a commitment to God and to one another. A group that lacks committed core members generally deteriorates into a support or therapy group, or it becomes superficial in character and irregular in meeting. It is helpful if this commitment is expressed tangibly. A few groups covenant with one another by means of a written statement. Two examples follow.

Cedar Community Mennonite Church

As members of the Cedar Community Mennonite Church, we believe the following understandings are ways to express in our lives the lordship of Jesus.

1. Active participation in worship services and "Life Together" meetings is expected.

2. Close personal relationships with fellow believers are essential to the Christian life. We encourage participation in a small group of the church.

3. We see ourselves as mutually accountable to both give and receive counsel in the body of believers (Matt. 18:15–20).

4. We commit ourselves to be peacemakers and reconcilers in human conflict.

5. As caretakers of God-given gifts and material goods, we commit these resources for use in ways consistent with our faith.

6. We recognize children as gifts of God, cherished individuals with rights and privileges in our congregational life. We seek to model the way of faith in Jesus so that children may freely choose to follow him.

7. We welcome as associate members those persons who have their primary commitment in another congregation, but still want to identify with and support CCMC. Expectations for the associate membership will be worked out in writing with each associate member.

8. Our covenant commitment, both confession of faith and understandings, will be reviewed and renewed annually.

Covenant of Mennonite Church of the Servant, Wichita, Kansas

We commit ourselves to following Jesus Christ,
through whom God has made friends with the world
and in whom we continue the work of reconciliation.
We commit ourselves to each other, the church,
to love our brothers and sisters in God's family,
sharing our decisions, our talents, our time, and our possessions.
We commit ourselves to caring for the world,
to bringing good news to the poor and setting free the oppressed,
to proclaiming Jesus the Servant as Liberator and Lord.
We commit ourselves to the way of the cross,
to a life of simplicity and prayer;
in this is our joy, peace, and new life.[4]

Other home churches have a statement that merely indicates the general spirit of their relationship. Still others during their meeting say a sentence or pray a short prayer that expresses their commitment to one another in a meaningful ritual. Each home church needs to work out what is most appropriate for itself.

As long as this basic commitment is present, others can come into a group with all sorts of reservations about how much they wish to be involved. Such people should be accepted as they are and should be allowed to grow into a deeper level of commitment. Even the core group will be characterized by a high quality of voluntary involvement, not devotion to meeting a demand or standard.

An analogy may be helpful here, though it may not appeal to everyone and it has its limitations. The commitment that develops within a core group is in some respects similar to that which exists in a marriage. The quality of involvement between a husband and a wife provides the stable basis on which a family can be built. As children become part of the family (or as outsiders are welcomed into it), they are not required to make the same kind of commitment. But they do have the benefit of seeing a model of commitment that they can voluntarily emulate as they grow up and start their own families. Just as a commitment between a man and woman develops from friendship to engagement to marriage and then deepens within marriage itself, so the commitment among the members of the core group must develop over time. It is often unspoken or low-key at the beginning and slowly develops and deepens into something quite rich. The analogy between core group commitment and marriage can be pressed too far, but it does highlight an important aspect of home church formation.

A Framework of Belief

Some agreement as to the general belief framework of a home church is also necessary. A group that begins under the auspices of a mainline or evangelical congregation will already have a denominational tradition of some kind. Some nondenominational groups also start with people who have a common allegiance to a certain form of Christianity, such as evangelical or charismatic. This does not mean that people in such a home church are not permitted to reexamine such a tradition or allegiance. This is often a healthy exercise, and some people join a home church partly to find out what is authentically Christian about the tradition or movement to which they belong.

But there does need to be an agreement (expressed or unexpressed) that the group is going to operate within certain basic, yet not restrictive or detailed, Christian convictions. This is what the well-known apologist C. S. Lewis called "mere Christianity."[5] These basic convictions should not be the lowest common denominator of beliefs but a recognition of Christian essentials. What are these? They are the basic Christian distinctives that have been maintained by most believers throughout the centuries. These convictions include:

- the personhood and creativity of God,

- the divinity and saving work of Christ,

- the presence and guidance of the Holy Spirit,

- the communal and missionary nature of the church,

- the certainty of future judgment and transformation.

The Bible clearly provides the foundation and norm for such convictions, however people may define its inspiration and character.

If a significant number of group members radically question these convictions, it may be better to begin as a discussion group rather than as a home church. But it is OK for members to review such convictions with a view to refining them or to understanding them better. That happens quite frequently in a home church as part of a general search for authentic Christian belief and lifestyle. A home church can certainly include one or two people who are not Christians or have lapsed from their faith. But such people should be prepared to accept that most of the group will want to continue operating within the framework we have mentioned. The belief system must be strong enough for a home church to worship God together; its function is not to be an apologetics group. On other matters agreement is not necessary at the outset, nor will it come in the long term, even within the core group. We will examine this issue more fully later.

A Pastoral Center

What we like to call a pastoral center should gradually develop among the group of original core members or perhaps from others who join the group. This pastoral center consists of a few people who show evidence of exerting a presence that enables the group to reach its full potential. We are not talking about leaders or elders as those words are normally understood; what we have in mind is the Bible's meaning of these terms.

Groups differ as to how they identify the kinds of people we have described. Some, following the example of parts of the NT, regard them as elders, which in biblical usage referred mostly to older, wiser, life-experienced people in a group. The home church may recognize them by laying hands on them in some official way and reviewing their contribution every year or so. Others, noting that the NT sometimes uses other words to describe what such people do, may simply talk about them in terms of what they do, for example, as the group's main "visionaries," and may simply pray for them regularly as a mark of appreciation and encouragement. This is our own practice. Since the word "leader" is so popular today, some groups prefer it to refer to these core people. The danger with this word is that it tends to give permission to everyone else to settle back and become followers. Since the word "elder" is now used to describe a position rather than a set of personal qualities, there is also a danger in using it. Words like "leadership" and "eldership" are safe to use only when it is clear that they refer to several people in a group, not just one and that they do not refer to people who run the group, but to those who primarily draw out from others their growing capacity to encourage it and mature it in this or that way.

All this is very different from a pastor in a congregation or a church planter appointing one person (usually a man) to be the home church's leader from the beginning. Generally this leader is appointed on the basis of his organizational or teaching skills, not necessarily his capacity for pastoring others. It is far better for a pastor or a church planter to give the group a simple shared process for getting under way—similar to what follows in the next section—and then wait and see who emerges from the actual dynamics of the group as possessing the desired qualities.

So far we have identified four factors that are an integral part of a new home church: a solid foundation, a basic commitment, a framework of belief, and a pastoral center. If these are lacking altogether, it is very difficult for a group to weld itself into a home church. If they are even embryonically present, a group can work toward becoming a home church in the fullest sense of the word. This may only happen gradually; the group should take plenty of time and not rush ahead of its actual capacities.

If, over a period of time, these fundamental factors do not emerge, the group will need to settle for something less or disband itself and pray for something else to emerge. The group must have a realistic attitude to home church formation—one that recognizes the creative work of the Spirit in a group but does not abstract this from the concrete realities present in the group. Jesus' words about the importance of "counting the cost" before embarking on an important enterprise (Luke 14:20–30) or Paul's words about a "sober estimate" of what can be contributed and achieved (Rom 12:3) lay down a general principle that is relevant here.

THREE GUIDELINES FOR DEVELOPING A HOME CHURCH

Once people have come together as a group, what approach will give them the best chance of success? At this point, talk about group dynamics, discussion methods, leadership styles, and interpersonal techniques tends to rear its head. While these issues may provide some secondary contributions, they are not the place to begin. They tend to introduce a self-conscious, even artificial, note into gatherings. Anyone who feels that these issues are important should quietly embody them in his or her participation in the group, discerning as the group develops whether or not it will be enhanced by discussing such dynamics, methods, styles, and techniques more directly.

A home church is different from other types of groups. Its model is less that of a cell or an organization and more that of a family. This affects its goals, duration, size, and the nature of its leadership. Also, while the dynamics, methods, styles, and techniques of small group life echo some of the ways the Spirit works in the church, they do not exhaust them. The role of forgiveness, the centrality of love, and the presence of spiritual gifts add a dimension that is not always present in more formulaic approaches. But certain factors are crucial to the development of a home church.

Focus on Getting to Know Each Other

The less people know one another, the more necessary it is for them to lower the barriers between them. Even people who have rubbed shoulders in a congregation for years may have had only limited contact with each other. Most people come into a group with their guards up and their best foot forward. As Jean Vanier says, "When people join a community, they always present a certain image of themselves."[6] It takes time for them to feel at ease and allow their masks to drop. This process of breaking down the barriers can be assisted in certain ways.

Keep the Group Small for a Time

There is much to be said for beginning a home church with only a handful of people. While initially this limits the range of gifts within the group and restricts the effectiveness of certain group activities, like singing, it has some basic advantages. In a group that is smaller, people are more likely to open up to one another and to develop stronger relationships. Most people find this hard to do in a large group.

If twelve or more people are interested in beginning a home church, it may be better to start two smaller groups rather than one large group. We once formed part of a group that began with only five adults, a teenager, a child in elementary school, and a baby. We felt it was important to establish our relationship with each other and with God firmly *before* the group increased in size. Since we knew we would find it impossible to say no to anyone who wanted to join us, we asked God to hold people off until we were ready to receive them. This was rather like a young married couple deciding not to have children immediately after their marriage so that they could lay a proper foundation for their life together. Several months later, when we felt ready to widen the group, a few people began to ask if they could join.

Don't Rush into "Religious" Activities

Where people do not know each other very well, they need to learn something about each other before plunging into prayer, Bible study, and exercise of charismatic gifts. It's not that these are out of place. Of course they are not. But too extensive a concentration on them at the outset can sometimes get in the way of developing a profound group spiritual life.

One way of getting to know each other is to encourage one household (whether a family or a single person) each week to tell something about their life story up to their joining the home church. The first time we did this in a group we saw how it helped people understand where others were coming from, how it threw light on why they held certain beliefs or used a particular kind of religious language, and how it enabled all to begin to see what others' particular needs and contributions might be. The process gave us some clues for our first studies and helped people to begin to pray for one another more practically.

If the group had started with more traditional activities, some real concerns and situations may not have emerged, at least not for a long time, and (given the spiritual games Christians often play) the real nature of each person's relationship with God may have been masked. It would have taken longer to develop genuine openness and depth in the meetings. As so often is the case, the most direct route is not always the most effective.

Emphasize Activities That Bond Members Together

Strange as it may seem, we have found no better way for people to bond than by simply spending time together, or "hanging out." It may be that "hanging out" is a more appropriate modern translation of *ecclesia,* which means "gathering," than our word "church." It's very hard for many program-oriented people to see that this is a valuable exercise, not a waste of time. Again and again we have seen this simple strategy work its special magic—in time. This is not an exercise you can hurry. There are two effective means by which a group can facilitate the bonding process.

Make a Meal Central to Your Gatherings

We have seen that the early Christians' common meal was as much a social as a religious event. Indeed, the modern separation of the social from the religious, of fellowship from worship, of love from truth, shows how far we have strayed from a biblical perspective. The "Lord's Meal" is not only an occasion when we thank God that Christ gave himself utterly for and to us. It is also an opportunity for us in like spirit to give ourselves fully to another. The following excerpt describes the special role a meal can play in developing relationships:

> To our utter amazement, some old friends of ours (two couples and a twelve-year-old girl), who had steadfastly groaned at the idea of housechurch, have decided to try it during advent. We all went out to lunch one day and sat around a big round table. At the beginning, everyone was moaning about what a problem finding a good church is—by the end of lunch, people were talking about when a homechurch might meet. I guess one should never underestimate the power of a big round table!

Sharing a meal together, especially around a table, naturally opens us to one another. We talk about the things that have been happening to us, how we are feeling and coping, what is coming up, and how we are preparing ourselves for it. If a group tries to do this by formally setting aside a time for "sharing," many remain silent or find it difficult to say exactly what they want. A meal is a more conducive setting for such interchange, and there is nothing that is better designed to encourage it. That is why prayer for one another is always easier after a meal than before it. Quite apart from the content of what people talk about as they eat together, there is something about the character of a meal that binds people together in a unique way. It just happens! Presumably this is part of the reason why Jesus made a meal central to the gathering of church and gave it such a profound sacramental significance.

Be Willing to Ask Questions and Volunteer Difficulties

One reason people keep so much to themselves is that they do not have the skills or the confidence to open up to others. But they can open up to someone who asks them the right questions. Certain people have this gift. Others can acquire it, since it develops with practice. All it takes is a genuine interest in others. It is not only adults who need to have questions asked of them, but children as well. Between songs and during the meal, members of a group can ask the younger ones what news they have to share, what interests they have, and what they are thinking about at the moment.

The most precious contribution any of us can give to bonding a church is to share about some difficulty we are experiencing. This is a special gift. It takes courage. It is risky. You can never be sure how others will respond or if they will respond at all. We may do this in conversation with the group or in prayer with God. However it happens, it encourages and frees others to do the same and provides an opportunity for the body to work together for the sake of one of its members.

Open Up Room for Freedom and Flexibility

There are a couple of methods that are effective in bringing about freedom and flexibility.

Give Play a Regular Part in Group Life

Children are particularly important in helping us reintroduce play into our lives. They can help us recapture some of the unself-conscious and unreserved zest for life that God delights in. Indoor games and outdoor games, quiet games and noisy games, silly games and clever games, games for young children and games for older ones—all these have their place at some time or other in a group's life.

Now and then a group can hold a "game day" when both adult and children's games—noncompetitive, competitive, and sporting—can be enjoyed. In our own group we like to stage a biblical play, in which we act out a favorite Bible story. We always learn something new and have great fun as well. We have also found that playing games with other adults sometimes brings out sides to them that we never saw before! Scott Peck comments, "I'm not sure there can be a community that is truly successful when its members do not laugh and celebrate with frequent gusto."[7]

Encourage Nonverbal Communication in the Group

There are a number of possibilities here. Acquire simple instruments that children and adults can play as they sing (for example, percussive instruments). Others will enjoy clapping or moving to the music in ways they find comfortable. There is room for such "right brain" activities as drawing, painting, and making things with our hands, all of which bring out sides of us that might not appear otherwise. We can also join in a simple dance. Music and praise are intended for our whole bodies, not just our lips. Other nonverbal ways of relating will develop slowly, beginning with shaking hands at the door and possibly developing to greeting and farewelling one another with a hug or kiss, from praying for one another at a safe distance across the room to laying a hand on someone's shoulder or head, from reserved expressions of pleasure or sadness to public gestures of delight or sorrow when God or others touch us in an unexpectedly personal way.

There is one very practical way in which a new home church can begin to implement these three guidelines for developing a home church: a retreat. The earlier in its life a group can go away for a weekend together, preferably a long weekend, the better. But do not structure such a weekend as a house party or as a conference. Supply opportunity to worship and learn together, but keep the main focus on getting to know one another better, hearing each other's hopes and fears about becoming part of a home church, joining in games with the children, and appreciating God's world. More primitive conditions on such a weekend are better; people tend to get thrown together and to reveal some of their underlying attitudes and feelings. It helps us begin to see others as they are, rather than as they pretend to be or even as we would like them to be.

VITAL PRINCIPLES TO KEEP IN MIND

In our experience of getting home churches under way, we have discovered three principles that can help a group avoid potential mistakes and can enhance its potential to succeed. These principles stem from practical experience, but more importantly, they are rooted in the trinitarian nature of

God. They reflect the providential activity of the Father, the saving work of the Son, and the transforming operation of the Spirit in having something quite concrete to offer our attempts to develop Christian community. This reminds us of the fact that starting a home church, as well as maintaining it, is a divine, not human, process. Failure to recognize these practical theological principles weakens any attempt to start and develop home churches.

The Providential Principle: Build on What the Father Is Already Doing

The first principle is this: In forming home churches we must take into account those networks of personal relationships that God has already established between people. These networks are part of God's providential arrangement of people's lives. It does not matter whether they are based on geographical proximity, mutual interests, or spiritual affinity. What matters is that we recognize and use them. Building home churches on preexisting relationships strengthens the possibility of their success. Always work with what God has put together.

Do not attempt to create groups in an artificial, top-down manner, consulting maps, making lists of names, and flinging together people who hardly know one another. In these days one's neighborhood and one's neighbors are defined more by the telephone, car, and work situation than by locality. More localized groups tend to develop in time through growing contacts between people in home churches, not through force feeding at the beginning.

There is a corollary to this. God also works providentially in the lives of individuals, preparing them throughout the course of everyday life to make particular kinds of contributions in a home church. This complements the additional contributions that gifts of the Spirit enable people to make. For example, the list of qualifications in 1 Tim 3 for bishops (the first-century equivalent of those in the pastoral center of a home church) includes managing a household. Managing a household involved running a business and raising a family, both of which help train people for the kinds of contributions nurturing a house church requires.

All too often this kind of divinely-arranged training of people through the circumstances of everyday life is overlooked in favor of theological education, church leadership skills, or charismatic credentials. While people with these latter attributes may become good teachers, organizers, or prophets, there is no guarantee whatsoever that they have the relational skills and accumulated wisdom necessary to function in an effective and community-building way.

The Resurrection Principle: Follow Christ by Dying to Self

The second principle is this: As with Christ, in the church it is only through death that new life comes; renewal only takes place if we are willing to allow some of our attitudes and structures to undergo some radical changes. It is illusory to think that a new form of church life can spring up without our being open to changes in our long-standing methods of operating at the individual and church, that is, personal and structural, levels. Unless we are willing to question many of our previous views and procedures and allow them to die when they get in the way of spiritual growth in the group, a new home church will soon suffocate. The home church must not be allowed to become a place for exchanging set views and prejudices. Rather, it should always be a place where members genuinely search for the mind of God. We must continually test our beliefs and practices by what we learn in the Bible as we study it together in a common dependence on the Spirit.

There is another side to this. For home churches to take deep root and flourish in a congregation, some existing organizations may need to die. Otherwise key people in the church may not feel free to become involved or, if involved, may have too little time and energy to give to their home church. The home churches themselves may be overwhelmed by the plethora of organizations in the church if they are never given the centrality they deserve.

While allowing some organizations in the church to die is often painful, ultimately it is gain. The aims of some groups or programs in the local church are often better fulfilled through home church meetings. What dies comes back in a different form with renewed life. Entering a home church is like receiving the gospel in that neither is simply an extra something added on to the rest of a person's life. Both mean giving up part of what we have been doing and restructuring our lives on a fresh basis.

The Organic Principle: Discern the Spirit's Leading and Dynamics

The third principle is this: It is only as small churches grow from the seeds and the watering of the Holy Spirit that they will prosper and fulfill their proper role. All too often the development of home churches is based on managerial thinking and the application of techniques. While a certain amount of organizing is involved in growing a home church, and certain ways of doing things in the group are more productive than others, there is still a difference between sensing the ways of the Spirit in such matters and, on the other hand, relying on leadership manuals and understandings of group dynamics that have been derived largely from secular organizations.

Home churching, like raising a family or developing a friendship, is an organic rather than a contrived affair. Too great a reliance on written manuals and too self-conscious an employment of techniques for developing relationships makes the process too formal and too artificial. This hinders the way a group normally develops relationships and decides how to run its affairs. It is not that leadership manuals and studies of group dynamics have nothing to offer; it is just that their insights should be drawn in to illumine, not direct, what is happening.

Home churches must have room to grow at their own pace, in their own way, and basically out of their own resources. Those who have authority in a congregation (or have a tendency to exercise control in groups) may be tempted to step in and shape activities according to their own agenda, not the Spirit's. Too often home churches yield to this temptation by appointing a leader to run things, drawing up a schedule for the meetings, prescribing the content of studies, and so forth, all of which hamstring a group. The home church needs to be free to sense the mind of the Spirit on these issues, rather than allowing an individual to make decisions and impose procedures.

CONCLUSION

These guidelines to how home churches best come into being may seem too down to earth—too horizontal or relational in character and lacking the more vertical or spiritual dimension. But study of the Scriptures, prayer, and exercise of God's gifts have their full effect only when they spring from soil that has been well prepared through group members getting to know one another, bonding together, and opening up to God's freedom and flexibility. They accomplish the most when they are brought into contact with our innermost selves, are undertaken within an open, discerning, and loving community, and involve our imagination, feelings, and bodies as well as our minds and wills.

All this means that home church meetings should not be programmed or rushed. If they are too planned, there is little room for people to share deeper things or for the Spirit to lead the group in the most fruitful direction. If they are too brief, there is insufficient time for all that needs to happen to develop the fullest communal life. The activities of a home church should take place in an orderly way, but this does not necessitate a fixed order. While home-church meetings should take account of people's other commitments, this does not mean that they should accommodate everything else first. Freedom and form are equally important here. The day and hour of meeting should be convenient and open ended.

While certain patterns of meeting may be followed more often than others, there should always be room for the unexpected to happen. Some groups may have different patterns of meeting from one week to the next, including, for example, a breakfast meeting, a children's day, an evening meal, and a childfree gathering. Most groups find that the pattern of their meeting changes as the group develops.

Change can also typify the time at which meetings are held. Many factors must be considered when choosing a meeting time, including the ages of the children in the group, the number of people coming, members' work schedules or other commitments. Often, the meeting time needs to be renegotiated after the group grows larger or its constituency alters.

The location of a home-church meeting should be appropriate for the number coming, conducive to fellowship with

God and one another, marked by the spirit and gift of hospitality, and suitable for use by the children present. Most groups find that having regular meeting places is a decided advantage. Some groups meet mostly at one home; sometimes they gather in homes by turns, meeting in the same home at the same time each month.

In all these matters—format, time, and place—two basic principles should govern all decisions. Let everything be decided so that everyone can gain the maximum benefit from the meetings. This is the principle of edification. Also, let everything be decided by everyone in the group. This is the principle of consensus. Both principles are clearly seen in Paul's writings and are as relevant today as they were when he advanced them. So long as they are adhered to, however diversely they are applied, all decisions will serve the best interests of the home church.

NOTES

1. See further R. Wuthnow, *Sharing the Journey: Support Groups and America's New Quest for Community* (Princeton, N.J.: Princeton University Press, 1994).

2. On cell churches see principally R. Neighbour Jr. with L. Jenkins, *Where Do We Go From Here? A Guidebook for the Cell Group Church* (Houston: Touch, 1990); and W. Beckham, *The Second Reformation: Reshaping the Church for the 21st Century* (Houston: Touch, 1995). See also, with some differences, the metachurch model outlined by C. George, *Prepare Your Church for the Future* (New York: Revell, 1991).

3. Peck, *The Different Drum*, 159.

4. Both of these covenants are found in Barrett, *Building the House Church*, 38–41.

5. C. S. Lewis, *Mere Christianity* (London: Collins, 1952) 6.

6. Vanier, *Community and Growth*, 30.

7. Peck, *The Different Drum*, 150.

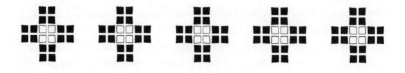

6

EXPERIMENTS IN PROGRESS

*Current Models of Home Churches
and Home-Church-Based Congregations*

In the last chapter we outlined the basic guidelines for starting a home church. The question that often arises at this point is What relationship should an individual home church have to other home churches? Another frequent question is How can congregational gatherings of home churches become more intimate, communal, and participatory? We will attempt to answer these two questions by presenting a range of methods that home churches within a congregation and independent home churches have employed to address them. There is a great deal of versatility in the way the Spirit of God works. Each group of people seeking God about entering or developing a home church should consider these models and discern which one God is leading them to follow. Our own preferred method, based on our particular calling we have from God, is described on pages 139–41 and 150–51, but we have helped churches develop other models as well.

MODELS FOR DEVELOPING HOME CHURCHES

As we survey the general religious scene, we see home churches developing in a variety of ways both inside and outside existing congregations. While we may have a preference for one or two of these over others, all are valid expressions of what God is doing today in renewing community and mission in the church. We will look first at the main forms they take. After that we will look at some alternative possibilities.

Starting a Pilot Home Church within a Traditional Congregation

Out of an Episcopal setting comes the following account of how a home church was begun as an experiment in the life of the congregation.

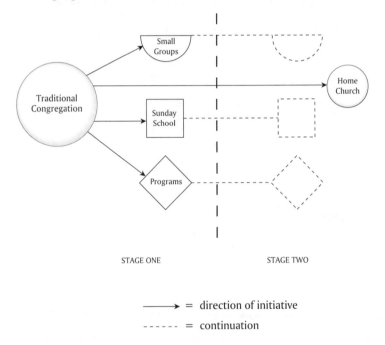

STAGE ONE   STAGE TWO

⟶ = direction of initiative

------ = continuation

Description

My husband and I had been attending a local Episcopal congregation for several months and were desirous of being a part of a smaller, committed group of families within the church. There were a number of small groups in existence, all quite different from one another. We asked to be a part of an independent home church for six months in order to participate in a new model of "church" and to learn some things that we might be able to bring to our local congregation. What we found in this home church was a seriousness of commitment. For the members this group *was* church. The groups in our congregation, in contrast, were far more casual; people came and went as they wished and, except for the core, the group's makeup was constantly changing.

My husband and I were interested in forming a group where people would make a more serious commitment to gathering together. First, my husband shared our desire with the pastor and asked for his blessing and input. The pastor gave us the names of two other families who were also new to the church. We asked these families if they wanted to join us. Six adults and four children ages two and under came to an initial meeting. We thoroughly enjoyed the time, especially as we considered the possibility of sharing our lives with these people. However, one couple called us later in the week to tell us they had decided to attend a congregation closer to home (they were commuting from forty miles away). We were disappointed but knew the decision was a wise one.

For the next two months we continued to meet with the other family. During this time we began writing down the commitments that we wanted to shape the group. We also learned of another family who would be moving to the Los Angeles area and wanted to attend our church. I called them to see if they would be interested in being a part of our home church, and they were. We also invited one more couple from the church who were not involved elsewhere. The process for each couple was the same: several weeks of participation followed by a decision to commit to the group. This allowed for group stability as we took time to know one another and to become more vulnerable in our sharing.

Comment

Developing a pilot home church within a congregation is not easy and may well run into opposition from traditional churchgoers who wrongly perceive it as elitist and inwardly focused. Further complications may arise if the group begins to question some of the basic goals, activities, and structure of the local church. Such a reappraisal led the members of a home church in one congregation to relinquish their positions on the parish council, in the Sunday school, and on other organizations in favor of more novel forms of witness in the suburb around them. This was seen as a betrayal by many people in the congregation. Although the minister had initiated the home churches and belonged to one of them, he found himself pulled increasingly in two opposing directions. But because the home churches produced new life and attracted new people to the congregation, he was prepared to live with this tension.

Transforming a Sunday School Class into Two Home Churches

This story springs out of a Sunday school class in a medium-sized Evangelical Covenant church in Los Angeles that consisted of about twenty-five members, mainly young marrieds, some with children.

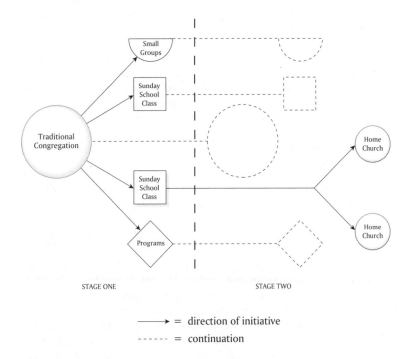

STAGE ONE   STAGE TWO

⟶   = direction of initiative

‑ ‑ ‑ ‑ ‑   = continuation

Description

Our Sunday school class of about twenty-five members had been meeting for some years but was beginning to dissolve. The main problem was that it no longer seemed to meet its members' particular needs. To find a way out of this impasse the class decided to study the theme of community. Over a nine-month period several books were studied, including Dietrich Bonhoeffer's classic text, *Life Together.* The people in the group felt they needed to take some tangible steps in the direction of community but were not sure about the most effective way of doing this. In order to work this out they set aside two blocks of Sundays to invite in people who had practical experience in developing communal groups. One team consisted of the members of an independent home church.

Over the next four Sundays the team led the class for about an hour each week, using a combination of brief presentations, role plays, interviews, storytelling, and visual displays. The presentations referred to Scripture and emphasized the church as a family and the home church origins of the Sunday school class's denomination. There was also time for discussion. On the next-to-last Sunday members of the class were invited to experience home church the following week. Since the class was too large to meet in one home, it was divided into two groups. Parents were encouraged to take their children out of junior Sunday school that day so that they could also take part. The meeting time of the class was extended, allowing the groups to have lunch together and celebrate it as the Lord's Supper. The theme of the meetings was announced so that everyone could reflect on it in preparation.

The team asked the pastor whether this proposal was in order, and he readily approved it. The following Sunday everything went as planned. The two groups met in the homes of members who did not live far from the church, half of the home-church team members going to one and half to the other. Team members were present for support and, if necessary, backup, as the meeting itself was facilitated by people from the Sunday school class. The two groups spent time singing God's praises, sharing and praying, reading a children's story, studying Scripture, and sharing a meal that began with communion. The occasion had some rough edges, but all were encouraged by how well it went. After evaluating the experience and with the pastor's encouragement, the class decided to turn the Sunday school class into two home churches. This method of developing community was designed to encourage people's gifts and meet their needs. All but a few class members opted to move in this direction.

In the two years since, these home churches have grown and two further groups have recently started. The pastoral staff has given support and has referred people to them. Some international students and their children have also joined. The pastor has publicly endorsed the value of what they have done and encouraged others in the church, if they should so desire, to follow the same course. Partly prompted by these home churches, a number of life-support groups have begun in the congregation. Though these do not include a meal or communion, they share some of the same features.

Comment

Given the continuing role of the Sunday school in North American churches, this story points a practical way forward for many congregations. This may be particularly true for African-American churches, where Sunday schools tend to have more than an educational role and often take on some of the characteristics of a communal group. This model applies equally to transforming a Bible study or other kind of small group into a home church. In either case it is essential, as was the case here, to have a core in the class who are committed to moving forward, to take enough time to explore the options together so as to allow as many people as possible to come on board, and to have the endorsement of a sympathetic pastor.

Developing Several Home Churches in a Long-Standing Congregation

Distilling the experience of a number of Mennonite congregations in which home churches developed as part of the normal life of the church, the author Lois Barrett provides the following general guidelines for any group of people who wish to do this.

Description

People in an existing congregation will accept new house churches more easily when they are seen as an answer to a pressing need. The church that says, "Something has got to happen. Too many people are falling between the cracks," has

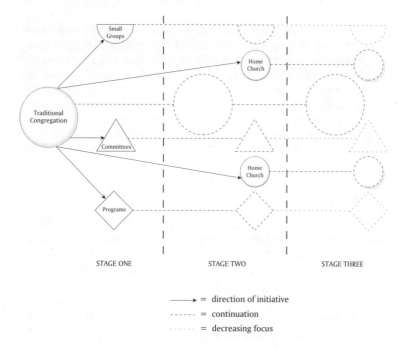

STAGE ONE   STAGE TWO   STAGE THREE

⟶ = direction of initiative

------ = continuation

······ = decreasing focus

a better chance at success of house churches than the congregation in which everything seems to be going smoothly and the house church is seen as an additional program in the church. . . . To begin house churches means a clear change in business as usual. People and churches do not make radical changes except under pressure or pain of some kind. If a congregation is able to bring its pain into the open, talk about its weaknesses, and be open to alternatives for the future, then house churches may be an alternative which can bring healing and new life.

To start house churches in a congregation where none have been is threatening because it implies that what was could have been improved. To those who do not want to deal with problems and pain, house churches seem like an unwanted criticism of the past. . . . But a change need not imply that the former was never good. It may simply mean that new situations demand new responses. We can celebrate the beginnings of our congregation and still be ready to move on to new structures that better serve the current needs.

To be the church to each other in a house church implies a strong commitment in time and emotional energy. If members are to give themselves fully to the business of being a house church, that may mean that the larger church will need to cut back the number of committee meetings and other activities in which people have been involved. The larger church may need to take some activities it has sponsored and turn them over entirely to the house churches, for example, pastoral care. . . . Clarifying what activities will happen in the larger church and what will happen in the house churches can be divided on the basis of what each group does best. Choirs and big musical events happen best in a large group. Discipling people who are struggling with moral issues happens best in a small group.

Decide also on the relationship of house church membership to membership in the larger church. . . . Will all members be encouraged to be part of house churches? Or will house churches be simply accepted or tolerated as an option for those who want them. What will probably work better for the success of house churches is to make them completely voluntary and allow people to choose which house church they want to be part of. But encourage people to join house churches and, in fact, expect that current members and new members will want to be part of house churches because that is where so much of the church life is happening. . . . Don't be afraid to spend time processing the decision to start house churches. Any time you spend now in reaching agreement over house churches will be saved later on when the house churches are actually operating. The person who is now opposed to house churches may be able to view them more favorably when he or she is convinced that you are listening and will take his or her objections seriously. . . . Take your time and give the Spirit time to work in people's hearts.[1]

Comment

The strength of this approach lies in its recognition of the misunderstandings about and resistance to home churches that exist in many congregations. Mostly people do not view them as really being church. They tend to be regarded as optional rather than central and interpreted as a judgment on earlier forms of small group life. Barrett suggests ways that pastors can advocate and complement home churches and notes the changes home churches are likely to bring to the other meetings of the congregation, including larger church services.

Moving a Cell-Group-Based Congregation to a Home-Church-Based Congregation

The following narrative comes from members of an independent church-planting team working among unchurched people in Rhode Island. Their story documents a new congregation's transition from being based on cell groups to being built on home churches.

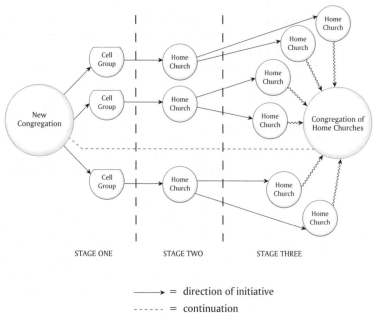

STAGE ONE   STAGE TWO   STAGE THREE

⟶ = direction of initiative

------ = continuation

⌇⌇⌇⟶ = coming together

Description

By the spring of 1989, a Christian Fellowship was meeting regularly at two locations on Sunday mornings and jointly on Wednesday and Sunday evenings. The church was combining small and large group activities. . . . We envisioned new members joining a particular house congregation where they would receive their basic discipling and shepherding. This would be their nuclear family—their church. Simultaneously they would develop allegiance to the larger community, their extended family. [Evaluating this a year later we observed that:]

1. The consensus was that the larger facility for Sunday evening was too sterile compared to the warmth of the home.

2. More and more energy was going into the large group meetings—meetings which required a great deal of planning (preaching, kids clubs, nursery, etc.). These maintenance activities had become so absorbing that little energy remained for growth activities (discipleship, evangelism, personal shepherding). The larger group was siphoning energy which the small groups needed for growth and reproduction.

3. The larger group effort showed a dramatic loss of flexibility. To meet the needs of the larger congregation, the meeting format and scheduling had become quite rigid. The leaders saw this as a tragic loss since the house church's flexibility was one of its greatest strengths.

4. In the larger group, interacting was easy among old friends from the different house churches; newcomers, however, tended to talk only to those of their own house group. The larger group meetings were not helping the small groups bond together.

As the leaders prayed and discussed these things among ourselves and the congregations, we saw that the cell house church model was not appropriate for our vision. *So a decision was made to put the weight on becoming a decentralized network of house churches.*

The practical effects were multiple. The Sunday evening meeting was dissolved; instead, each house church focused its energies on developing a written covenant and vision statement. A person could join a particular house church by signing its covenant and having hands laid on by the leaders.

In addition, all the house churches in the Fellowship started to meet as a large group [or home-church-based congregation] once monthly, on an evening—although during the summer a Sunday late morning or afternoon picnic became the norm.

The house church meetings were limited to two per week to allow members time to deepen their intra- and inter-house church relationships. Likewise, the members were encouraged to develop relationships with unbelievers—bridges for the gospel. The mid-week meeting was largely devoted to planning activities.

Sunday meetings were given to worship and Bible study. There was no formal preaching.

We have been excited with the number of people engaged in the expansion of the Kingdom and about the house church fellowships' part in the broader world of missions. Financially, the fellowships have been very involved; 50% of the offerings routinely go toward outside mission endeavors.[2]

Comment

The move from what have been called "program-oriented churches" to "cell churches" is a significant feature of present congregational life. It is taking place particularly among evangelical, ethnic, and charismatic churches. Here there is a move toward a more organic, flexible basis, one that gives more freedom to the home groups on which the congregation was built and frees up resources and energy that so often go into maintaining a large weekly meeting and round of programs. A question that remains is how much the carefully patterned approach to beginning new home churches, originating with a team of male church planters and focusing on male gatekeepers, will result in a male, leader-oriented structure within the home churches and congregational gatherings based on them.

Planting a Congregation of Home Churches

The following is a Mennonite congregation's description of its beginnings as a home church in a small southern Virginia city.

Description

In the winter of 1986–87 a core group of people came together to look at planting a new church in the community. The group included a couple from a mission board exploring new ideas about evangelism and church planting, a local pastor considering church planting as an alternative to building expansion, and a small group of people meeting for a home Bible study. Though people's views on how to establish a new church were diverse, both fellowship among members of the group and interest in outreach deepened.

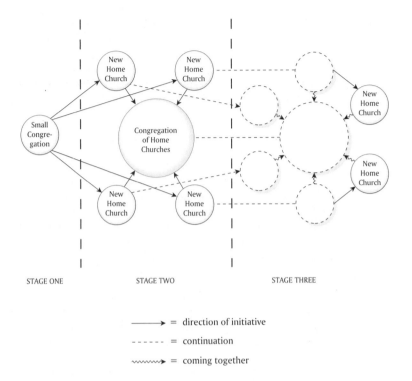

STAGE ONE   STAGE TWO   STAGE THREE

⟶ = direction of initiative

------ = continuation

⤳ = coming together

After being exposed to the needs of the poor at a motel in the area where they wished to plant the church, the group plunged into a ministry in the motel and began to hold its regular meetings there. For a time social justice issues took precedence, and church planting was put on the back burner. This led to some conflict of expectations within the group, which the mission board was asked to resolve. But out of this period of being "in the wilderness," a more appropriate vision developed for the area they were seeking to reach, new plans started to formulate, and new families began to join the group. One of the families had an alternative model for planting churches and was engaging in demographic and economic investigation of the area.

The group committed itself to exploring the possibilities of establishing a network of home churches as a foundation from which to build effective ministry. They decided to work with a trial six-month covenant, discerning their gifts and resources and studying Scripture on who they were in Jesus Christ and what their functions were in his body. They included a mission planning time in the meeting and began to discuss ways of being church together. They also began to share a meal together as part of their fellowship. The pastoral core of this group started to meet together weekly to brainstorm and to hold each other accountable.

Out of this initial group several home churches began. Each home church is limited to approximately twenty persons, including children, and functions as church in the fullest sense of the word. Each meets weekly, at a time agreeable to its members, in homes rotated among those able to host the meetings. Each meeting includes worship, teaching, eating a meal, and a mission focus. As these churches grow, and with prayer and discernment, the existing groups send people out to start new home churches.

At least once a month all churches meet as a home-church-based congregation for celebration and business. These meetings, which are held in a rented facility, are meant to encourage more formal teaching, creative large group worship, unified vision, and communication and decision making among all members. There is also a monthly joint social activity, quarterly retreats, special outreach projects, and a number of interest groups. A common family budget attempts to reflect the network's commitment to holding the tension between nurture and outreach.

Comment

The experiences of this group underline the time it often takes to do something new in a traditional setting, the advances, detours, and withdrawals that are part of the process. They also underline the importance of having a few people who can provide vision and define reality for the group, as well as give spiritual encouragement and model spiritual priorities. In this case the support of a denominational agency and the openness of some local congregations was also a help. The outcome is a vital new church that is pioneering for its denomination an alternative method of planting congregations. Recently this church played a major role in hosting a national consultation on house churches for groups and other interested people from all over the country.

Founding a Cluster of Independent Home Churches

The following example comes from outside a denominational setting and describes the origins of the original home churches to which we belonged. They have now been in existence for over twenty-five years. They attracted mainly people who felt burned out or excluded from standard churches, people from countercultural backgrounds, and unchurched people.

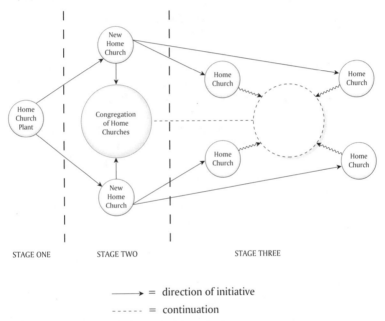

= direction of initiative

------ = continuation

᠁᠁᠁➤ — coming together

Description

These home-church groups owed their vision to two seminary-trained people who had advanced a new paradigm for the church. These two began by offering teaching sessions. They eventually started a home church when those attending the sessions requested it. This move was initiated partly by what was being taught and partly because the teaching sessions developed into times of corporate worship and fellowship that many found exceeded their experience of Sunday church. The group provided a partial income for the person who had set up and continued to lead the teaching sessions. But we neither desired nor needed a full-time pastor, so the teacher was encouraged to develop a ministry outside the group in any direction he chose.

Although some of the original people did not continue, the group grew to around twenty-five adults plus children within a year; it was well past time to divide into two groups. The members had established strong relationships with each another, and it was difficult for us to split the group. But the group agreed from the beginning that we would not grow through accumulation, that is, we would not allow the home church to become as large as the number of people who wanted to join it (which would have meant moving into a larger building). Rather, we would grow through multiplication, that is, as soon as the group became too large to meet in a living room, it would divide into two, and as those groups grew, into three, and so on. Within a year of the first meeting a second group was formed. The home churches met together in congregational meetings. Eighteen months later the second group had given birth to yet another home church. Some time later a monthly pastoral meeting group was established, open to any who wished to come, where the particular concerns and common issues of the individual home churches could be discussed and prayed over. Though this drew in key people from each group, it was not a decision-making body except in certain minor matters.

Occasionally members from the different home churches came together to discuss other matters of common concern, for example, evangelism, Christian education, and youth ministry. These discussion groups did not form organizations or programs. Most members found that the most effective way of fulfilling some of their responsibilities in these areas was by joining and supporting existing groups of Christians in parachurch movements or other existing institutions and movements. Occasionally they partnered with other Christians who wished to develop some experimental form of ministry. Once a year some people joined in a combined service with members from most of the churches in the city, as well as in other common acts of witness. Some home-church members have formed teams to assist traditional churches develop home churches within their own framework and have encouraged home churches in other cities to network with one another and come together as larger groups. This congregation of home churches later hosted the country's first national consultation for home churches.

Comment

The strengths of this model are its strong links between the individual home groups, the sharing of personnel and other resources when appropriate, the possibility of one group helping out another when the situation arises, the existence of people who have a more general ministry outside of the various groups, and the links the combined groups have developed with other home churches in the city and elsewhere. Such a model requires strong lay involvement, with all members playing their proper part, both within and between the individual home churches. This approach has increasingly become the dominant model for independent home churches. It is similar to the method that some denominational church planters are pursuing. It may well be the evangelistic and church planting wave of the future, a bottom-up, low-cost approach to church growth that values the role of especially gifted and trained people rather than the top-down, high-cost approach that is largely building centered and pastor driven.

Developing Home Churches in a Denominational Context

Can home churches be developed in a denominational context? Certain contexts appear to be more conducive to the development of home churches than others. On the whole, home churches within denominations are most easily established in decaying inner-city churches, in new churches in recently-built housing developments, and in churches located on the fringes of cities. These settings tend to be characterized by a willingness to experiment, a lack of tradition, and a quest for community, respectively. Of course, this does not mean that it is impossible to develop home churches in other settings. An older suburban area that has retained a sense of community can also lend itself to the development of home churches.

The success of a home church within a traditional church also depends on the pastor. (There is more on this at the end of the chapter.) It goes without saying that when a pastor is not open to the development of home churches it is more difficult for members of the congregation to move in this direction. While this should not prevent them from trying, they should be sensitive to the difficulties involved and the tensions that might arise. In the case of a pastor who desires to move toward home church structure, the pastor must be willing to stay at that church for a significant period of time. It is conventional wisdom that it takes five years for a minister to implement any changes that he or she most deeply wishes to see. Unless a pastor is prepared to remain double that number of years, the home churches may not consolidate properly. If the pastor leaves before this has happened and the incoming minister is less committed to the home-church approach, the congregation may revert to its original structure.

Whether a home church can develop in a denominational context also partly depends on the character of the denomination—how institutionalized, bureaucratic, or hierarchical it is. Our experience has shown us, however, that these qualities can vary, even among churches in the same denomination. Given the nature of institutions, in general it is more difficult for them to do something new and to restructure themselves in a far-reaching way along the lines of a home church or an interactive congregation. One congregation that did move to home churches decided to return its building to the denomination, and its pastor voluntarily became a part-time elder. Although the whole congregation voted in favor of a home-church structure, the denomination could not accept the direction the member church had taken. Consequently, it struck both pastor and congregation off its books.[4] The problem here was one of wineskins: the old wineskins could not contain the new wine that was being poured into them. On the other hand, now that there is a move in some denominational circles toward church planting by home churches, we may be entering a new era. Only time will tell.

It should be noted that those who join or plant independent home churches should not think that they have complete freedom just because they are not bound to a denomination. While they may be able to more quickly fulfill their vision for home churches and home-church-based congregations than their counterparts elsewhere, they also operate under certain limitations. These limitations mostly arise from the existence of the institutional church itself—its ongoing (if declining) prestige, attraction, and influence—and from the scattered, independent nature of home churches and home-church-based congregations, which sometimes makes establishing helpful networks among themselves difficult.

OTHER CONTEXTS FOR DEVELOPING HOME CHURCHES

Apart from the models described above, there are several other valid ways of developing home churches. Some of these additional possibilities are context specific. Because they tend to be rare or temporary forms of home-church life, we deal with them more briefly; we have not included narratives or diagrams with them.

Establishing a Solo Home Church

Sometimes a group has little choice but to go it alone. The people involved may live in a new housing area, may not know of any other home churches, or may not have a connection with a local church. A group that finds itself in this situation must begin on its own. This presents no problem so long as in time it multiplies into a cluster of home churches, discovers and links up with another home-church network, or develops some relationship with a congregation. Finding even one other home church with which to connect strengthens and enhances its efforts.

A home church should not be intentionally established to remain as a solitary assembly. Such groups, which are often structured around an authoritarian figure or among a group of friends, tend not to reach out sufficiently, hold people long enough, or retain their own children in the group. While God will undoubtedly bless these groups, and some have informal links with other Christians and are strongly involved in mission, they miss out on the advantages of meeting regularly with larger groups of fellow-believers for church, never achieve a broader dimension of church, and do not reproduce themselves. They run the risk of becoming one dimensional or withering through lack of cross-fertilization with other groups.

Forming a Parachurch Home Church

This kind of group sometimes develops out of a campus ministry. Students who graduate sometimes find themselves at a loss in their local church. They miss the strong experience of community, even if it was mainly among their peers, and look unsuccessfully for this in their congregation. Out of this situation a home church develops, at least for a time. A home church can also develop when a group of graduates become committed to some needy group and find that they need a strongly communal ecclesial base such as a home church provides in order to minister effectively.

This kind of home church has a positive contribution to make to its members but tends to be transient. Unless it ultimately attracts a wider range of people, it is too homogeneous to last for long. Interestingly, homogeneous groups tend to have a shorter life than multigenerational ones; when members begin to marry, move, and have children, the group begins to disintegrate. If it is the only group around, it can also suffer from some of the same difficulties as the long-term solo home church. There are several instances, however, of such a home church developing into a more broadly-based independent cluster of home churches or (less frequently) of its being instrumental to introducing home churches to traditional congregations.

Turning a Small Rural Church into a Home Church

All over North America denominations are shutting down rural churches. This is due to a gradual decline in the rural population and to the decreasing number of clergy outside urban areas. Initially this meant that rural church members had to settle for services only when the pastor was able to make it to the area, perhaps once every two weeks or month. Then it meant traveling to town for church. Now it often means people have to drive to a provincial city up to a hundred miles away. Although they may assume that the pastor is indispensable, there is no reason why lay people cannot gather together and sustain themselves as a church on their own.

Now and again a rural church realizes this, generally when it is between pastors. Church members discover that they have the resources to survive, at least for a while. Running the church as a formal affair that depends on a prepared sermon each week does tax the congregation. But when the church shifts to a home church form—and often the number of members is comparable to that of a home church—all sorts of gifts and experience begin to emerge. Only in isolated cases, however, are denominations beginning to see in home churches the possibilities not only for survival but also for growth. In the past, congregations in isolated parts of the country were often founded by lay people and initially met in people's homes. In a sense these new rural home churches are only returning to their origins.

Transforming a Traditional Ethnic Gathering into a Home Church

Judaism has always placed a strong emphasis on the family and the home. As we have seen, this emphasis has deep roots in the OT. Today this tradition continues in the role played by the household in celebrating the Passover and the weekly Sabbath meal. Apart from these gatherings, Jews traditionally have tended to meet for religious purposes only in ways that are officially sanctioned and organized by the synagogue. Against this grain, various unofficial meetings held for different purposes, called *chavurah,* have become increasingly common. Among these are *chavuroth* encouraged by rabbis as an appropriate expression of synagogue life. As a result many Jews are now complementing their synagogue meetings with gatherings for worship and study in the home. They organize and lead the meetings themselves.

This wider Jewish practice has been caught up into the life of some congregations made up of converted Jews (often known as messianic Jewish congregations). Within such congregations an interest in encouraging home churches has occasionally emerged. As a result, some messianic Jewish congregations have begun to develop home churches within their local church structures, using the *chavurah* as a model. One unexpected byproduct of forming home churches is the discovery that unconverted Jews are sometimes willing to attend.[3]

DEVELOPING HOME-CHURCH-BASED
CONGREGATIONS

You may wish to develop a home-church-based congregational meeting that is non-hierarchical and very participatory. Though this large meeting cannot be as informal or as inclusive as a full-blown home church, it can become an occasion that draws significantly on the gifts and the fruit of its members. Just as there is value in families coming together in both a nuclear and an extended group, so it is in the church. Small and large meetings complement and reinforce one another.

There are two basic forms that these large interactional congregational services can take. The first occurs when home churches elect to come together in a larger joint meeting, called the home-church-based congregation. The second occurs when a traditional congregation moves its large Sunday morning worship service in the direction of the interactive, flexible, participatory worship seen in a home-church-based congregation. One difference in the second case is that there are no home churches as a foundation to the larger congregational meeting.

Decentralizing a Larger Church into
Home Churches

This illustration concerns a three-hundred-member Mennonite church in a midwestern city. The pastor and elders came to the conclusion that something was lacking from the life of this otherwise vigorous church. The small groups in the church were producing many good results, but they were not going deep enough into member's lives and were not drawing out all the members' gifts. After study, prayer, and thought, they decided to sound out the congregation about basing its life on home churches rather than on small groups. Over a period of time agreement was achieved, and the transition took place successfully. Most members of the church, including the children, joined one of the midweek home churches.

After a year the leadership of the church evaluated the experience. They were pleased with their progress but sensed that something was lacking. As they studied, discussed, and prayed together, they decided that the problem lay with the large Sunday gathering. It was too big. Only a few could contribute or lead, while others who had gifts from which the wider church could benefit did not have opportunity to minister. So they suggested that the church divide into three smaller congregations, only coming together as a whole body for a celebration several times a year. This was accepted on a provisional basis for a year.

They were left with one issue to resolve: How large should their newer groupings be? How many home churches should make up a congregation? Their thoughtful, indeed profound, conclusion was that each congregation should be no larger than one that enabled everyone in it to know the name of everyone else and something about them, including the children. In other words, the group should not be too large to function as a unit. This enabled everyone to acknowledge visitors and strangers who attended their meetings. These congregations had no need of name tags or visitor cards!

The Sunday gatherings of the three new congregations met weekly in community buildings in different parts of the city. They were organized by a representative group of people from the home churches associated with each. Because the numbers were not too large, there was opportunity for many gifted people to contribute to the meetings, as could various groups among them who had special expertise. What this church had learned was an important principle: just as home churches are, like extended families, made up of people who get to know each other intimately, so the next level of meeting, the congregation, should be like a clan, comprised of people who all know each other to a degree. The occasional large meetings of the whole church were like meetings of the tribe, made up of people who all had something in common, even though they did not all know one another.

Starting a Denominational Congregation Based on Home Churches

In the face of swelling urban centers, rapid demographic changes, and expanding unchurched populations, we must continually ask ourselves, How can we start the congregations we need to impact our diverse mission context? A new movement of church planting is emerging that is powerfully simple and reproducible: relational-based congregations that grow and multiply as the gospel is shared throughout networks of relationships. They are being started by busters, boomers, and boosters from diverse ethnic, educational, and economic backgrounds in rural, urban, and suburban settings. Such congregations are not limited by the supply of buildings, money, or seminary graduates. They need little, if any, start-up money, they can meet anywhere (homes, apartments, community centers, public places, etc.), and they can be started by any group of people God so calls.

There is a young Southern Baptist-affiliated church plant that is a cluster of six Christ-centered, relationally based, and mission-driven churches (what we call home churches) that meet in members' residences. During its two-year pilgrimage this congregation of six churches and seven evangelistic groups has sent three church-planting teams out of the area and has catalyzed three other church starts. Similar movements are beginning in many other states.

Each new church start moves through four stages. This process is not a formula for church planting, but rather a description of various processes and activities that have been used to start new churches.

Sending

The focus of this phase is to call out and send out the church planting teams of two or three believers (Acts 13). The new team will focus on "having the same love, being in one spirit and purpose" (Phil 2:2). They should covenant together to affirm their mission, purpose, individual roles, and how they will relate to one another on and off the field. The team members' primary functions at this stage are intercession and building new relationships with seeking unbelievers. In a context of prayer they begin to make contact in the community through a variety of means to discover people who are open to the gospel and people who will open their homes for a seeker group.

Gathering

The team goal is to start seeker groups to which unbelievers or new believers can bring their family and friends to hear the good news of Jesus (Acts 16). It is best for the group to meet on their "turf"—any place unbelievers will gather. The church planting team prays and works toward two or three family units who put their faith in Jesus, are baptized, and desire to form a church. Throughout this stage the team helps the group develop a sense of ownership through their active involvement. They also begin to identify potential leaders— even future pastors—who are equipped to serve the emerging church.

Covenanting

As a group comes into relationship with Christ, the church planting team immediately begins talking about what being the body of Christ means. The focus of this stage is to affirm the nature and purpose of the church as a missionary community. This is done through creating a covenant. A covenant defines how members of the church relate to Jesus, one another, and our world. Both the function of the church and the function of its ministers is discovered. The church planting team needs to be careful that everything they do is easily understood and reproduced by even the newest of believers. When a group of believers realizes the presence, power, and purpose of Jesus Christ in their midst as community, they become a church. At the same time they realize that they are "on mission" with Jesus and begin to look beyond themselves, seeking to bring others into relationship with Jesus and his church.

Reproducing

The goal in this fourth phase is to build momentum for continued church growth and multiplication. In addition to growing larger, the church must also send out teams that will continue the church-planting process. The church develops a vision statement affirming God's direction for the church over the next several months. This includes strategies for both evangelism and edification. Evangelism strategies may involve prayer walks, surveys, block parties, community seminars, or whatever may lead to starting new seeker groups and churches. Edification involves equipping and empowering the congregation to reproduce at every level of church life: disciples, leaders, churches, and church-planting teams.

Creating a Congregational Meeting of Home Churches

This continues the story of the home churches with which we were originally involved (pp. 139–41). After the first group had multiplied into two groups that were meeting separately each week, we continued to meet together once a month, initially in a larger home. There we maintained a similar pattern to what took place in the smaller groups. Soon we realized that the larger number of people functions somewhat differently than our small home churches do. Nevertheless, we were committed to the meetings' being as participatory as possible and gradually developed ways of achieving this. Everyone participated equally in some aspects of the meeting, for example, in fellowship over the Lord's Supper (which was still celebrated as a full meal in a leisurely way) and in singing together (though this meeting gave opportunity for those with special musical gifts to share them with a larger number of people).

The time of sharing was, of course, less personal, but this gave greater opportunity to focus on broader concerns shared by the two home churches as well as by the city as a whole. The meeting also provided the opportunity for those who had particular gifts of teaching to use them, though always with ample time for feedback from others. At other times visiting groups or speakers were drawn in, including a group from other churches from whom we learned something about celebration, and a Christian dance group that helped everyone learn how to take part in religious dance. These meetings lasted up to a full day and later were sometimes held in a park, community meeting room, interdenominational church center, or other convivial space, even a restaurant!

After a time third, fourth, and fifth home churches developed and joined in these combined meetings. Initially the combined meetings took place once a month. Since other events drew people together at about the same frequency (for example, farewells, baptisms, weddings, fiftieth birthdays, and important visitors), combined meetings were held every six weeks. Originally individual groups took turns organizing events. Later the pastoral meeting took responsibility for some of the logistics, worked out a schedule for involving each home church, and occasionally planned a combined gathering. These cluster events often involved several members from a particular home church contributing to the meeting, which was organized around a common theme (for example, one teaching a song, others doing a dramatic reading, perhaps a couple organizing something for the children, and another leading us in a dance). At other times individuals or families across the groups shared with the rest in a wide range of ways (for example, Scripture readings, stories, songs, testimonies, and so on).

As this combined meeting grew, people began to realize that a large gathering, just like a home church, loses something vital when it gets too big. As the members were considering the possibility of dividing into two combined meetings or congregations we came into contact with folk from the Mennonite church mentioned above. This clarified for us the principle of not allowing such meetings to grow so large that people lost track of each other. We decided that once the home-church-based congregation grew beyond eighty to a hundred people (including children) it was time to multiply. This is what we did. The whole body of people still meets together a few times a year to celebrate major Christian festivals. These larger celebratory meetings, planned by each of the participating home-church-based congregations in turn, are now attended by another cluster of home churches in the city. There are also "home church enrichment days" for anyone in the city who is involved in a home church.

Developing Home-Church-Based Congregational Worship without the Home Churches

Some congregations, while not based on home churches, may wish to have a large congregational meeting that is similar to that of the home-church-based congregation. A community church in Massachusetts wanted to become more flexible and participatory in their Sunday morning service. The following is an excerpt from someone who was involved in this church's move toward a home-church-based meeting style.

In the end, each church and tradition must determine for itself exactly what changes will renew worship according to New Testament principles. . . . What follows is one proposal for such changes.

First, churches should tear out all pews and pulpits. In place of pews, churches should buy padded folding chairs and set them up in concentric circles with aisles, so participants face each other. . . .

Second, churches should have facilitators, not worship leaders/ directors. Instead of having the same person lead the service week after week from the front (in a circle there is no front), various members should take turns as meeting facilitators.

Facilitators sit *with* the congregation. Their role is not to direct everything that happens in worship. It is to keep an eye on time and to facilitate transitions when needed. They might say, for example, "Perhaps now we should spend some time in prayer," "Now Joe has a teaching to share with us today," or "It's almost time to end. Are there announcements?" . . .

Third, churches should let flexibility, not rigid preplanning, be their guide. Churches oriented toward radical renewal should abandon or pare back preplanned programs of worship. Churches should not determine only ahead of time, with paper and ink, exactly what will transpire during meetings. They should leave meetings flexible and open-ended. . . .

Such changes inspire a worship atmosphere which invites the appropriate participation of all. The structure and tone of worship ought to encourage members to share testimonies, insights, fears, prayer requests, confessions, Scripture passages, and song requests. The schedule of teaching and preaching should be opened to whoever has such gifts.

Other changes could also be helpful. Churches might spend time discussing the meaning and practical applications of teachings immediately following input, either in small groups or together. Through these discussions, questions can be asked, and the teaching's practical implications further explored. . . .

Churches should also cultivate an atmosphere where it is acceptable to let our hair down and physically express worship of God. . . . Try learning and writing some new Scripture songs, hymns, or choruses. Try introducing new accompanying instruments—such as guitars, percussion instruments, recorders—in worship. Instead of didactic teaching, try presenting a drama skit now and then for the congregation to reflect on or discuss. Occasionally try orienting the activities of the entire church meeting around the children of the congregation. On a nice day, try holding the meeting outdoors in a local park.

Church renewal that makes a difference catches a vision of worship that is communal, open, participatory, Spirit-led, God-centered. The worship service, if judged at all, is evaluated not by the oratorical brilliance of the sermon or goosebump-raising performance of the choir, but by the deepening faith of the saints and the glorification of God.[5]

IS THERE A ROLE FOR THE PASTOR?

What is the role of the pastor when home churches are being developed in a congregation? The more the pastor supports a home-church structure, the more likely it is to come about. The more the pastor is willing to teach on home churching, open up discussion among members, and encourage the church to move in this direction, the easier it is. Many pastors have done this. Should they take the further step of becoming involved in a home church themselves? The answer to this is Yes!

First, as much as anybody else a pastor (and the pastor's family) needs such a group for the practical aid it provides. Many pastors can testify that belonging to a home church has supported them through difficult times and has helped them identify their real, as opposed to expected, gifts. We realize that in some denominations pastors are warned against or even forbidden from getting too close to their church members. In other cases it is church members themselves who expect their pastor to be different or to not relate more to one group of average church members than to any others. This separatist attitude is not only grossly unbiblical—just think of the intimate connections Paul forged with members of various churches he founded and spent some years with—but betrays a false attitude toward ministry. But often the main obstacle to ministers' belonging to such a group is fear of something that puts them on the same level as others and asks them to open up to others about their inner weaknesses and doubts.

Second, belonging to such a group enables the pastor to learn along with the congregation whatever God wishes to teach its members through the pastor. It would be a pity to miss out on some of the best things God has to offer in terms of new understanding, particularly learning the art of love and pastoral care. Even pastors—sometimes especially pastors—may have much to learn here, for their expertise and skills often lie elsewhere.

Third, if pastors wish to give some leadership to their congregations in this area, they need to be a vital part of a group. Of course they may visit other home churches from time to time to see how they are faring, but if their involvement is limited to administration, they do not engage in the deep learning that comes from being primarily involved in one group. One pastor who did not become involved with a group told us, in the middle of the second year that home churches were developing in the church, that he realized he had made a mistake in not joining one. "When the key people in such groups get together," he said, "I find I have less and less to say that is of any help. They are now leading me in understanding how to handle what happens and where we should head from here."

Where pastors encourage the congregation as a whole to get together in more interactive ways, they will begin to experience some redefinition of their role. They will find that others begin to share in and take on (even handle better) some of the functions for which they felt mainly responsible. They find themselves less at the controls of what is happening in the church, partly because so much is going on in an organic way and partly because others are developing gifts of leadership. Most of the pastoral work is now conducted in and through the small groups, or through members of the congregation who are developing skills in this area because of their home church involvement. Some pastors fear these developments, thinking that they will do them out of a job. More likely, they will be freed to focus on the things that matter most, which normally they do not have time to give themselves to sufficiently. Or they may be freed to initiate ministry outside the church in new areas that the church feels are important and wants to support. For the pastor willing to take some risks the whole enterprise can become a real adventure!

This raises a related question. As home churches begin within denominational churches, more denominational facilitators with the vision and the ability to encourage them will be required. Some pastors have already begun to engage in this after having helped home churches develop in their own congregation. It would be encouraging indeed if some denominational organizations or representatives saw the importance of this and looked for people with experience in the area whom they could draw on or in some cases fully employ. This would constitute a new form of apostleship.

But independent clusters of home churches need such people too. While their number will expand as groups continue to multiply, there is also a need for some people to be engaged full-time in evangelism and church planting. This kind of apostolic work is crucial. Such people exist here and there, and their numbers are increasing gradually. As well as having the capacity to preach the gospel or, where working among ex-church people, to reinvigorate their faith or give them a new vision for church, they are able to discern which persons are best placed to draw others around them. These "people people" then become the prime vehicles through which a new home church, and eventually a home-church-based congregation, is formed.

Such "apostles" are also important for the contribution they can make to helping individual home churches, or a cluster, to establish contact with others who are meeting in the same way. At the very least they may be able to help them connect with one or two people who have long-term pastoral experience in such groups, however informal or intermittent the link might be. As Jean Vanier points out:

> No community, whether large or small, can cope on its own. Very often its members are not able to resolve their tensions. They need help to grasp the way community is evolving and to find new structures for the different stages of its growth. Every community seems to need regular visits from a friendly outsider . . . above all someone who can counsel its leaders, so helping the community evolve and discover the message of God in its tensions.[6]

NOTES

1. Barrett, *Building the House Church,* 160–61.
2. D. Sloggins, "Planting House Churches in Networks: A Manual from the Perspective of a Church Planting Team" (Warwick, R.I.: n.p., 1992).
3. We owe our knowledge of this to Stuart Dauermann, a pastor in a messianic Jewish congregation in Los Angeles, who has written extensively on this phenomenon. His writings are as yet unpublished.

4. The church in question is the subject of two books by R. Girard, *Brethren, Hang Loose: or, What's Happening to My Church?* (Grand Rapids: Zondervan, 1972) and *Brethren, Hang Together: Restructuring the Church for Relationships* (Grand Rapids: Zondervan, 1979). See also Girard's more personal statement, *My Weakness His Strength: The Personal Face of Renewal* (Grand Rapids: Zondervan, 1981).

5. Smith, *Going to the Root*, 85–87.

6. Vanier, *Community and Growth*, 110. See also p. 93.

7

GATHERING TOGETHER

*A Conversation about the Art and Craft
of Home-Church Meetings*

We now turn to the main components of home-church meetings. How can we best spend our time together? What can we do that will most help us to be the church? What matters most to God when we are in each other's company? How do we go about praying, learning, sharing our gifts, and celebrating communion in ways that will deepen our lives with God and with one another? What do we do about decision making, leadership and pastoral care, and multiplying groups, all of which are basic to the life of a home church?

A CONVERSATION ABOUT THE DYNAMICS OF MEETING TOGETHER

A helpful way of looking at the principle and practice of gathering together is to view it from different angles. This is partly because there is no one way of doing things: what suits one group will not necessarily suit another. It is partly because often we can think through issues most lucidly when several perspectives are presented to us: this helps us work out what we find most persuasive and what will benefit us most. For these reasons we have constructed this chapter around a conversation between several people. Alan and Pat are a married couple involved in a home church within a denominational setting; Carol and Tim are single people attending a newly established home church that sprang out of a parachurch background; Ruth and Graham, also married, have belonged to an independent cluster of home churches for many years.

Praying and Praising

Alan: I don't know about your group, but ours sometimes has real difficulty praying aloud together.

Graham: Why do you think that's so?

Alan: I'm not really sure. Perhaps it's because few of us are used to praying aloud in a group.

Pat: In my home we had family prayers of a sort when we were young, but we never seemed to move into praying together as adults. I don't even know if my parents prayed together as a couple.

Alan: We have used a sort of litany in our group from time to time. Whoever's leading the prayer time says something like: "Let us pray for the world." People then simply state things they'd like to pray about and the leader says, "Lord, hear our prayers," and we all answer, "And grant our requests."

Ruth: Occasionally we do something similar, especially when a new home church develops out of an existing one. For a time we limit prayers to one or two sentences. We also found something else helpful. As various things came up in the evening, we would stop right there and ask who would like to pray briefly for the person or for the item in question. We found that doing things this way made prayer a natural part of the group's life and made it more likely that someone close to the person or issue would be willing to pray.

Alan: We seem to manage OK at the level of minimum involvement in prayer. What we find difficult is going beyond that.

Carol: There are some good books of prayers around, so encouraging individuals to read those might help. Perhaps the group could also have some Bible studies on prayer.

Pat: I'm sure that books and Bible studies can help. But I have to confess that they didn't do a lot for me. I think I really learned to pray in a healing group.

Tim: What made the difference?

Pat: It was partly the bond that developed between us. The concerns of the others became my concerns, and mine theirs. I found I couldn't help praying about them, if that makes sense.

Ruth: For me that happened through being in a home church. But what I found after a while was that I started to view prayer differently. I began to see it as a group conversation with God rather than a collection of prayer made by members in the group.

Tim: I don't understand what you mean.

Ruth: Well, it's what happens when we go beyond asking God for this and that, or even claiming answers for certain things, to wrestling with God together over how best to pray for someone, searching for a direction and then exploring it, discerning how far to travel along it and whether there are side paths to be taken. Another way of putting it is to say that it involves praying into . . . around . . . and through a situation rather than simply praying about it. Does that make sense?

Pat: I understand what you're saying. That's what happened in our healing group when the Greens' teenager—it was the Greens' house we met in and we used to see a little of her—developed some physical and psychological problems. Some extraordinary times of prayer came out of that.

Graham: It suggests that when the chips are down, the more a crisis hits someone in the group or someone close to a member of it, the more prayer will rise to the occasion.

Pat: That makes sense to me. But what if you don't have any crises in your group, if people just have the usual ups and downs or illnesses. Are you suggesting that we pray for something really bad to happen so we can all learn to pray better?

Graham: Of course not. You can't manufacture it. They're bound to come sooner or later. But it could be that there are things going on in people's lives—not necessarily some crisis, maybe some new opportunity—that they're not talking about in the group. This is where core members in a group have a special responsibility. When the going gets rough for them, they should open up to the group about it. That gives permission for others to do the same.

Alan: What do you suggest we do in the meantime?

Carol: I wanted to say something about this earlier, for I wonder whether praying effectively doesn't partly develop out of praising God first. We always have a time of singing before we pray—Scripture choruses, charismatic songs, and some older hymns—and this draws us into worshiping God together in a more general way. In my experience this tends to draw us out of ourselves, helps us to begin thanking God for all sorts of things, and lays a good basis for other kinds of prayer.

Tim: We do something similar. I find that the pressures and demands of the week often push to the background the regular blessings I receive from God, sometimes even the specific ones, so that I forget to be as grateful as I should. When we get together in church and start to sing, many of those blessings come back to mind. Some people choose songs that express what they're grateful for. Then the very songs we sing become a form of personal prayer for some members of the group, one that we can all enter into in our own way. We also encourage people to interweave the songs with personal prayers in which they can give God thanks in more specific ways.

Alan: Do you think that sometimes singing becomes too individual, even in a group? For example, people may choose only the hymns or songs that are meaningful to them. Or sometimes people close their eyes and do not even look at one another.

Graham: You may have a point, but I still like what Tim is saying. Mostly our singing and praying are at separate ends of the evening. We don't move from singing into prayer as much as we could at the start of the meeting, and perhaps we could introduce our time of prayer later with a song or a psalm to help us do that.

Carol: We find that the children sometimes want to thank God for something too. They enjoy the singing, of course, especially if we have lots of instruments they can play, and we include some dancing along with the music.

Ruth: I'm all for that!

Tim: We also keep a note of all the requests that people make in prayer, and then each week we thank God for answers received. It's been a great revelation to us about the way God works, even though our prayers aren't always answered or answered in the way we expect.

Ruth: God's greatest gift to us in terms of prayer was sending Arthur. He was an older man with a very natural way of relating to God. Whenever he prayed, you felt as if God were there in the room, sitting in an armchair and listening. And it wasn't "chatty" in the wrong sense. It was just that Arthur simply accepted that God was present and, in one sense, could be talked to like anyone else. He wasn't afraid to tell God that he didn't understand or that he was angry about something. His honesty with God helped us over our hang-ups about using the right words or only praying about certain things.

Alan: Like the fellow in *Fiddler on the Roof?*

Graham: Exactly! But I guess the most significant thing I've learned from our discussion is just the importance of doing it together. I find that the more the group gives time to prayer the more I pray in it and the more I pray outside of it as well. It's a bit of a paradox, like so many aspects of the Christian faith.

Carol: We all seem to have been assuming that none of our groups have a problem with finding time for prayer.

Alan: We set apart time each week, but it's mostly a pre-scribed time. It's not all that flexible.

Graham: Well, we're often so flexible and get so engrossed in what we're studying or learning that sometimes prayer, which we tend to leave to last, gets squeezed out. Though it's quite unintentional, it can happen several meetings in a row.

Tim: That's happened once or twice to us, and one of our members suggested that one way of handling it would be to compensate every so often by giving over most of an evening to prayer.

Ruth: Why not? I think that's an excellent idea. What counts is whether we are giving appropriate time to prayer over the long term, not whether we are spending a specific proportion of time in prayer every time we meet.

Learning Together

Pat: Can we turn our attention to teaching?

Tim: Teaching! That's what we need—not just about prayer—good biblical teaching about everything!

Carol: No one in our group has had any serious theological training. One or two have some Bible college background, but that's about it. Some of our members are concerned that we might end up with "the blind leading the blind"—or drift off into some heresy.

Alan: I'd be concerned about that too. It's important to have a solid talk or Bible study at the heart of each meeting. How can you grow if you aren't receiving solid teaching and studying the Word?

Pat: Alan and I often have disagreements over this. It's not that I feel that biblical talks or studies are unimportant, but I feel there's more to it than that.

Ruth: I agree, Pat. In our group we've come to see that God is more concerned about the quality of the learning than the quality of the teaching. And learning is not confined to that part of our gathering officially designated "teaching." The whole meeting is a learning experience.

Tim: Would you like to say more?

Graham: A good example is what we were saying about prayer. We learn to pray as much by listening to others pray— and by simply praying together—as by listening to people talk about prayer. That has its place, but it's not everything. We learn about serving others by having it modeled to us in the group, not just by doing Bible studies on servanthood.

Ruth: It's the same with learning how to love and how to minister to others. I appreciate studies we've had on this, but I'm continually being challenged by the caring that I see others giving to someone in need. I often find myself saying, "Why didn't I think of that?"

Graham: We have come to see that teaching of one kind or another is going on through the whole meeting. A home church, as much as anything else, is what one influential writer calls a "learning organization," and we should be alert to how we can grow in understanding and in doing through all that happens.[1]

Tim: I can see that your attitude toward "teaching" is different from mine. I like what you say, but isn't it important to have some exposition or study of the Word each week?

Carol: I'd be interested to hear what the rest of you have to say about something that happened in our group last week. While we were eating our meal, we became involved in a discussion about sports. One of our young people began talking about the lowering of ethical standards in sports generally. Then Jenny mentioned some problems she was having in this area in her sports team. At that point Tim reminded us that time was moving on and we'd better get started on our study for the night. Alice said she felt we ought to abandon the study in favor of addressing Jenny's problem. I've had this niggling doubt ever since that perhaps God really wanted us to focus on her problem and trust in God that significant learning for all of us would come out of that.

Alan: I think you made the right choice. The Bible study is too important to drop.

Pat: This is where Alan and I disagree. Dropping the Bible study is precisely what you should have done. It's a matter of discerning what the Spirit is saying, isn't it?

Ruth: More than once we've begun talking during the meal in our home church about some issue affecting one of our members, and then we decided to pursue that subject rather than the study planned for the evening. These are always special occasions as people draw one another out with questions, share experiences of similar problems, remind each other of relevant scriptural passages, and learn by praying in and through the issue in the way we were talking about earlier. And somehow there's always some element in other people's issues that overlaps with our own.

Tim: Occasionally we use a book as a guide—say Jacques Ellul's discussion of the difficulties modern life raises for prayer.[2] But since we're not a study group as such, we don't work through books like these in a systematic way but rather use them as a resource for our own exploration of the subject, if you see the difference.

Graham: Sometimes we have meditations. One of the members of our group leads us through reflection on some biblical image, personal experience, deep longing, or encounter with creation . . .

Ruth: . . . and we mustn't forget Joe's parables. Joe loves to garden, and when he is out in his yard God often gives him parables, some of which he senses are intended for the church. Sometimes we've spent a whole evening unpacking a couple of Joe's parables and found them extraordinarily helpful. They provide us with further insight into the ways and values of God's kingdom. Remember the time we talked at length about the fact that there are few "straight lines" with God, just as there are few in the shape of the creation or, for that matter, in the stories of people's lives in Scripture?

Graham: People found that so helpful. "No straight lines with God" has become a catchphrase in our group!

Ruth: The beauty of it is that it's such a simple picture to remember and yet it says so much, like "I am the Good Shepherd" or "You are the salt of the world."

Graham: We also encourage a person in the group to tell us his or her life story every couple of months. This is always very informative, not only helping us to understand that person better, especially where he or she is coming from, as they say, but also broadening our knowledge of how God works in people's lives.

Pat: I like the sound of that, though I can't imagine Alan being too enthusiastic.

Alan: You might be surprised.

Ruth: We've also had meetings out in the forest or mountains and shared what we can learn about God from being attentive to the creation, drawing on some psalms or other passages from Scripture as we do so. And we've attended a film or rented a video and then talked about its implication for us. I still have strong memories of what came out of seeing *Schindler's List* and *Babette's Feast.*

Carol: Even though we tend to place more emphasis on study, we've begun to explore creative ways of approaching it, like putting ourselves in the position of the characters in the Bible account. We ask ourselves how we'd feel or react if we were, for example, the prodigal son, the elder brother, a servant, or the father. It's amazing how such a familiar passage comes to life when approached this way, and how much you learn from playing one or more of the characters. The children also are able to join in and to contribute to such a discussion.

Tim: Occasionally we encourage people to volunteer, in the form of a talk, something that God has been teaching them over a period of time. Once May shared how much she had learned from the sense of isolation and abandonment that she experienced during a lengthy illness and what it taught her about suffering generally and even about Christ's experience on the cross.

Graham: We've also begun to explore another way of sometimes teaching one another. We refer to these, half jokingly, as our "Quaker meetings." We don't plan for a talk or study but encourage everyone to give thought and prayer during the week to something they'd like to share with the group. It could be a Scripture passage or a hymn, a poem or a prayer, a story or an object, or anything else that God impresses upon them. When we reach that point in the meeting, we have a time of silence, after which people are free to sense what and when to contribute. I can say that these have been stimulating and often moving meetings.

Ruth: What I like about all this is that though we can't all give formal talks or lead studies at the same level, all of us can find the way we can best help others in the group learn what God wants them to know.

Sharing the Lord's Supper

Alan: Maybe I'm getting ahead of things, but your views on teaching are so different from what I've understood by it, that I'm wondering what you think about Holy Communion.

Ruth: Is that part of your home-church meeting, or is it only celebrated when the home-church-based congregation meets?

Alan: We have it in our home church about once a month.

Graham: Do you have to follow one of the orders of service in the prayer book your church uses?

Alan: Not necessarily. We can if we wish, but apart from citing Jesus' words of institution we have freedom to devise our own way of doing it. This tends to have a liturgical form but also includes extempore elements. The balance of one and the other largely depends on who is presiding.

Ruth: And who is able to do that?

Pat: It's usually one of the elders in our group, although they can choose to involve others.

Carol: Does that include women as well as men?

Alan: Yes, we don't have any difficulties on that score.

Tim: Our celebration of the Lord's Supper is rather different, though we still have our own questions in this area. Some of the ministers in the congregations to which we belong are a little suspicious of our home church, especially when it comes to our holding the Lord's Supper. We're anxious to keep good relations with them, so we've tried to find a way of not alienating them. We have a common meal each week that we call an agape meal. Although we bless the food and drink before us, linking them with all that Christ has done for us, we don't necessarily use bread or wine or use the words of institution. This is why we call it an agape meal rather than the Lord's Supper.

Carol: Certainly some of the members in our group regard it as the Lord's Supper, regardless of what some of the pastors think. In any case, I come from a nonchurch background, and I think we bend over backward too much so as to avoid offending others. I sense that the ministers' monopoly on celebrating the meal is threatened. I am not sure that their main concern is that we are acting in a divisive way. I may be wrong, but that is often the impression I get.

Ruth: I can't judge that, but I do find some pastors' reactions quite contradictory. They are happy to let laypeople gather to study the Bible in their own homes, without a theologically trained person leading, yet they refuse to allow the Lord's Supper to be celebrated in homes with ordinary church members hosting it. When I've asked them for the biblical basis of what they're doing, they can never give me a clear answer. I'd have thought there was more danger in letting people interpret the Bible in their homes than in allowing them to celebrate the Lord's Supper there.

Graham: Mind you, when we first began to have the Lord's Supper regularly in our home, we had some difficulties knowing how to approach it.

Pat: What kinds of difficulties?

Graham: We became convinced that the Lord's Supper should be an actual meal and that the experience of real fellowship with one another was a vital part of it. Originally we introduced bread and wine, as distinct from the other food, at some point during the meal. But we found that doing this altered both the atmosphere of the meeting and the way people related. Instead of bringing us into greater contact with the reality of God and leading us into a deeper fellowship with one another, it tended to make us more stilted and artificial with respect to both. It was as if we were trying to put new programs into an antiquated computer. It just didn't work.

Pat: What did you do?

Ruth: We concluded that somehow, despite ourselves, we were still regarding the bread and the wine as sacred in a wrong way. So we decided to dispense with them and use whatever food and drink made up the meal on a particular evening, since that would be more natural to us.

Graham: In fact, we also found we had to forego communion-type prayers over the food and drink altogether for a while, since they too changed the complexion of what we were doing and seemed to inhibit the meal's having its full significance for us.

Ruth: So for a while we just said a general grace over the food and drink. Then we added specific references to the death and resurrection of Christ and, when people brought bread and wine, integrated that into what we were doing. Over time people felt free to draw into the grace, or introduction to the meal as we began to call it, not only parts of Scripture but relevant readings from other books, poems, and hymns. In other words we developed a way of introducing the meal—as well as our fellowship around the table—that grew out of the life and experience of the group, and the whole meal began to take on a special character: not just a social event, but not just a ritual either. In one sense it was quite ordinary, in another quite extraordinary. In one sense it was about fellowship, in another sense about worship. It became a seamless web in which Christ's giving himself for us and our giving ourselves to one another, as well as our receiving physical and spiritual nourishment, blended together beautifully.

Pat: You express that very eloquently.

Ruth: Thank you.

Alan: Who undertakes this introduction?

Graham: Mainly the person in whose home we have our meeting. Often a married couple will do it together, or, if they wish, they may delegate this responsibility to someone else.

Tim: In our group we pass around a roster each month, and people just sign up for it as they wish. Since we haven't been going that long, we offer to help them if they want some assistance in knowing what to do. But mostly they learn by observing others, particularly those of us who have thought about it more and have had a little more experience.

Alan: Do children take part in Communion?

Graham: Yes.

Alan: We come from a tradition in which children at least accompanied their parents up to Communion and received a blessing and in which they were often confirmed at a young age. So it did not take us long to include the children. In that tradition children often assisted the clergy as servers in the Communion, so in our home churches we sought to involve the children at that level as well. Often they are the ones who pass around the bread and the wine to the adults. Of course you can imagine how much they love doing this! We never have any problem getting volunteers. Even the younger ones want to help carry the dish and the cup. I must say that I find this a very touching way of celebrating the meal. It reminds me of the passage in the Bible that says, "A little child shall lead them."

Ruth: That's a beautiful idea. I thought we were very inclusive in our group, but it hadn't occurred to me that children could be drawn into serving the Lord's Supper as well as taking part in it.

Carol: Children are allowed to take part, then?

Ruth: Yes. We reason that just as they come to know the word of God by listening to it from their earliest days, so they come to know the meaning of the Lord's Supper by participating in it as they grow up.

Alan: Can I go back to the elements for a moment? Do you simply bless all the food and drink? Or do you say something specific over part of the food and drink, not necessarily bread and wine, but whatever happens to be designated as elements on that day?

Graham: It varies. In our old group those who were introducing the meal mostly took some bread and wine and distributed to others at the beginning of the meal. Some people liked to do this quite formally, much as you would do if hosting a banquet. Others, like Paul in 1 Cor 11, left saying anything over the wine until the end of the meal, using that as a way of reflecting on the fellowship people had enjoyed and anticipating the even greater delights awaiting us in the coming kingdom of God. In our present group some people just bless the food and the drink in general, believing in Quaker fashion, I guess, that everything God has made is sacramental. You can see that we try to make room for a variety of approaches to the meal, though we wouldn't tolerate just anything.

Carol: We did something very meaningful recently. Instead of having our agape meal before the rest of the meeting, we structured a whole meeting around the meal, interleaving the main course, dessert, and coffee, with singing, teaching, fellowship, and finally praying, concluding with a blessing over a final drink. It was quite a remarkable and profound experience.[3]

Exercising Gifts

Ruth: Tim and Carol, you mentioned that many of the people in your group come from a charismatic background. I'd be interested to hear more about that and how it has shaped what you do when you come together.

Tim: Well, some of us grew up in Pentecostal churches, and others came in touch with charismatic Christians during our college days. Most of the people we associated with took it for granted that prophecy, healing, and speaking in tongues were intended to be a normal part of church and Christian life. So when we formed our group, we looked for some indication from God that it was OK for us to go ahead along these lines. It was Carol, actually, who had a dream whose interpretation was plain to us all. There was also a prophecy from one of our members to similar effect, which we weighed and found to be God-given. So we took these as confirmation that God wanted us to proceed.

Carol: I found it quite encouraging that the dream came through me, not through one of the men in the group. It affirmed the role of the women from the outset.

Ruth: I can see that.

Tim: In our meetings we always include a time when people can contribute any charismatic element to the meeting that they sense is appropriate. Often this is in conjunction with our singing. Sometimes we all end up singing in the Spirit, you know, all singing in tongues but in a way that harmonizes quite beautifully. But that only happens occasionally. The time of exercising gifts may last only a short while, or it may be longer. We are also open to responding with a word of knowledge, a prophetic statement, a prayer for healing, or whatever is most appropriate at any suitable time. So, although we don't want to place undue importance upon them, charismatic contributions of these kinds are a real dimension of what we do.

Carol: Would you call your home church charismatic?

Ruth: It depends on what you mean. If you are referring only to the more dramatic gifts or to the more dramatic exercise of the gifts, then not in any substantial way. We do have people in our group who believe in prophecy and healing, as well as speaking and singing in tongues. But if you came to our meeting, you would not see much visible evidence of these in operation. That's not to say I don't think they have their place. In fact, I think we would benefit from their having a greater presence. But they are not the gifts on which we would tend to place the most emphasis.

Carol: What did you mean by gifts then? The ones that are mentioned by Paul, such as helps, giving, and administration?

Graham: We'd certainly include all of those as well as teaching. These are all very beneficial. We need people who have a knack of helping others in very practical ways, who are generous with the extra money that they have, and who possess organizing abilities. Any church needs such people. But we'd define gifts more broadly than that. It seems to us that the ones Paul mentions are not the only gifts that are available. They were simply the ones that were highlighted most by the people to whom he wrote.

Tim: What else would you include?

Ruth: Well, such things as hospitality, which he does mention in another context, listening in a way that really hears what people are saying, asking the appropriate question that will lead people into a deeper awareness of what they are seeking to learn, a sense of wonder at what God is doing and an ability to catch the whole group up into that, the gift of laughter—I mean just ordinary laughter, not necessarily the Toronto kind—which breaks down people's inhibitions and opens them up to see all things in a new way.

Graham: Even, as is the case with one of our members, the capacity to make great cheesecakes that lift everybody's spirits and put them in a mood of gratitude toward God and outgoingness toward others!

Alan: As a connoisseur of fine desserts, I can say "Amen" to that!

Pat: Don't you think the best gift we bring to the church is ourselves, with all our complexity?

Ruth: I couldn't agree more. And it follows that sometimes our greatest contribution to the church is admitting our weakness and need.

Pat: It never ceases to amaze me to see God at work in such a situation. Our group still has a way to go in relating to one another and to God, but now and again something happens that takes us a step or two forward. A couple of weeks ago, when a few of our more reserved members were away, one of our teenagers broke down in a flood of tears. She's under a lot of pressure at the moment. She's worried about final exams coming up at school, she doesn't know what she wants to do in the future, and, as if these weren't enough, she's just broken off a romance that has been going for eighteen months.

Alan: Who'd be young again!

Pat: It was really encouraging, Alan, wasn't it, to see the way various people in the group sought to calm her and draw her out.

Alan: Even Colin, who's somewhat renowned for putting his foot in it, went over and gave her a bit of a hug.

Pat: But especially Edith. She's our group grandmother. Someone like that is a tremendous boon, a wonderful gift to our church. We may not have known how best to pray for the girl, but she certainly left that meeting affirmed and loved. It was her tears that drew affirmation and love out of the group.

Carol: Well, I can see that lots of gifts were involved in dealing with that situation. But do you think that either of your groups experience what you called "the more dramatic gifts" in your meetings?

Ruth: Yes, now and again, though you could come on any given night and not witness any, at least not in a way that you might immediately recognize. When they do turn up they tend to be exercised in a rather matter-of-fact way.

Tim: How do you mean?

Ruth: Well, someone who has something to say to another from God will tend to just say it, perhaps prefaced by "I think this might be important" or "I sense that God is saying to you," or some such expression, not so much "thus saith the Lord." It's a kind of conversational prophecy, I suppose, that might just as much occur in someone's prayer or sharing as in a direct statement. We also get involved in laying hands on people in the group. This happens whenever anyone has a birthday, is about to take on something important, or is going through some real difficulty.

Graham: The group also laid hands on us before we took that weekend for St. Bede's on the importance of home churching.

Ruth: It also happens when people are ill and we gather to pray over them for healing. But this form of laying on of hands is not really treated any differently. Mind you, at times I think we are in danger of taking it a little too casually. It's almost as if it's not cool to pray too enthusiastically for someone, or to ask God for something really out of the ordinary, or to demonstrate our concern for a person too expressively!

Alan: I find this helpful, for at one stage the charismatic issue generated real tension in our group between the "haves" and the "have nots." Those who'd had the experience began to demand that everyone in the group seek it. Many of us needed more time and convincing and felt that, in any case, there should be room in the group for differences of opinion. But the group did not move as quickly as the enthusiasts wanted, and they eventually left us.

Pat: It took the group months to recover. Even a year later certain people felt very vulnerable about it. But what you are saying, Ruth, about a broader definition of gifts helps me see that we are more charismatic than I had imagined, and it may point a way forward that will help us take a further step in this direction.

Ruth: Tim, how is it that people in your group discern what gifts they have?

Tim: Partly through undertaking a spiritual inventory that helps them identify their gifts and partly through other people in the group identifying what they find most helpful.

Pat: What about in your group?

Ruth: We've been influenced by Paul's comment that if you're eager to see the Spirit manifesting himself among you, then you should strive to build up the church.[4] We take that to mean that we should get on with responding to the needs around us as best we can instead of focusing on trying to determine what our gifts are, which may be a bit like putting the cart before the horse. In other words, "concentrate on the needs and potential of people in the church and you'll gradually discover how best you can assist them," partly, as Tim said, because they will tell you what was helpful and partly because you will gradually see for yourself the contribution you make. A pattern will gradually take shape and become more obvious to you.

Graham: Exactly.

Carol: That's very helpful, actually. I've always tended to look at gifts the other way around.

Decision Making

Pat: I've often wondered how you make decisions in your home churches. Do you have a leader who works out what to do or does the majority have the say?

Graham: What sort of decisions are you thinking about?

Pat: Things like how you organize your meetings, what you're going to study, how to deal with problems that arise.

Tim: In our group one couple is appointed to handle those matters, although they may check certain things out with someone else first or possibly with the whole group.

Pat: In one sense that's similar to what we do. In our home church the pastoral staff appoints someone, or perhaps a couple, to take charge. But, as you say, they don't decide everything on their own. The more the decision affects the whole group, the more they'll seek the group's opinion before deciding what would be best for us.

Graham: I can see that having certain people take on such responsibilities is very efficient. But do your groups ever chafe under this arrangement?

Alan: Not as far as I'm aware. Many of our people are very busy, and some tend to be rather unorganized, so they appreciate having people in the group who can keep its act together.

Carol: We feel that God gives certain people a gift for organizing. But that's not to say that lots of smaller decisions aren't left to other people in the group to make or to the group to make as a whole.

Pat: What about your group, Graham?

Graham: Well, we seem to go about making decisions rather differently. Everything we do—for example when and where we meet, how we proceed during our meetings, what we shall learn or study, who will introduce the meal, whether the group should multiply—is decided on by everyone.

Pat: You mean you discuss these issues and then take a vote?

Graham: We came to the conclusion quite early on that we should decide all major issues by consensus.

Alan: You mean everybody has to agree before you can go ahead and do something?

Graham: Well, yes and no. When an issue arises, we're all encouraged to think and pray about it and then share what we feel should be done about it.

Tim: Does that include fairly new members as well?

Graham: Yes. It's rather like the parable of the laborers in the vineyard. Even those who begin work at the end of the day receive exactly the same treatment as those who were there the whole time. But even though all take part in making decisions, we don't always all have to reach the same conclusion before we can go ahead.

Pat: Isn't that the same as a majority vote?

Graham: No. But let me say first that working by consensus tends to bring full agreement most of the time—far more than you'd normally expect. When it doesn't, we only go ahead if those who disagree are happy to trust the judgment of the rest. Even if only one person has a serious reservation, we will hold back until those misgivings disappear or until the remainder come to see that the decision is well taken.

Alan: That would drive me crazy! If I ran my firm in that way, we'd take ages to get anywhere. In fact, some things would never get done at all!

Graham: I agree. Sometimes it can be frustrating. But then we're a church, not a business. I understand that there's a lot more consultation and consensus building in business today, in addition to top-down management, isn't there?

Alan: True, but only about some matters, not everything.

Ruth: I have to say that sometimes I feel we're too scrupulous in this area. Some of the decisions we have to make hardly seem worth all the effort of getting consensus. I'd rather we just appointed someone competent to look after them and let that person get on with it. If they make a mess of it, we'll just ask someone else next time.

Graham: Maybe, but how would you know where to draw the line?

Ruth: Just use your common sense . . .

Tim: . . . and a little charismatic discernment.

Ruth: Yes.

Graham: Well, maybe.

Ruth: Sometimes, Graham, you're too much of a purist. The new group that recently came out of our group has simplified decision making by leaving some aspects of meeting planning—introducing the meal, looking after the children, taking responsibility for the music, bringing food and drink—to individuals to sign up for. We can waste a lot of time on such matters.

But I agree with you about the importance of consensus generally. While striving for a consensus may take longer to come to a decision, in the long run it's far more efficient. It helps people to grow in discernment more quickly and therefore gradually enables them to make decisions more quickly too. Because people feel that their views really count—that no one, even the majority, is going to ignore them—it's sometimes easier to reach a decision anyway.

Alan: I can see the wisdom in that. People who feel that their opinions don't count will tend to feel resentful and dig in their heels even further. I've seen that happen all too often at our annual church meeting when it's clear that a vocal minority is going to be overridden by the majority, especially if they've had the better argument.

Graham: True. The other thing I was going to say is that when disagreements arise, some in the group haven't learned to respect the wisdom of others enough to trust their judgment.

Carol: You've spoken of all this in rather human terms, Graham. Where does the Holy Spirit come in? Aren't you still dealing with these issues on the horizontal level rather that the vertical one?

Graham: That's a good question. I do believe the Spirit is involved in the whole exercise, but maybe we need to intentionally seek to discern the Spirit rather than just assume the Spirit's involvement.

Ruth: And we need to be sensitive to a prophetic word or vision that is directed to us. When we reach a stalemate, it's best to abandon discussion and ask God to give us some fresh light. Sometimes a new possibility emerges that resolves the issue.[5]

Leadership

Pat: Obviously the issue of decision making is tied into the question of leadership in our group, as well as in Tim and Carol's.

Graham: Ours too. I think we just come at it from different angles.

Tim: I'd like to talk about that more. As I said earlier, we feel it's very important to be very up front about it in our church. You need leadership for anything worthwhile to happen.

Graham: I think I can agree with that, but we might differ on how we define leadership. But tell us first how you appoint leaders—or do you call them elders—in your group and how long you appoint them for.

Carol: Yes, we call them elders, following the NT. We all give some thought as to who has demonstrated the attitudes and

the capacities we most need in a leader. Then we wait on the
Lord for further direction or confirmation. Once we have that,
we lay hands on the one who is identified and commission that
person to fulfill his or her responsibilities. We would review the
appointment only if that individual was not working satisfacto-
rily or had received our blessing to move on and begin a new
group.

Ruth: What about your group, Pat?

Pat: Our leaders—we call them church pastors—are appointed by the pastoral staff of our church, who place people in
a group for a year. They give some training to the house-church
pastors, monitor their performance, and then at the end of the
year sometimes reassign people and change leaders. Not always though: Richard and Alison have been in our group since
it started and seem quite happy to stay. They come from the
neighborhood where most of our people live, so it makes sense
for them to remain with us.

Alan: I think Richard and Alison are a real boon to us. They
work so well together as a team. He's got some good pastoral
skills, but she's better at hosting meetings and teaching. Not
that they're the only ones who function in those capacities, but
they provide a first-rate model. He often defers to her, even
when it makes some of our more conservative members
wince. We have a few people in our group who are strong on
this "headship" thing. I suspect that this is a control issue for
them more than a role issue.

Pat: What I like about Richard and Alison is that they're not
into power games in our group either. As soon as they find
someone who has something to offer the group, they offer encouragement. Encouraging others is one of their real strengths.
They never seem threatened, even when others start to develop the capacity to do some of the things they're best at. On
the other hand, when nobody is willing to contribute, they take
control and make things happen.

Ruth: I'm not so sure that taking control is really a good
thing. Scott Peck writes in his book on community that, although he's often tempted to maneuver toward what he wants
to have happen in his group, it's really better to sit back and
allow the group to work it out. Otherwise, whatever is achieved
represents only the will of one person.

Alan: But surely sometimes you have to take charge?

Ruth: I think there's a difference between catalyzing a group and doing the work for it.

Alan: You're the leader of your group, aren't you, Graham?

Graham: Ruth and I are certainly the oldest members, but we're not the leaders. The others would be very upset if they thought anyone regarded us in that way.

We all tried to be very egalitarian when we started. No one wanted to be more prominent than anyone else because of past experiences in groups where there was a clear, almost authoritarian, distinction between the leaders and everyone else.

Ruth: But it didn't work. After a while we began to see that in our zeal to get away from a model where one person called the shots, we'd fallen into the opposite trap of thinking that everyone was the same. Even in a situation like that some people are calling the shots more than others, simply because they're more vocal, older, or more qualified in some way. This isn't always recognized, but it's present nevertheless.

Tim: I'm lost. If you don't have a leader and yet you're not all leaders, what do you do?

Graham: I didn't say we weren't all leaders. I said we weren't all *equal*—we are equal as persons, in Christ—but we are not equal in our functioning. If each person is regarded as an equal contributor, you soon get confusion. No one is quite sure what to offer, or everyone offers even when they're not good at it. But as we said in talking about participating in the meetings and decision making, the one who is contributing is the one who is leading the group at that moment. This extends to those whose role seems to be in the way of anything happening. The person who always plays devil's advocate helps ensure that alternative views are explored; the one who tends to be a bit of a dreamer reminds us that sometimes we're too pragmatically focused; the one who is often resistant to change forces us to make sure that we're not forgetting something important. When all major issues are resolved by consensus, everyone helps lead the group. So we do view leadership as involving everyone in some way.

Ruth: It's a matter of discerning what each person has to offer and being prepared to listen to and respect one another accordingly.

Graham: For example, say we're meeting at the Smiths' place, and they're the hosts for the night. But Mary is busy with

the children and Bruce is talking to someone, and they don't realize that they should be moving things along. We don't just
wait around for them. Anyone in the group could say we ought
to get on with it, perhaps offering help in doing so.

Tim: So you don't have elders?

Ruth: What we've said doesn't overlook the particular maturity and gifts that certain people bring to the group and the
need for others to acknowledge their contribution. Every group
needs a few people like that. But we don't call them leaders,
and they would be the last to want us to. Because of unfortu-
nate past associations, no one likes the word "elder" either. We
use a variant of it by referring to such people as a group's pastoral core.

Carol: On what basis do you identify those who belong to
the core? Is it their ability to organize and teach the group?

Graham: We've talked a lot about that. Initially we wondered whether the ones who were the best organizers or teachers in the group were our leaders. But we operate quite well
when they're not there. A little less efficiently and thoughtfully
perhaps, but we still meet and learn together. Then one of our
group had a real insight. She said, "Instead of asking who are
our leaders, wouldn't it be more helpful to ask who we would
miss most if they weren't there?" This set us off on a new tack,
and it didn't take people long to work out that there were three
people whom we would miss most. There was Ruth here, who
has a wonderful capacity to accept everyone, even the most
difficult members in the group, to sense when people are
needy or have something to contribute, and to get alongside or
mediate between members when they are in conflict.

Ruth: And there was Graham, who maintains a quiet,
steady confidence that God is present, at work, and bringing
good things out of what is happening. This is a good balance
because I tend to feel overwhelmed by all the problems in the
group and to identify too much with the people who have
them.

Graham: Finally there was Maureen, who could see beyond the present and catch glimpses of where God was taking
us, sometimes as individuals and sometimes as a group, a
sense of vision if you like.

After we'd identified these three people, one of our members asked if we'd realized what we'd done. "What?" we
asked. "Well," she replied, "Ruth embodies love, Graham faith,

Maureen hope: faith, love, and hope, don't you see?" The central virtues of the individual Christian are the same for the group. But in the group they are embodied in more than one person.

Ruth: And when those people are operating as they should—modeling God's fidelity, mercy, and purpose—then those who are good at organizing and teaching have a framework within which to do that. When necessary, the group can also select other people to take responsibility for specific tasks. As long as they're doing the job, they're exercising leadership. But those tasks tend to come and go or to rotate around various members.

Pat: All that's very interesting. I'd like to think about it for a while and then maybe come back to you on it.

Multiplying Groups

Tim: What is the optimum size for a group, and how you go about starting a new one? Our group has grown to a point where some of us are wondering whether we're beginning to get too large.

Alan: How many of you are there?

Tim: We've got twelve adults, several younger children, and a couple of babies.

Carol: And there are one or two other people inquiring about joining.

Ruth: You wouldn't want to get too much larger.

Pat: We have a rule: when we reach twelve adults, we automatically divide into two, half the group staying put and the other half starting a new home church.

Ruth: For us there's no magical number. It varies from group to group. But you do reach a point where the quality of relationships begins to diminish, people aren't able to contribute as freely as they did before, and there's just not enough room to put everyone.

Carol: When we have visitors in the group, we're aware of some of these things now. But I hate to think of losing the fellowship of people I've come to love and value.

Graham: The trouble is that you'll start to lose that anyway if you just keep growing larger. In any case, we should always be wanting to "extend the table," as one of our people put it, so that new people can begin to enjoy what we've been experiencing. While that involves a certain degree of loss for us, it's a very real gain for them.

Carol: I see that: a kind of dying to self so that others may have life.

Ruth: Exactly. But precisely because a certain amount of dying is involved, we shouldn't pretend it's not painful.

Tim: Do you think it's ever right to say no to someone who wants to join your home church?

Ruth: We've certainly felt it right to pray at times that God would not add anyone to our group for a little while, particularly when we've been going through a time of reappraisal or have been dealing with some crisis. We've also occasionally referred people to another group that we felt would be more helpful to them. I once encouraged another group to redirect someone in our direction. The group concerned was very fragile at the time, and the inquirer was a dominant and rather insensitive person who had been a key factor in the break-up of a previous group. By and large, however, we accept people as they come.

Graham: We find it helpful to invite people who express an interest in our church to a meal with another couple from the group, not to screen them, understand, but to find out if our kind of group is really what they are after. But the main thing, as I see it, is that we don't say no to people simply because they're different from us or may introduce problems into our group.

Tim: Getting back to dividing a group . . .

Alan: . . . since "dividing" had too many negative connotations—although it's a lot better than "splitting"—we decided to call it "multiplying."

Tim: OK, multiplying then. How does it work?

Pat: It's only happened twice. Once it seemed to work reasonably well. The other time it didn't work well at all: our half of the group took quite a while to recover from being split down the middle, and the other half lost members and eventually folded.

Ruth: That doesn't surprise me. We had a similar experience ourselves some time back, although the new group managed to limp along for quite a while. We decided that there had to be better way of starting a new group.

Tim: All the books I've read about dividing groups advise following the model you just described. They say that cells divide in that manner and furnish a model of the way groups should divide as well. In other words, it's a pattern of God's working in both creation and the church.

Ruth: Far be it from me to take on the experts, but the Bible compares the church to a body or family, not a cell. You don't just slice a body in two and expect it to reproduce itself. You have to take a small branch and plant it separately with considerable care. And you don't just take a family and slice it in half—although that is happening a lot today. Rather, a member of the family joins with somebody else and goes out to start a new family. Surely these are better analogies for methods of multiplying groups.

Pat: That makes much more sense to me. I've always felt the other way of doing it was too severe. It caused a lot of upset when we went through it.

Alan: But surely it's good for a group to be shaken up a bit every now and again. Otherwise, it becomes too inwardly focused and complacent.

Graham: No one wants a complacent home church. But we find that groups get shaken up enough in the normal course of events, with people leaving the district and moving interstate, new people coming in, children growing up into teenagers and wanting to be fully involved in the group, and so on. In fact, there's so much mobility among people today that we appreciate the stability of long-term relationships with a few people. And you can maintain this if a home church multiplies in the way we described.

Tim: I can understand that. In the past I belonged to small groups that stayed together for a year or so, and then everyone had to play musical chairs. We had to keep saying good-bye to people and starting all over again with a new group. After a while I just wanted to hold myself back so that I didn't suffer so much when the breakup occurred and a new group began.

Alan: But even if you follow a different model, how do you determine who ought to form the nucleus of a new group?

Ruth: We learned the hard way, I'm afraid, partly because we were following the cell model but partly for other reasons. The first time our groups multiplied, we did it along purely geographical lines. But that separated a number of people who had much to give one another, including a few who had strong prior relationships. The second time around we simply allowed people to choose which group they wanted to join. But this resulted in an imbalance of gifts between the two groups, making it difficult for one of the groups to establish itself properly. The third time we gave careful thought to the issue of gifts and asked if anyone would volunteer to become part of the pastoral core. One couple did, but we made the mistake of taking their word for it rather than looking at their involvement in our group to that point. They hadn't showed much practical shouldering of responsibility and that didn't really change when they moved into the new group. The group did manage to survive a number of years, but eventually decided it didn't have enough resources to continue.

Pat: So what did you do next time?

Ruth: Our group discerned that two couples were already moving into the pastoral core, so we talked with them and encouraged them to think about forming a new group. Initially they felt they weren't quite ready for the responsibility, and our group remained too large for a while. Later they consented and went out. Once so many people wanted to join at the same time that our group and another group loaned out couples to help the newcomers get on their feet as a church. Six months later the couple from our group returned, although the other couple decided to join the new group permanently.

Alan: Here's another possibility. Together with Alison and Richard, a few of us from our group led a meeting with members of the church who weren't in a home church to try to persuade them to join one. A number wanted to do so, and they formed a new group. The pastoral staff appointed two of our laypeople to get it under way, and the group seems to be doing quite well.

Tim: Our group was started by someone from our parachurch organization who felt God was calling him to start house churches. He had stayed with us for a little while when he felt called to found churches elsewhere. He is even considering doing it overseas. He now has a couple of others with him in the work. They're particularly interested in working among unchurched people, so they are preaching the gospel and then looking for the kind of person or couple who are gatekeepers to whom people naturally gravitate, using them as the basis for a home church. One of the church planters stays with the new group for a while. After a few months, when the church is consolidated, the team moves on and starts all over again.

Alan: I suppose one of our pastoral staff does something like that, though mainly among people who are already in the church or new people joining it.

Graham: I've felt for a long time that we need something like that in our home churches, in addition to simply multiplying groups. What you're talking about is planting rather than multiplying them. I would like to see us identify one or two people who show signs of being able to do that and then commission and support them to get on with the job. Not as a substitute for what we've been talking about, but as a complement to it. Surely we need both if we're to fulfill the Great Commission properly.

CONCLUSION

As this conversation has showed, there is a variety of approaches to being a home church. While each style will appeal to different individuals, in practice no one group ever contains the whole experience and so each group needs to learn from other groups. This only underlines again how important it is that individual home churches come together regularly as a large group and that home churches in different denominational or independent settings occasionally meet together to learn from one another.

NOTES

1. P. Senge, *The Fifth Discipline: The Art and Practice of the Learning Organization* (New York: Doubleday, 1990).
2. J. Ellul, *Prayer and Modern Man* (Grand Rapids: Eerdmans, 1972).
3. On celebrating the Lord's Supper in a way similar to that of the early Christian times, see R. Halteman Finger, *Paul and the Roman House Church: A Simulation* (Scottdale, Pa.: Herald, 1993) 154–86.
4. 1 Cor 14:12.
5. On a consensus approach to decision making, see Barrett, *Building the Home Church*, 99–112.

8

GROWING PAINS IN THE FAMILY

Tensions in Home-
Church Life

Just as a baby grows to maturity through various stages, so must the church. This growth entails a certain amount of pain and struggle. Community does not come cheaply. It requires that I give up my life for the sake of the group. It requires that I forsake control of my life and be prepared to change in order to bring community into being. It requires that I stop demanding others to think and act like me and that I give them permission to be themselves. It requires that I give up anything that stands in the way of community.

Scott Peck has described the four stages of a community's life.[1] There is a transition from "pseudo community," in which we attempt to create instant community by ignoring differences, to "chaos," which is when our differences begin to emerge and we realize that the honeymoon period is over. This usually leads us to develop chaos-containing strategies that do not work and that result in what he calls "emptiness." The only way forward from this lies in a willingness to abandon our preconceived notions and desires in order that out of chaos the Holy Spirit may create "genuine community."

POTENTIAL PROBLEMS

New groups usually go through a "honeymoon" period that lasts about six to nine months (but it might be as short as a few weeks or as long as a year). During this period the freshness of home-church life—its freedom and relevance, opportunity and intimacy—tends to carry the group along. But as the novelty wears off, problems start to surface. These may emerge slowly and gradually, or they may appear suddenly and unexpectedly.

Some problems spring from differing views about the nature of Christian faith and life or about the importance of long-standing Christian practices. Others have to do with varying perceptions of spirituality, community, and ministry. Occasionally there appear personality conflicts or differences over the discipline of children. Fortunately, none of these conflicts are terminal, although they can create considerable anxiety and lead to some disruption in the group.

Disagreements over Doctrine and Ethics

Many home churches include people from different denominational backgrounds. Even when a home church is part of a local congregation, not all members will share the same denominational upbringing or viewpoint. Increasingly Christians are shaping their own pattern of belief, irrespective of the particular denominational tradition to which they belong.

Though doctrinal differences may arise as soon as the group gets started, generally they take a little while to come to the forefront. The reason for this is that initially the more concrete needs and desires of the people in the group take precedence: people join the group for pragmatic reasons. Most average churchgoers are less preoccupied with traditional doctrinal disputes than people who are theologically trained. Only where doctrines bear directly on everyday problems do most church members take a serious interest in them. But there will always be certain people who consider such issues highly important, and there are some current issues, for example, charismatic gifts, prosperity teaching, abortion, etc., about which believers hold differing opinions.

One early home-church cluster, made up of people from different backgrounds, found a creative way of dealing with this difficulty:

> We differed over such matters as predestination and free will, the time and character of the Second Coming, and the nature of the Lord's Supper. Christians have quoted Scripture backwards and forwards at each other on these issues, still without coming to any conclusive solution. If this is the case in Christendom, it is only with some difficulty that we are all likely to come to one conclusion in our groups. What do you do when you have in one church people with strongly held beliefs that have some different practical outworkings?
>
> We had some friendly disputes at the beginning, but then gradually evolved a methodology applicable to these "historical areas of dispute." We endeavored to respect one another's opinions even if we couldn't fully understand or agree with the position others took.
>
> After this initial acceptance, there was a much greater readiness to listen without prejudice to other's point of view. This helped people to appreciate different positions better. Quite often we were then able to sit down and discuss these questions afresh. On some we have come to a mutually agreeable decision, while on others we have agreed to disagree and have recognized that such differences of opinions are no barrier to fellowship. People are not really interested in arguing among themselves; their ongoing fellowship becomes more important to them. Part of Christian freedom is accepting those whom God has accepted and accepting each other "without disputes over opinion" or questions regarding spirituality and Christian orthodoxy. If Christ has received us, then we must receive one another. That is really the basis of our fellowship—a common experience and love of Jesus Christ.

Members who hold strong convictions about a particular issue have the freedom to ventilate them but not to indoctrinate others. If the issues are personal "hobby horses," people should leave them at the door and not insist that they dominate regular discussion in the group.

Disagreements over Practices

What about other issues that require the group to make decisions about how it is going to operate? Can it function effectively in the presence of significant differences of opinion over basic practices like baptism, the Lord's Supper, and charismatic gifts, or more contentious issues like divorce and sexual orientation?

Baptism may become an issue dividing those who favor infant baptism from those who prefer believer's baptism. Accepting a plurality of approaches instead of insisting on one can unite those who hold differing views. When a baby is born, members can ask the parents how they would like their new child to be accepted into the church. If the parents prefer the baby to be baptized, the home church can arrange a baptism. If the parents prefer some form of dedication, then this can be organized. When the parents are uncertain about this matter, the group can examine the relevant biblical passages and help them reach a clear decision.

There may be a broad spectrum of opinion in regard to the Lord's Supper. Some members may hold a more symbolic, others a more dynamic, view of its operation, and some members may desire an informal, others a more liturgical, celebration of it. A good solution here is to encourage the family hosting the gathering to decide what form the Lord's Supper will take. This allows the Communion Meal to be celebrated in different ways. Most people find that this enriches their understanding of Communion. Allowing variation also prevents the Lord's Supper from becoming a repetitive ritual.

Some Christians prefer traditional hymns, while others prefer Scripture choruses, or charismatic songs, or Christian folk music. There is a place for all these expressions in church—as well as for compositions that are written by members of the group. We do not have to like certain songs to enter into them with a brother or sister who does. The principle of "including diversity of expression" can be applied to a wide range of issues about which people differ.

All members of a home church need not agree on the value of every gift of the Spirit for gifts to be exercised in church. Can we not exercise openness and tolerance here? There is room for those who speak in tongues and for those who do not, for those who pray for healing by laying on hands and for those who just pray, for those who are given some direct prophetic message and for those who simply share their experiences.

Groups may experience difficulty in connection with contentious issues such as marital breakdown and sexual orientation. While people who are engaging in adultery or promiscuous gay activity seldom express a desire to join a home group, there are many people who are experiencing personal dislocation, emotional stress, and moral confusion. A group does well to open its arms to such people, accepting them as they are and helping them work through their issues. In time God will clarify how those in difficulty can best proceed.

God has called us to unity, to love our neighbor as ourselves. This requires a costly commitment to hang in there and work at issues unless it becomes obvious that there is no achievable solution. Unfortunately, when disagreements occur, we usually try to deny the conflict, exclude the offender from the group, or withdraw ourselves. All of these behaviors are detrimental to community. True community only develops as we learn to face the reality of our differences and work through them together.

Other "problems" arise from the varying perceptions people have of their role in the group more than from particular doctrinal or practical matters, with what goes on in their imaginations and feelings rather than what goes on in their thoughts. The chief hindrances to our becoming a genuine Christian community lie within us: in our basic attitudes, expectations, and motives. These are so intrinsic to our way of looking at others that we are often unaware of them. Yet they govern our relationships with each other, the way in which we seek to serve our fellow members, and our view of what our home church should become.

False Expectations

A person who joins a home church has already formed an image of what the group should be like. This image may be derived from a number of sources: sermons or books on the nature of Christian community, previous experience in a small group, or projections of personal needs and aspirations. Holding preconceived notions is quite natural—no one goes into a new situation with a completely open attitude. It is what people do with these notions about community that matters. The following three things must be understood in order to deal with our preconceptions in a positive manner.

First, any individual notion of the ideal Christian community is bound to be incomplete. No one person can have the whole truth about this. The Spirit distributes various insights into the nature of community life to different people, and a fully rounded portrait of community can only emerge as everyone shares their insights.

Second, any individual picture of community is bound to be partly wrong. We are too affected by self—too vulnerable to the danger of creating a community in our own image—to have an undistorted view. We need each other not only to fill out our one-sided views but also to correct our false ones.

Third, we must not be too attached to our preconceptions. We may find home church wanting if it doesn't develop in the direction of our ideal picture. This may result in our distancing ourselves from it and blaming it for not living up to our expectations. In doing this we further undermine any chance the group has of deepening its communal life.

As Bonhoeffer points out, God wants us to recognize the real world and work with the actual situation before us rather than dream about an ideal, hypothetical one. The home church is made up of people who are imperfect, imbalanced, and immature, although God can change them. As Bonhoeffer writes:

> Just as surely as God desires to lead us to a knowledge of genuine Christian fellowship, so surely must we be overwhelmed by a great disillusionment with others, with Christians in general and, if we are fortunate, with ourselves. By sheer grace, God will not permit us to live even for a brief period in a dream world. He does not abandon us to those rapturous experiences and lofty moods that come over us like a dream. God is not a God of the emotions, but the God of truth. Only that fellowship which faces such disillusionment, with all its unhappy and ugly aspects, begins to be what it should be in God's sight—begins to grasp in faith the promise that is given to it. The sooner this shock of disillusionment comes to an individual and to a community, the better for both. A community which cannot bear and cannot survive such a crisis, which insists upon keeping its illusion when it should be shattered, permanently loses in that moment the promise of Christian community. Sooner or later it will collapse.
>
> Every human dream that is injected into the Christian community is a hindrance to genuine community and must be banished if genuine community is to survive. He who loves his dream of a community more than the Christian community itself becomes a

destroyer of the latter, even though his personal intentions may be ever so honest and earnest and sacrificial.[2]

What are some of the false expectations we can have about community? One is the feeling that the community is primarily there for us: to encircle us, to support us, to love us. Certainly community involves all of these, but it also calls on each of us to encircle, support, and love others as well. It is true that some people in a home church may have to be carried for a time by the remainder, receiving rather than giving. But eventually the time comes for each of us, in Jean Vanier's words, to move "from community for myself to myself for the community."[3]

Another false expectation is the belief that the home church exists to solve our problems. These problems may arise from serious personal, family, or vocational difficulties. The community is certainly there to listen to us, talk with us, pray for us, and help us in any way it can. But it is not primarily a therapy or welfare group that will resolve all our difficulties for us. As one of the members of our home-church cluster put it, "We are not here primarily to solve each other's problems, but to provide the supportive context within which members, with God's help, can begin to work through their own problems."

A further false expectation is that everyone in the home church will become friends or that we will find our closest friendships there. We may make one or two friends in the group to which we belong. But sometimes we will have little in common with those among whom God places us. There may even be some people we find difficult to like. This is not an easy situation to be in, but it is one that promotes growth. We need to allow the Holy Spirit to teach us to love as God loves us. The genius of a home church is that it brings together the most unlikely people and calls them to form a community. This means that you should not expect the group to meet your basic friendship needs, and you must not judge it when it doesn't. If it does, God has given you a bonus.

Foregoing expectations does not mean abandoning any vision for the group. But this vision should be shaped by the life of the community, the gifts of its members, their level of maturity, and the focus or mission that develops in the group. Its sense of identity and direction, its sense of becoming and doing must be derived from the work of the Spirit in and through the community itself. Real development takes place only as we forsake our idolatrous absorption with an ideal and seek to serve and enhance the community as it is. This is the basic gospel principle in new dress: only as we are prepared to lose our ideal do we have any hope of finding it.

At this point another distinction becomes useful: the distinction between expectations and hopes. It is one thing to have expectations about the progress of a group. Expectations are demands that are placed on the members and on the group as a whole. Expectations amount to a kind of law for others, and they only produce disappointment and frustration when they are not fulfilled. Hopes are another thing altogether. They do not insist on having their own way, but they recognize that at times people are bound to fail. Indeed, the person who has hopes rather than expectations realizes that in order to go one step forward it is sometimes necessary for a group to take a step to the side—or even a step back. Many individuals who criticize a community for failing to meet the requirements of their ideal are unwilling to face up to their own flaws and weaknesses.

Self-Righteous Attitudes

When people first join a small community of Christians, they may not know anyone very well and may feel uncertain of themselves and unsure of how to interpret what others say or do. As time passes, however, they begin to settle into the group and feel more relaxed. Their feeling of strangeness recedes as they become better acquainted with the others.

As more time passes, the members begin to know each other a little too well. They come to know their taste in clothes and their facial expressions. They recognize each other's mannerisms—the way they tap their fingers or rub their eyes—as well as other habits. They become familiar with the attitudes, prejudices, and hobbyhorses of the others. Sometimes they can predict exactly what others are going to say before they have spoken a word!

In particular, members begin to notice all the differences, for example, different class backgrounds, different lifestyles, different politics, or different attitudes toward childrearing. It is all too easy to look down on others and feel superior to them.

When that happens, there is a temptation to give those who are different less time during the meetings, focusing rather on those who are like-minded. People may even find themselves passing sentence on others because they fall short of unnamed requirements. In that moment any basis for a strong bond is lost and, with it, the hope of the whole group's becoming a genuine community.

An important distinction needs to be made here. It is permissible to recognize the differences that exist between ourselves and others, even their weaknesses and failings. Paul constantly urges his readers to exercise discernment in all their dealings: with God, one another, and the wider society. Some members of the church have a gift in this direction—they see people's weaker points more quickly than the rest of us. In a way such people are the conscience of a group. But all discernment should include awareness of the factors that may give rise to personal differences—family upbringing, disappointing experiences, present difficulties—as well as a recognition of our own weaknesses and failings.

It is not discerning the truth about people that creates problems, but yielding to the temptation to judge them because of their differences. We have no right to do that; we have too many failings ourselves and lack sufficient knowledge to come to a proper decision. Only God has the knowledge to pass sentence in this way. In any case, has not God created us to be individuals—in looks and temperament, in interests and abilities—and called us in other areas to complement and correct one another? And does not God in Christ accept us as we are, with all our weaknesses and failings, indicating how we are also to accept and forgive, rather than reject and condemn, one another?

Members of a group sometimes find this hard to do. Consider the following letter from a home church that was facing this problem:

> The difficulty we seem to be battling with is the different ways we all have of relating to God. Stephen once said to me it was as if he and Jenny had two different Gods, they approach him so differently.
>
> In church, this is magnified ten times over. . . . Those whose relationship with God has much in common tend to gravitate towards one another, with an accompanying sense of enthusiasm in their

sharing of the benefits they find. Then come various forms of judgment on those not so like-minded.

This has time and again provided a problem for the institutional church. How much more is it felt in a home church? We cannot underestimate how deeply threatened people are by those whose approach is different and how desperately they seek the security of those who think the same way. Because we are not sure how to go about tackling this problem, we are inclined to avoid it by finding the "lowest" common denominator of agreement and sticking with that. This seems to entail just meeting together, sharing our concerns and interests, and trying to be involved in one another's lives as far as we are able.

I write "lowest" in quotes because I don't really consider this "low." In fact, it has the potential to be the "highest"—if anyone sees the possibility contained in it. But at present people feel without anchor, insecure, with vague feelings of "there should be something more," "is this enough?" . . . The answer I'm gradually finding for myself (not without considerable difficulty and heart searching) is that God does not have to be approached in only one way. We can delight in all the various ways people find God working in their lives.

While we know something of the power of a group of like-minded Christians praying in agreement, we have yet to experience the greater glory of unlike-minded people genuinely loving, respecting and encouraging one another in their differences until God brings about an undreamed-of unity in spirit. Our home church sits on the brink of this possibility because of the unique opportunity it offers for this unity to develop.

Accepting personal differences and forgiving others' failings are crucial to developing more than a limited or superficial community life.

Failure to Give Credit Where Credit is Due

Many people, when they come into a home church, have a relatively low estimate of themselves and their gifts. There are various reasons for this low self-esteem. It may stem from the kind of Christianity in which some people were nurtured. Certain forms of Christianity revolve around numerous positive and negative rules—read the Bible every day, witness at every opportunity, pray at all times, don't drink or dance, don't mix with certain people, don't listen to certain kinds of music. The person who fails to live up to these regulations is considered a second-rate Christian. Internalizing this judgment results in low self-esteem.

Low self-esteem may also stem from the wider cultural ethos. White males in general often praise their children for certain "masculine" attitudes and endeavors such as grit and sport. Females find praise when they exhibit certain "feminine" traits such as sensitivity and serving others. They are generally encouraged to feel inferior to males and to believe that they make a less useful contribution to society. The advertising industry and the structures of our society tend to reinforce these attitudes.

As a result of all this, many people who join a group come with a relatively low self-esteem and with a weakened capacity to encourage others. This leads to a catch-22 situation. Most people are looking for affirmation, but few are in a position to give it. Indeed, those who have low self-esteem, may be the very ones who contribute to the low self-esteem of others—with a tone of voice, a raised eyebrow, or a knowing exchange of smiles with another. After a while this inability to show appreciation for others or to encourage the development of each others' gifts produces stagnation in the group. It can even cause those who had the courage to express their needs to withdraw even farther into their shells.

The irony of this situation is that every Christian is of inestimable valuable—a daughter or a son of God. What higher status is there? However unworthy people may feel at times or however much they may fail to reflect their Father, God only ever sees them in and through Christ—as the sinless, mature, perfect person that they will one day fully be. The Spirit has given them gifts to share with others. However little people may understand these gifts and however unsure they may be about how to exercise them, God has made a present of the gifts to each person for the church. In time each individual will be able to make full use of their gifts.

Once again, we need to draw an important distinction. We must learn the art of focusing on the strengths of others, not their faults, and of discerning potential strengths in even their weaknesses. God does not so much take away our shortcomings as transform them into capacities. So we have to ask God to help us view others from a divine perspective rather than our own. While we can still be aware of others' faults, we will sense the potential in even their most fragile qualities.

What a difference it would make if people saw each other in terms of their potential and treated each other accordingly! Instead of concentrating on each other's inadequacies, we would be thanking God for the privilege of knowing one another. We would also be building up one another through praise and encouragement of each other's strengths and efforts. C. S. Lewis captures the essence of this attitude in one of his most eloquent passages. Although it deals with people in general rather than Christians in particular, it is very relevant here:

> It is a serious thing to live in a society of possible gods and goddesses, to remember that the dullest and most uninteresting person you can talk to may one day be a creature which, if you saw it now, you would be strongly tempted to worship, or else a horror and a corruption such as you now meet, if at all, only in a nightmare. All day long we are, in some degree, helping each other to one or other of these destinations. It is in the light of these overwhelming possibilities, it is with the awe and the circumspection proper to them, that we should conduct all our dealings with one another, all friendships, all loves, all play, all politics. There are no *ordinary* people. You have never talked to a mere mortal. Nations, cultures, arts, civilization—these are mortal, and their life is to ours as the life of a gnat. But it is immortals whom we joke with, work with, marry, snub, and exploit—immortal horrors or everlasting splendours. This does not mean that we are to be perpetually solemn. We must play. But our merriment must be of that kind (and it is, in fact, the merriest kind) which exists between people who have, from the outset, taken each other seriously— no flippancy, no superiority, no presumption. And our charity must be a real and costly love, with deep feeling for the sins in spite of which we love the sinner—no mere tolerance, or indulgence which parodies love as flippancy parodies merriment.[4]

The more a group puts this into practice, the more each person values the other, the more all grow into the kind of people God wants them to be. And the more gratitude and encouragement we express, the more everyone's gifts are identified and developed.[5]

Settling for Too Little

Most people who first link up with a home church are enthusiastic about this new way of meeting and want to make it work. But after a while some of the novelty wears off. There are many reasons for this—outside pressures and difficulties or personal problems. Any of these can sap people's initial optimism and vitality. But serious problems can occur if people begin to settle for less than they or the group can actually offer.

Today many people have the tendency to take on too many responsibilities. As a result, the home church often has to fit in after everything else. Overcommitted people may not have the time to pray for others in the group or to make any contact with them during the week. They may not have time to consider what contribution they can bring to the meeting or whether there is someone in the group who requires their special attention. They may come to the group worn out by their many other commitments.

Some people are burdened with heavy responsibilities. Think of mothers with preschool children, individuals experiencing intermittent periods of intense busyness at work, or those suffering personal dislocation due to circumstances outside their control. In such situations other members of the home church should take on some of the burden. But a person who is weighed down by habitual busyness and long-term overcommitment needs to reassess his or her priorities.

The drift toward a lower level of functioning in a group may come more from the dynamics of the group itself than from outside pressures. The presence of one or two strong personalities who are overly skeptical about their faith, hypercritical of others, or generally lax in attitude may inhibit others. Or some members may be so preoccupied with sharing their problems or supporting those who are struggling that they never move from focusing on the negative to celebrating the positive.

What can be done about this? There is a key role here for the members of the pastoral center of a group. They can act as a counterweight to such tendencies and create a climate in which others feel less inhibited. But sometimes this means challenging the dominant influences in the group.

One factor in particular causes a group to settle for a low common denominator: ourselves—our own level of involvement and commitment. In the last analysis, the quality of a home church's life will be reflective of the quality of the lives of its individual members. Allowing the values and the pressures of secular society to control us will diminish the vitality of the groups to which we belong. Whenever we do not contribute to the best of our ability, everyone loses something. If when we come together we focus more on what others can contribute to us than on what we can contribute to them, then we all will be the poorer for it.

The attitude we should strive to have is captured by Francis of Assisi's prayer that begins, "Lord make me an instrument of thy peace." When we gather together we should

not so much seek to be consoled as to console;
to be understood as to understand;
to be loved as to love.
For it is in giving that we receive;
it is in pardoning that we are pardoned;
· and it is in dying that we are born to eternal life.

If only two or three attend a group in this spirit, the remainder will be encouraged to follow their example. To come in this spirit is to come in the Spirit of Christ, reflecting in our attitude toward others his commitment to and involvement with us.

Finally, we need to distinguish between our general calling in Christ and our specific stage in our personal pilgrimage. All of us are at different levels of maturity and at different points in our life cycle. Some are young in faith, some older; some are free of family and work demands, some not. Some want to fully identify themselves with a group, others are newcomers or in transition. Some find that life is going smoothly for them at the moment, some are passing through a crisis of identity, vocation, or relationship. Given these differences, we should maintain realistic expectations of each other.

For instance, a home church that is made up mostly of young marrieds with children will not have much energy, and meetings will reflect this. Children will be distracting and demanding, further affecting the quality of the gatherings. Members of the group who insist on the ideal of a quiet, spiritually charged church will feel frustrated. Young marrieds who come expecting others to assume the burden of their children will be disappointed. Both must adapt to the actual situation, creatively making the most of it and attempting to minimize its difficulties. They could ask God to bring others into the group to share the overall responsibility. But they may simply have to grit their teeth and carry on, appreciating the good things that come out of their being together despite the difficulties.

The bottom line is to be content with what you have. This was Paul's attitude toward the varying circumstances in which he found himself. "I know what it is to be in need, and I know what it is to have plenty. I have learned the secret of being content in any and every situation, whether well fed or hungry, whether living in plenty or in want. I can do everything through him who gives me strength" (Phil 4:12–13).

But the spirit of contentment—like the spirit of acceptance, service, encouragement, and responsibility—cannot be produced at will and does not reside fully in any one individual. It is a fruit of the Spirit. Only as we come together, making up for each other's weakness, can a peaceful attitude develop in the group.

POTENTIAL POINTS OF TENSION

In addition to disagreements over "larger" issues such as those discussed above, home churches will also experience a number of disagreements over "small" issues such as those discussed below. Even seemingly insignificant differences, if they are not handled wisely, can do much to threaten the health of a home church.

Tensions will eventually emerge in any home church, where people come into close contact with one another. Genuine fellowship does not eliminate problems; it brings them out into the open, intensifies them, and creates the possibility for their resolution.

Punctuality

Flash points can arise over seemingly minor issues like punctuality. Some people regularly fail to show up on time! They seem to find punctuality constitutionally impossible and tend to be late for any type of meeting or appointment.

People may avoid addressing this touchy subject, since no one likes to offend others. When the matter is finally raised, the offending person may apologize for their habitual lateness. For two or three weeks everything is fine, but then the old behavior pattern reasserts itself. Even giving helpful hints to the latecomers, such as to prepare their meal contribution the night before or to set their clock early, rarely has the desired effect. The problem is too deeply rooted. Only coming alongside them with practical advice and developing strategies in the group that help them become more accountable, together with a considerable dose of patience, will help move them in the right direction.

Discipline of Children

The discipline of children can be a very touchy issue. Families have different approaches to discipline, arising out of their different backgrounds and different philosophies of childrearing. It is not uncommon to find one family in a group exercising a very tight rein over their children while another largely lets theirs do as they please. Some parents believe in disciplining their children physically, others do not.

The potential for tension and conflict over this issue is considerable, especially when there are several children in the group. At first members of a home church tend to let each family handle problem situations in its own way. They do not wish to intrude on what is a very delicate area. Today many parents feel insecure about their ability to raise children. Or, especially in two-career families, they feel guilty about not spending enough time with them. Their general anxiety about childrearing makes them touchy when they suspect someone is criticizing their children. They interpret it as a direct criticism of themselves.

How does a home church come to terms with these situations? It is hard for anything positive to happen until trust is built among all the members in the group and a relationship is established between children and other members of the group. An older couple may be able to step in and help even before general trust is created. Their experience and seniority will generally enable them to get away with calling an unruly child into line or freeing an overprotected one from its parents.

Those who have previous experience in a home church can sometimes influence the situation. Once other members have gotten to know the children, they can begin to circumvent some difficulties by creating positive alternatives, e.g., redirecting the child's attention, placing them on their laps, or occasionally taking them out to play.

Gradually all the parents in a group need to reach the point where they can allow others to discipline their children in the way most natural to them. This takes time and may only come after some heart-stopping moments. In some measure differing attitudes about childrearing will remain a challenge, only changing in form as children get older. However, this process is enormously maturing for both adults and children alike.

Demanding Individuals

If a home church includes members who are particularly demanding, this can also create difficulties. We are referring here to people who tend to be obsessive or to feel insecure about themselves, not to those with specific needs, whether long-term (e.g., chronic illness) or short-term (e.g., a personal crisis).

Without realizing it, these people sometimes attempt to manipulate the group into accepting—or even rejecting— them. They can make intrusive, at times overwhelming, demands on particular people, or even on the whole home church. They may expect the entire group to focus on them, to shoulder their responsibilities, perhaps to focus meetings on their particular needs.

Another kind of demanding individual may attack the group intermittently or withdraw from it periodically in a attempt to win attention. Some people in the group may find it difficult to accept such a person. It is always easier to accept those who accept you, always harder to accept those who do not. When a problem of this kind arises, a home church can only bear with the unwarranted demands or criticisms, carefully scrutinize its own motives and attitudes, and work to demonstrate a practical love for these people. Unfortunately, this will not always solve the problem, although years of patient, prayerful commitment can bring about change. As this begins to happen, some members may be able to speak up more about such a person's occasional overly demanding or overly critical attitude. Not everyone can do this, but someone who has counseling expertise or someone who has a close relationship with the person may be able to help.

Mini-Messiahs

Those who are overly generous in helping others can also create difficulties. Appearances can be deceptive. Sacrificial service to others can spring from a variety of motives. Giving time to people, listening to their concerns, and sincerely praying for them may be motivated more by a searching for love than by a sharing of love. Giving makes such people feel needed and valued, lovable and loved. But they may also have a tendency to control others, to try to mold others into their own image rather than to free them to find their own destiny. People who demonstrate this attitude must be dealt with firmly—sometimes in private, occasionally in the meeting—always with gentleness and respect. But even addressing the issue may represent a challenge to these people's sense of selfhood. Only when controlling people learn how to receive the love of the group do they begin to lose their compulsion to dominate.

Sometimes a person who is good at helping others finds it difficult to accept any help in return. This leads to one-sided relationships. Sometimes the person concerned treats the whole group as an object of mission rather than a body of friends. Only patient encouragement can bring such people to see themselves as co-members of a common body.

CONCLUSION

The road to community is not an easy one. It is fraught with unavoidable difficulties and tensions—we are not in heaven yet. Experiencing such difficulties does not mean that we are somehow less spiritual. No, difficulties and tensions are the necessary milestones that mark our progress on the road to community. At times the journey can be exhilarating, at times it can be nerve-racking. It includes high moments and low ones. There are times when you feel you could not survive without

your home church, and there are other times when you wonder whether it is really worth the trouble.

A helpful analogy to this situation is provided in the bio-
logical family into which we were born. We did not choose
our relatives; neither do we choose those with whom we are
involved in church. We do not necessarily have a great deal in
common with our relatives beyond the natural bond that
unites us; nor may we have much in common, except spiritually, with others in the church. We experience occasional tensions and embarassing moments with our relatives, just as
we do from time to time with people in the church. To expect
a troublefree passage, a succession of pious experiences, or
constant in-depth relationships is to have an unrealistic and
romantic view of the church.

Tensions in home-church life can only be tackled in a
spirit of thankfulness and patience. Dietrich Bonhoeffer speaks
about the importance of gratefulness. He reminds us that only
if we give thanks for the "little things"—even in the midst of
problems—will the "big things" we desire from God come
our way:

> We think we dare not be satisfied with the small measure of spiri-
> tual knowledge, experience and love that has been given us, and
> that we must constantly be looking forward eagerly to the higher
> ground. . . . We pray for the big things and forget to give thanks for
> the ordinary, small (and yet really not small) gifts. How can God
> entrust great things to one who will not thankfully receive from
> Him the little things? If we do not give thanks daily for the Chris-
> tian fellowship in which we have been placed, even where there
> is no great experience, no discoverable riches, but much weak-
> ness, small faith and difficulty; if, on the contrary, we only keep
> complaining that everything is so paltry and petty, so far from
> what we expected, then we hinder God from letting our fellow-
> ship grow according to the measure and riches which are there
> for us all in Jesus Christ.[6]

Not only individuals but the community as a whole should find
ways of regularly giving thanks. There are many things to celebrate, e.g., birthdays, special happenings, promotions, success
in exams, reunions, etc. We should develop little rituals around
these occasions that express our gratitude in ways that reflect
the distinctive character of our church.

For the rest, as Jean Vanier says,

We shouldn't get discouraged when things go badly and there are tensions. Each of us has to grow, each of us has the right to a bad patch and to weariness, to months of doubt and confusion. We have to know how to hold on through these difficult times and wait for happier ones.[7]

If we have come to terms with the fact that our individual Christian lives will be full of ups and downs, advances and retreats, delights and difficulties, why should we expect communal Christian life to be any different? It is more to the point to learn how to defuse times of tension. Someone needs to know the moment to produce a bottle of champagne or a chocolate cake. The visionary in a group may play an important role in helping to lift the group's eyes to its high calling in Christ.

The central place occupied by thanksgiving and patience in NT thought becomes very understandable here. Paul tells us that he learned to be content in all circumstances, whether he was receiving much or little (Phil 4:12). He also lists patience as the first characteristic of Christian love (1 Cor 13:4). Without thanksgiving and patience as its constant companions, a home church—or any other form of Christian community—has little chance of survival.

Over a period a time, as the home church experiences and grows through tensions, there develops a quiet trust in the providence of God—a realization that God really has brought it together, that God has the interests of the church as a whole at heart, not just the interests of individuals. A vital trust in God provides the courage necessary to face the next round of tensions and difficulties.

NOTES

1. Peck, *The Different Drum*, 86ff.
2. D. Bonhoeffer, *Life Together* (SCM: London, 1954) 16–17.
3. Vanier, *Community and Growth*, 26.
4. C. S. Lewis, *The Weight of Glory and Other Addresses* (New York: Macmillan, 1949) 14–15.
5. On the importance of encouragement generally, see the helpful book by L. Crabb Jr. and D. Allender, *Encouragement: The Art of Caring Community* (Colorado Springs, Colo.: NavPress, 1984).
6. Bonhoeffer, *Life Together*, 19.
7. Vanier, *Community and Growth*, 220.

9

THE IMPORTANCE OF INREACH

*Ministering to Children
and Adults*

In this chapter we will look at the potential of home churches for drawing in people who are on the edges of a local church but are not fully integrated into it. Home churches naturally attract such people and help connect them more fully with Christ, with other believers, and with God's purposes in the world. This is what we mean by "inreach," and it is as important as "outreach," which has been referred to in previous chapters and which will be examined in chapter 10.

Despite the fact that local churches include many interest groups, certain people still tend to miss out. Consider, for example, the diminishing numbers in junior Sunday schools and youth groups. Whatever benefit these groups bring, they fragment the family and keep younger people segregated from the total community of the church. This is one reason that a large proportion of children in junior Sunday school never join a youth group. It is also part of why the majority of teenagers in such groups do not become adult members of the church.

In many cases single people miss out, as do those married to a nonbelieving spouse, those who are separated or divorced, and those who are widowed. A singles' group may provide acceptance to divorced people and support to the widowed, but it does not provide an opportunity for all to meet and mix in a substantial way.

People who are physically, psychologically, or developmentally challenged need to belong to a small group where they can minister to others in special ways that only they know. Women in the church are still disadvantaged, despite making gains over the last two decades. Sunday school classes or Sunday services that cater to aged church members also tend to segregate the elderly from, rather than integrating them into, the range of people in the congregation.

INREACH AMONG CHILDREN

The place of children in a home church has always been a matter of considerable discussion. No one claims to have the answer, but we do have the right question. In the middle of a discussion about this issue some years ago, one of the women asked, "Don't you think that what we do for our children in a home church should be as different from the typical junior Sunday school as worship in a home church is different from a typical Sunday service?"

We all recognized the truth in her words, but what did they mean in practice? Most people did not want to repeat the school activities children experience during the week. But what to put in their place? We began with unanimous agreement on two basic principles. First, the responsibility for the Christian education of children lies primarily with the parents.[1] Second, as a small church we can become God's family in a real sense and make the children as much a part of all that we do as everyone else. It is important to find new ways of integrating children into the life of the church. But to do that requires a new way of looking at Christian formation or education of children.

Some Basic Convictions

Behind our efforts to include the children lie certain basic assumptions regarding the character of each child's relationship with God and the nature of the Christian life. First, every child is a unique individual, created in the image of God with a capacity to choose whether he or she will respond to God's love. Because of this capacity God relates to each child individually. There is no blueprint available to us that explains the course of that relationship, i.e., the manner in which it develops or the period of time that it involves. This means that we, as parents and as churches, endeavor to introduce our children to God as the creator and sustainer of the universe and the Father of our Lord Jesus Christ—someone whom we love and seek to honor with our whole lives, someone who loves the children more than their parents and teachers do. While we encourage a relationship to grow between the child and God, we do not force it. We seek to discern the state of a child's relationship with God, and then we actively encourage its development by prayer and "specific input."

We are not surprised when our children begin to question and to doubt, since we recognize this as a necessary precursor to new growth and understanding. Of course, it is our earnest desire that our children grow into a mature relationship with God. For some this will be relatively easy, for others exceedingly difficult. For some it will come early in life, for some later—and for some, maybe not at all. Our searching of the Scriptures, for all the promises that we came across, unearthed no support for the belief that the children of believing parents will *necessarily* become believers themselves. Distressing though this is, we recognize that God does not coerce anyone into a relationship and that we should not attempt to do this either. Our responsibility as parents or the church is to be faithful: to do and to become all that God asks of us. The rest is up to God and the child.

A second basic assumption has to do with the character of the Christian life. The Christian life has at its heart a trinitarian relationship—with God, through Christ, in the Spirit. This assumption involves beliefs, but it is not *primarily* an acceptance of certain doctrines. Jesus commanded us to "love the Lord your God with all your heart . . . and your neighbor as yourself." The danger with placing too great an emphasis on doctrines is that they tend to become all-important. They can lower our eyes from God to human formulae, and they can create divisions between people who are sisters and brothers in Christ. Putting the emphasis where Jesus does reminds us of our need for God's forgiveness—even of our doctrinal errors—and that we are all at different stages in our relationship with God.

This relationship is not just an occasional one. It permeates the whole of our lives, leaving no aspect of our personalities, work contacts, circle of friends, leisure, or church life untouched. It is dynamic: constantly changing and constantly growing. But the character of that growth is not a straight line that progresses from one experience to the next. Sometimes we take one step forward and two steps back before we surge into new understanding and deeper commitment. We cannot attain these periods of growth through our own determination and effort. The patterns and rhythms of our spiritual growth lie in the hands of God.

Young Children

The child's relationship with God begins at the moment of birth. This is why the responsibility of introducing children to God is laid on the shoulders of parents. It is they who are closest to their children during their early formative years.

How can a little child actually learn to relate to God? An illustration may help. For several years when our children were babies, we lived in England. Their grandmothers, uncles, aunts, and cousins were in Australia. However, the boys did not have to wait until we returned to Australia to get to know and love some of their relatives. We told them stories of our childhood, sent and received letters, parcels, tapes, and photographs, and frequently talked about these people. When we did eventually return and the boys saw the relatives for themselves, the bonds they formed were all the stronger for the way in which they had learned to love their relatives through us. So it is with children and God. They first learn to relate to their heavenly parent through us, their earthly parents.

Deuteronomy 6:20ff. emphasizes the responsibility of parents to explain the law to children. Unfortunately, when we become parents very few of us are sufficiently mature as Christians to be confident about our capacity to do this. We are aware of our shortcomings as models for our children,[2] yet we tend to set extraordinarily high standards for ourselves in this area and regard ourselves as failures when we do not reach them. But does God expect us to be people who have "arrived," who have all the answers? Or does God want us to be people who are learning to love God with all our heart, our mind, and our strength (Deut 6:5)? We are to be people who make mistakes but are not afraid to ask for forgiveness; whose understanding is not perfect, but who seek to grow in knowledge and wisdom; who are learning to love ourselves and our fellow creatures; who find it hard to trust, but are gradually gaining confidence in a God who is totally dependable. Can we really ask more of ourselves than this? We permit our children to share our pilgrimage, learning that the Christian life is not necessarily lived on an even keel but is very much an up-and-down matter full of doubt, despair, and uncertainty as well as confidence, joy, and assurance.

Fortunately for parents, the responsibility for children does not solely lie with them. The church has a secondary, but vital, role. Home churches and congregations should take their responsibilities to children very seriously. A home church begins its ministry to children through ministering to their parents. It encourages their growth to maturity in all areas of their lives, including parenting. The latter happens naturally through observation, shared anecdotes, and questions. It also occurs on a more organized basis through the searching of Scriptures on issues like discipline and the reading of appropriate books or the viewing of videos prepared as aids to parenting. Of course, sometimes we learn what not to do as much as what *to* do!

A home church ministers to children through the prayers that it offers for each child from the moment the group hears a baby is on the way. After the birth it is important to welcome the child into the church in some tangible way. In home churches attached to denominations this welcoming usually takes place at a regular service and follows the tradition of that denomination, whether child dedication or infant baptism. The home church in such a congregation should welcome the child as well. In independent home churches this welcome can take the form of either a baptism or a dedication and can involve the whole cluster in a creative and moving way. In some home churches all adults accept the responsibility of becoming godparents to the child.

Since children are a regular part of home churches, they have additional models to the ones provided by their parents. From a very early age they learn that there is no set way of relating to God. They learn that different types of people are Christian—middle class, working class, intellectual, practical, mainstream, or counterculture. They also learn the dynamics of God's family, its responsibilities, tensions, and struggles. They learn the costs as well as the rewards. And rewards for children can be great. It can be wonderful to have many "uncles," "aunts," "cousins," "sisters," "brothers," "grandmothers," and "grandfathers" in the Lord with whom to celebrate Christmas, Easter, and birthdays, with whom to play and have special outings, chat on the telephone, and exchange letters. Of course, some rewards are not always perceived as such by the child. It can be very trying to find oneself with people, be they adults or children, with whom you have little in common. Sometimes a child finds it difficult to accept others as they are and to begin to love them. Yet that is what being part of a home church means—for children as well as for adults. A home church is a unique social laboratory in which children come to understand the central meaning of the gospel.

Teenagers

During the teenage years the quality of relationships between young people and adults becomes increasingly important. As young people begin to separate themselves from their parents, they find others in home church to whom they can turn for advice about careers, friendships, and romances. There are people with whom they can discuss politics, sports, music, literature, and faith. There are people with whom they can talk if they sometimes feel misunderstood at home. The absence of rigid separation of age groups in a home church facilitates teenagers' transition into adult status in the group. It is good to mark this significant transition with some "ritual" appropriate to the young person and the situation. In a tangible way this marks a commitment by both the teenager and the church.

Very young children may join in certain parts of the meeting—the singing, playing, storytelling and eating. School-age children may remain with the adults longer, entering into prayer, study, and discussion, particularly if the church modifies its activities to encourage their active involvement. As the youngsters become teenagers, they generally begin to participate in the entire meeting, as part and parcel of their desire to join the adult world.

Naturally some teenagers find it easier to make this adjustment than others. It depends on the group's attitude toward them, their relationship with their parents, and their own developing convictions. But even if one of them decides to drop out of the group, the relationships that have been established with other members ensure a continuing link with the home church and all that it stands for.

The peer group issue is a difficult one, and different home churches resolve it in different ways. Those attached to denominational churches usually have youth groups that teenagers can attend, as do some clusters of home churches. Such groups can be gathered around a common interest, such as photography, backpacking, or biking.

Our experience with teenagers in home churches makes us wonder if a Christian *peer* group is as important as some parents tend to think. Whenever the question of the peer group is raised, we ask, "Isn't the average Christian teenager more deprived of quality relationships with adults than with peers? Aren't those relationships ultimately more significant?" It is too easily forgotten that for nineteen centuries young people in Christian families matured in faith without the benefit of Christian peer group organizations.

How It Works Out

Including Children in Gatherings

How do children participate in a home church gathering? This depends on the number of children in a particular group, the age range, and the imagination and skill of the adults. To begin with, most children love to sing. It is not difficult to include special songs that children like, for example, "Away in a Manger," "All Things Bright and Beautiful," "He's Got the Whole World in His Hands," or even "Humpty Dumpty"! Percussion instruments, clapping, and dancing make it possible for younger members to participate even when the songs are more "adult." Some children will be confident enough to present a song, a dance, or a mime. Or they may play an instrument, read a story, or recite a poem. In any case, it is good to spend time collectively with the children at some point in the gathering. This may take the form of a story (either told or read, biblical or other), a mime, or a play. It can include games and a time of prayer in which the children participate.

Children should also be provided with the opportunity to relate to one another on their own level. Most often this means playing in another part of the house or outside, with one or more adults present. As the children get older, they can be included more often with the adults, especially when the learning time draws on the imagination. This can be done by asking people to identify with the characters in a biblical story or by role playing followed by a discussion in which both adults and children participate.[3]

Here is a description of how one home church folds children of varying ages into their gatherings.

Each week a different family is responsible for conducting the meeting and anyone from the family may read or pray or initiate the Lord's Supper. Often the older kids are eager to do this and they readily read and lead prayer. They also participate in our conversations as we fellowship, and they sing with us as we worship. It is usually the case that they stay for the teaching as well.

When we are studying Scripture we usually do so with everyone until the youngest children become restless, at which time they may go out to play or go off somewhere else in the house for games or videos. The older kids will sometimes join them and care for them by playing with or reading to them.

The teenagers enjoy the special privilege of being able to float between the two worlds of adult and child as they so choose, with an occasional suggestion from their parents or the host about a special task like finding the chairs, setting the table, or helping with the younger children. They do consistently avoid clean up. We collectively engage them in conversation and prayer, remembering their concerns about schools and jobs and what college to attend. The budding romances in their lives are followed and they are free to share with us about them. They receive a lot of encouragement in expressing themselves verbally and creatively. We solicit their opinions regularly. Their friends are always welcome to join us. (And they do.)

In the normal course of our life together as a community, there is very little segregation according to age. We tend to all pile in on whatever the event is and then sort ourselves out according to our interests, which often cross the lines of age. The teenagers are given responsibilities as we discover their individual talents and strengths. They are hired for babysitting, lawn work, odd jobs, and as taxis when they begin to drive. We include them in our social events as much as they will tolerate us. But there is a strong affirmation that each child is an individual and not just a part or extension of the parent. (For that reason, from a very early age, relationships are cultivated with the children by all the members of the community so that by the time the teen years roll around, there are many relationships of trust already in place.

Many of our teenagers express extreme self-confidence in their dealings with adults even outside of the community.)

When people join the community with teenage children, the family is welcomed in as a whole and each person is engaged by others in activities of interest to them. It's a fitful process at times, and it is easier with some than others, but it is consistent with our convictions about church being our whole life together, not isolated events, our relationships being fluid rather than contrived and our organization being people- not program-driven. The teenagers receive special recognition as straddling the two worlds of child and adult in a world that offers little support or integration. We do our best to make them feel a part of the larger group, we are specific about the meaningfulness of our life together with God at the center, and we try to communicate a context for the events of daily living. It is our hope that we stand in opposition to the meaninglessness and self-indulgence offered by the culture around them.

The parents receive encouragement from the other adults regarding their children's strengths and individuality as well as having a place to share their trials and frustrations.

A few years ago we were introduced to a young woman who had grown up as a member of an underground church behind the iron curtain. She spoke most eloquently of the nurturing she and the other children had received. From the age of eight they were encouraged to lead Bible studies (suitably instructed and aided by an adult) because in their persecuted situation the children could be left without adult mentors at any time. Her story challenged us and showed that our understanding of nurturing children's faith and gifts has been severely limited.

Some groups allocate one day a month as "children's day" when they have a picnic and play games or engage in some activity like baking bread, painting a mural, or making a set of puppets. A picnic should not be regarded as mere entertainment. Approached in the right way, it is an important way of getting to know the creator of the universe, celebrating God's world, and celebrating the life and energy God gives us.

Recently a friend of ours had one of "those revelations" in his understanding of how to include the children in home church. Here is his own description of what happened.

This past Sunday I had an experience that I think taught me something very important about doing-with-the-kids. Something unusual happened. No, that's not strong enough—something "unprecedented" happened.

Sunday was our network meeting (when all the home churches in our network get together at one place), and it was my home church's turn to be responsible for facilitating the meeting and providing a teaching. I agreed to teach and was going to do something typically erudite, complex, and detached from real life. But one member of my home church suggested that, since the last two network meetings had involved erudite and complex teachings, I do something that included the kids.

I was crushed but agreed that is was the right thing to do. After all, our home church has made what I thought were substantial strides over the last two years in including the kids. We call it "integrated Bible study" since we do our teachings in a way that integrates all ages, but that's another subject. In any case, "including the kids" became my job in preparing the teaching.

My subject was community and church. But I began by helping the whole network make four lists:

• What I like most about church.
• What I like least about church.
• What I would like to do more of.
• What I would like to do less of.

The under-eights went first and said what they liked and disliked about the way we did church. Then the under-sixteens went, then it was a free-for-all. Naturally, one of the things the under-eights and under-sixteens put on the "like least" list was teachings. Don't worry. I wasn't the least bit offended. But it was a rollicking good discussion, and I believe we came to some helpful things about what God is doing with us here and now. Then we prayed and ate and went home.

And then the unprecedented thing happened. I got a phone call from one of the kids. The message was: I really enjoyed your teaching. Thanks. Good-bye.

Now, in twenty-five years of teaching that had never happened to me. Oh, the grown-ups are normally good-natured and make kind comments about how they learned something or were touched or ministered to, etc. Sometimes, at least, they are sincere about it. But *never* had I heard that kind of praise, unsolicited, from a kid. Pretty fluky.

Later in the day, I got a second phone call from an unrelated kid. The message was the same: I really enjoyed your teaching. Thanks. Good-bye.

I was flattered. Not flattered—flattened. That second phone call changed it from a fluke to a landslide consensus in my mind. What on earth had I done to bring out this kind of response? It was especially mystifying in that our home church had been working on including the kids in teachings and pitching them to be inclusive for years.

So I began to ponder, and here's what I think I'm learning: there's a big difference between doing something that includes kids and including the kids in doing something.

It's the difference between participating as an actor and participating as a director. In our "integrated Bible studies" we grown-ups had picked the subjects and made certain that we drew the appropriate morals from the Bible stories we used (since Bible stories are notoriously dangerous from a moralist's point of view). We had gone out of our way to include the kids, but we had never included them in setting the agenda.

I think that what the kids picked up on in my teaching last Sunday was that they were really getting to "direct" the course of things. We weren't just presenting them with something they could participate in; we were opening ourselves to learning with them by learning from them.

I'm still trying to process this. I don't quite know what it means for our ongoing life together. But I do know that I'm not going to be quite so complacent about thinking we have "included" the kids just because we have done something that requires their participation. I think they want (and deserve) a bigger role than that. I know that as a parent, one of my constant struggles is to remind myself to really "listen" to my kids. They need direction and discipline, but the danger we grown-ups face is getting trapped in that directing role so that we can't effectively do *with* our kids because we're so busy doing *for* them.

Ministry to the children need not stop here. It can include occasional outings with adults, opportunities to play with other children, group visits to movies, museums, or concerts, as well as overnight (or weekend) stays with adults and other children.[4] Adults' relationships with children should not be purely social. Here is a wonderful, God-given opportunity for discipling on a one-to-one basis. In some home churches this discipling develops naturally. In others it needs to be encouraged by alerting adults to the possibilities and perhaps deciding together who is most suited to mentor this or that child. Where a home church exists as part of a cluster or denominational church, it is possible for the mentor to come from the wider community.

Including Children in the Lord's Supper

Whether or not children participate in the Lord's Supper varies from group to group. Some home churches attached to denominational churches are reluctant to include children. Some people may feel that, where bread and wine are separated from the other food and drink, the children should take part only in the actual meal. There is room for considerable latitude here. The situation in independent home churches can be different, since most people regard the meal to which everyone brings a contribution as the Lord's Supper. Children take part in this quite naturally, gradually learning as they do so what Jesus' death means to them and how we can share our lives with one another. It goes without saying, we hope, that adults talk and relate to children and young people in the context of the meal in the same way that they chat with one another.

We are currently helping a new group get under way. One of the members is a delightful two-year-old girl. Each week she watches as we pass around the loaf of bread, breaking off pieces to give each other in Christ's name. One week she picked up the basket with the remaining bread and proceeded to move around the circle, giving to each of us in turn a small piece of bread. She has begun to learn what the Lord's Supper is all about!

Celebrating Children's Membership in the Home Church

We have already discussed the options open to parents when a new child comes into the family. A dedication or infant baptism in a home-church setting is a moving and challenging occasion for all concerned and particularly encouraging for the parents. In later years, depending on the denominational allegiance of the group, opportunity will arise for young people to declare their full consciousness of God's commitment to them and of their commitment to God. This may be through baptism or some other ceremony. Once again, the home-church setting lends special significance to such an occasion. The atmosphere of an extended Christian family, plus the freedom to construct a form of service appropriate to the individual, adds much to what happens. When an eighteen-year-old was baptized at a favorite fishing spot on the edge of a quiet mountain stream, encircled on the sandy shore by the members of his home-church cluster, it was a very special event.

What Children Provide

Our discussion of home church ministry to children should also consider what the children contribute to the life of a home church. Just as the adults provide "uncles" and "aunts" to the children, so children become "grandchildren," "nephews," "nieces," "brothers," and "sisters" to others. It is marvelous to have a baby come into a home church. The baby gives the adults something: the opportunity to watch her grow, developing her own personality, form relationships, enjoy the world God made for us, and learn to be part of our Christian family. The simplicity of children's prayers, questions, observations, and love can be profoundly moving and encouraging. The searching questions—and provocative arguments—of teenagers may cause us to think afresh or may remind us of our own faith struggles. There is great joy in seeing them make real strides in their relationship with God as they find their niche in the church.

Children also help us learn—one of the reasons that Jesus held them up as a model to his disciples. They show us how to unbend, play, give of ourselves emotionally, and celebrate more freely. Their uninhibited responses encourage us to be more direct and spontaneous. They teach us patience. But perhaps the most important contribution children can make is just being there, helping create a genuine family atmosphere, stretching our feelings, imaginations, and ideas to the limit as they demand our consideration and love.

Two final thoughts. The first child in any family is disadvantaged in that the parents have to learn their parenting skills as they go. The second child gets the benefit of parents who are more confident and competent. So, too, in a home church. The first children in home churches are, in a sense, the guinea pigs. The second generation then receives the benefit of what we have learned. We would rather it had been otherwise, but unfortunately there have been no models to follow.

We would be remiss in not emphasizing the important part prayer plays in our ministry to the children. We pray for the children in all facets of their lives. We also pray for their parents and for ourselves as a church in relation to the children so that they may come to know and to love our Father in heaven.

INREACH AMONG ADULTS

Within any group there are likely to be adults who are in particular situations that render them needy, marginalized, or simply requiring of a little extra sensitivity. We are thinking here of some single people, lone attenders, the physically or mentally challenged, seniors, members with varying ethnic backgrounds, and many women.

Single People

People are single for a variety of reasons. Some have made a conscious choice to remain single—to pursue a vocation unhindered by family ties, to care for another person, or to avoid relating to the opposite sex. Other single people want to marry and have children. No church, large or small, can guarantee the right match for a single person. God may provide a suitable mate from the congregation, but matchmaking is not necessarily a function of the congregation, let alone a small group or home church within it. The church is there to provide support and encouragement while *God* assists people in this area. God may or may not involve other members of the church in this process. Whatever the reason for their singleness, single people need to find a wider community than friendship can provide: they need some kind of family to which they can belong. Indeed, all of us—married and unmarried— need this to develop into fully mature persons.

A home church is well equipped to provide the secure, accepting environment in which the single person can find a home and in which the married couple can break out of the limitations of the nuclear family. First, the home church provides a set of committed, familylike relationships that many singles in our society lack. These relationships include not only the emotional support but also physical contact. The hugs, kisses, knowing looks, and nudges that are a genuine expression of life together are vital to the single person.

Second, the home church provides an opportunity to discuss the issues raised by being single within the context of these relationships. These issues may include sexual longings, lack of companionship (especially around the holidays), the priority of work, coping with friends who are married, not having children, and home ownership. Daily life raises a myriad of issues that it is so helpful to talk through over cups of coffee and via the telephone with members of the extended home-church family. Some within the church will develop a common social life around shared interests like movies, dancing, photography, or hiking. It may also be possible to celebrate holidays together.

Third, precisely because they are single, some people have time and energy to give to a home church that marrieds with children lack. Some can contribute by preparing talks, facilitating Bible studies, or performing music. Some singles relate particularly well to children and teenagers. Outside the gathering, singles may contribute to the welfare of a family by taking the children on outings, visiting the home, or babysitting while housebound parents pursue some personal interest. The very fact that singles are not preoccupied permanently with children introduces a different perspective into their conversation and helps those with children maintain a broader interest in the world around them.

Lone Attenders

Not all lone adults are in fact "singles." Some have non-believing spouses at home, while others are separated, divorced, or widowed. These people are sometimes accompanied by children. The needs of fractured family units are great, especially those that are trying to come to terms with a divorce or separation. They greatly need love and acceptance, which a small group is able to provide better than a larger gathering. Not that any group can meet all their needs—only God can sustain them ultimately. So how can linking up with a home group in the church lighten their load?

Many unbelieving spouses are more open to attending a home church than a traditional service. Friendships can develop between the spouse and other members of the home church as they meet socially for dinner parties, picnics, or birthday celebrations. More than one unsympathetic spouse has eventually joined a home church because the barriers were broken down in this way. But this does not always happen. The church has to help the Christian partner accept the unbelieving spouse, while actively praying that God will continue to work in the other's life. In our experience, where larger church gatherings are more participatory, such spouses are also more likely to come. This enables them to connect with other people and enter into what is taking place.

What about those who are bereaved? A home church is well placed to provide a caring group of people who are not just there for the initial grieving period, but for the long haul. This is important because the need for a supportive network and a family circle does not diminish as time passes. The home church provides a context within which the life of the deceased person can be remembered and celebrated. The group creates a safe place where the bereaved can work at discovering his or her new identity and role as a single person.

What about those who are separated or divorced? The home church can accept them just as they are. Caring for their many hurts and unresolved conflicts can be costly and time-consuming. Some families dare the church to love them, warts and all. Others demand (perhaps unconsciously) that the church make up for the absent spouse and parent. It is not uncommon for a deserted husband or wife (or widow or widower) to expect the church to satisfy their needs for affection. Their children may also expect the church to provide the attention they crave from the missing mother or father. Yet even a very familial group cannot fully compensate for such a lack. Precisely because such families draw out the concern and prayer of the church, they are a gift from God. The caring is not a "one way street," from the group to the needy family. The lessons that people in the group learn from the needy family's circumstances and struggles can be enormously helpful.

In all of these situations the home church can give practical as well as emotional and spiritual assistance, e.g., providing meals, minding children, offering financial aid, mowing lawns, and so on. The amount and nature of the pastoral care a group can give depends on a home church's particular resources and personnel—and the number of needy families already within its ranks. Where such a group is part of a wider cluster or congregation, additional resources lie ready at hand.

The Challenged

In the church all worldly distinctions of gender, class, and race are overcome (Gal 3:28). This includes distinctions based on differing abilities. We all meet as equals in the sight of God, each with a special need and a special gift to share. As Jean Vanier, founder of the L'Arche communities for the handicapped so eloquently reminds us, all of us are "handicapped" in some way.

For a variety of reasons home churches tend to attract a disproportionate number of "challenged" people. Perhaps these churches have a flexibility that makes it easier for such people to fit in without drawing attention to themselves. For example, someone who suffers from a chronic bad back finds it more acceptable to lie on the floor in a living room than in the aisle of a church sanctuary! A deaf person can lip-read more easily when facing the speaker. The needs of someone who is blind or someone who has a learning disability can be more easily accommodated in a home church than in a large congregation.

The group that welcomes differently abled persons into its midst must remain sensitive to their needs. As Jean Vanier points out,

> When a community welcomes people who have been on the margins of society, things usually go quite well to begin with. Then, for many reasons, these people start to become marginal to the society of the community as well. They throw crises which can be very painful for the community and cause it considerable confusion, because it feels so powerless. The community is then caught in a trap from which it is hard to escape. But if the crises bring it to a sense of its own poverty, they can also be a grace.

> There is something prophetic in people who seem marginal and difficult; they force the community to become alert, because what they are demanding is authenticity. Too many communities are founded on dreams and fine words: there is so much talk

about love, truth and peace. Marginal people are demanding. Their cries are cries of truth because they sense the emptiness of many of our words. . . . But sometimes marginal people can become a focus for unity, because they . . . can force the community to pull itself together.[5]

That would be the testimony of one home church that we know of. For the past twenty years they have had as a member a woman who could be described as a person with limited intelligence. Alice became acquainted with one of the women in the group through a community endeavor to help those who were unable to read or write. In time Alice became a part of the woman's extended family, sharing weekly meals, babysitting, participating in special events and occasional holidays. Eventually she was drawn into the life of the home church to which the woman's family belonged.

Alice has been a precious gift to that church. Her warm heart and willingness to admit that she doesn't understand everything has endeared her to the adult members, and she is much loved by the children, who appreciate her simplicity and childlike demeanor. But that is not to say that Alice has always been easy to live with. She can be very demanding at times, obstinate and fearful because she doesn't always understand what is happening around her.

While the Hughes family has been her major support, others in the church have included her in dinner parties, outings, and holidays. Some have shared the responsibility of getting her to and from doctor's appointments. In many ways she has been a group "project," although that is certainly not the way the home church would talk about her. As Alice describes her experience as a member of the home church, "When I made contact with the group I didn't know nothing. I was dubious about going to a house church—but when I went they gave me such confidence in myself, although I'd had no chance in life. The house church helped me a lot. That's all I can say."

Seniors

We live in a society that tends to separate those who are older from those who are younger. Seniors are grouped together in retirement homes or villages. Senior citizen clubs and tours provide a wide range of leisure activities. Many seniors live a long distance away from their children. Age segregation is also practiced in local churches.

People visiting the West from other cultures, especially those coming from non-Anglo or third world countries, are often shocked by this age segregation. It makes no sense to them. In their own settings older people may get together for certain purposes, but the importance and value of the extended family remains deeply embedded in the culture. Older people are regarded as having a unique role to play in the nurture and direction of younger people, indeed, of the whole group.

Home churches, and congregations based on them, seek to reclaim some of the benefits of these arrangements. They wish to affirm the distinctive contribution that older people can make to the life of a group. In a home-church setting there is much such people can contribute. They have accumulated a wealth of wisdom over the years, and they provide a model for younger people, present a different perspective on life, and create a sense of continuity with the past. They can establish relationships with children who are deprived of regular contact with their grandparents. Children need this kind of relationship with older people—and vice versa. Seniors have more time to visit and be visited, to talk and to listen, to reflect and to pray. They often have more patience. In these and other ways they add much to the life of a home church and gain much from it themselves.

Older people, like everyone else, have their weaknesses and failings. They can be hard of hearing, forgetful, repetitive, overbearing, or demanding. They can become set in their ideas and find change difficult to handle. They may also depend on others for transportion and personal support. It is exactly here that we learn what it means to be a genuine extended family that spans several generations and what it means to accept the idiosyncrasies as well as the accumulated wisdom of such people. Isn't this what being the body of Christ is all about?

Varying Races

It has often been said that ten o'clock Sunday morning is the most segregated hour in the week. People gather in different churches according to their color or ethnic background.

Two or more congregations of people from different races or cultures may occupy the same building on a Sunday, but they do so in turn, not at the same time. Genuinely multicultural churches do not exist in large numbers. There is no simple answer to this problem of segregated church groups. Some people, such as recent immigrants who do not as yet know the common language, may have a need for them. Ethnically homogeneous home churches may have a role within a multicultural congregation, allowing people to reap the benefit of both contexts. Where two or more congregations made up of people from different races or cultures use one building, it would be possible for home churches to cut across those boundaries and provide people with face-to-face contact with each other. In other settings multicultural home churches can be established right from the very beginning. For example, we have spent a year with a new group that includes people from four different countries and three different ethnic groups.

Research looking for what enables people from various ethnic and racial backgrounds to come together and develop good personal relationships has identified four main factors.

1. These relationships involve the whole person; that is, we do not separate business from pleasure but include and acknowledge our personal sides (such as family, interests, hopes, and dreams).

2. A sense of shared history over time is developed in these relationships; we've been through good times and bad times with each other. We've laughed and cried together and learned from one another.

3. These relationships are collaborative rather than competitive. Each person has certain strengths that can be counted on and well-known weaknesses that have to be taken into account.

4. There is a strong sense that each person affirms and values the other. We are one another's supporters and admirers.[6]

These four characteristics are a perfect description of what takes place in a home church. Other research has demonstrated that people in a racially mixed marriage have a low rate of church attendance. They experience difficulty finding a church in which both partners feel at home. The segregation in so many congregations makes one partner feel uncomfortable.

(A similar difficulty is experienced by couples whose partners come from different religious traditions, for example, Catholic and Protestant, or mainline and nondenominational.) Once again, a home church provides the setting in which such people can help create a new culture or environment that is genuinely diverse where each can feel at home, contribute in appropriate ways, and enrich the common life of the group.

Women

There is considerable controversy concerning the role of women in church meetings, but our view is that all women and all men ought to be able to participate in both smaller and larger gatherings of the church according to the gifts and maturity God has given them. Experience has shown us that both are equally able to give talks, lead discussions, exercise pastoral gifts, baptize, introduce the Lord's Supper—as well as pray, read Scripture, choose hymns, mind children, prepare meals, and do dishes. Although not every member will have exactly the same function in church, one half of the body cannot say to the other, "We have no need of you" or "You have less to offer."

Differentiation of gender roles is not normally a major issue in home churches, perhaps because of their informal setting and relational character. The issue arises only when a particular interpretation of Scripture intrudes, although, even there, people's practice is normally more inclusive than their doctrine. It is also true that even those who espouse the equality of men and women carry some cultural and theological baggage. This means that women are not always allowed to contribute all that they can. For example, men may still end up doing more of the teaching. This could be due as much to women's lack of experience and confidence in this area as to the men's assumption of the role. All women and men who are capable of "teaching," in the more traditional sense, should be encouraged to do so. In addition, it is important to recognize that learning can take place in a variety of ways, only one of which is the more traditional teaching method. Women and men both need to be encouraged to explore a variety of ways to facilitate learning in accordance with their particular gifts.

Home church opens up the possibility of the nurturing gifts of women being affirmed and developed as they take up pastoral responsibility in the group, which in the past has normally been reserved for men. This is as true within the wider cluster or congregation as in the individual home church. In general, home-church groups encourage women to minister in ways still denied them in most church circles. Many women are attracted to home churches precisely because they find opportunity and encouragement to be all and to give all that God intended. Such groups provide an excellent setting for both women and men to discover their individual gifts, develop the fruit of the Spirit, and work out their divine complementarity.

Other Groups

There are some additional subgroups of people for whom home churches have much to offer. For instance, many women who stay home with young children are largely housebound. In our society such women often live a long way from their parents. Because so many women are in the workforce today, those who stay at home usually have few neighbors to call on during the day. The kind of help a home church can give is typified by a middle-aged woman who took three children off the hands of their mother for a few hours each week. This gave the mother a real luxury—some time to herself. Eventually the mother found opportunities to help other women in that situation.

Another group to whom home churches have much to offer is the so-called baby busters or Generation X. As Joseph Higginbotham says in a recent article:

> With the possible exception of the "cell church model," none of the emerging Boomer-style churches—"Seeker," "Shopping Mall," "Seven-Day-a-Week"—are likely to appeal to Xers. On the contrary, this intimacy-driven crowd could well become the "House-Church Generation." Relational, participatory, egalitarian, and non-authoritarian, the growing house-church movement might find a generation of twenty- and thirty-something Christians ripe for its efficiency and intimacy. The first generation since the Great Depression to expect less prosperity than their parents, Generation X may see virtue in the cost-effective, streamlined efficiency of the house church. Since house churches require no special facilities, they can be started anywhere at virtually no cost. The confines of private homes and apartments make large groups impossible, so the intimacy and caring relationships Xers

desire find fertile soil in such mutually accountable interdependent communities of believers.[7]

We have also found that a home church provides a sensitive base of support for those who become unemployed or are struggling to make ends meet. Because of the close bonds that develop in a home church, members become aware of the needs of those who are less well-off. They then determine the most appropriate ways of alleviating their distress and helping them deal constructively with their situation. Examples of assistance that home churches can provide to their unemployed or low-income members include paying the rent for a couple that was branching out into a new venture, giving financial assistance to an unemployed father who could not support his family, giving practical assistance (such as tidying up the garden, providing vegetables, paying for a family outing to the cinema or a restaurant, doing babysitting, and covering unexpected expenses) to a deserted mother and children. In these days of growing unemployment and single-parent families, there is much that a small, committed group can do. In particular it can shore up faltering self-confidence. In the long term the loss of self-esteem is more difficult to endure than living in poverty.

As we have already noted, home churches are ideal for newly-arrived immigrants or for visitors spending some time in a different country. Such people face many hurdles, for example, understanding how a different culture operates, establishing contact with people in it and developing relationships with them, knowing where to go, whom to see, or what to do in certain situations, and coping with feelings of homesickness, loneliness, or confusion. A home church can provide a setting in which all of these difficulties and challenges can be addressed effectively.

Final Thoughts

Occasionally the need of a particular person or marginal group is so great that it comes to dominate most of what happens in a home church. For example, there may be so many children that very little occurs that is not child-oriented. The plight of a lonely, deserted, or bereaved person in the group— or of someone experiencing acute physical, psychological, or economic distress—may be so overwhelming that meetings tend to revolve around their concerns. A home church has the flexibility to focus on any of these for a time. But allowing one person or family to preoccupy the group for an extended period of time undermines the health and sometimes the viability of the group. It can become a therapy group, and this is not its primary purpose. Constantly focusing on the need of one person or one family drains the group of most of its resources. Others with lesser needs, which nevertheless require attention, will begin to look elsewhere for support. A balance needs to be struck between the needs of the various people in the group. A balance also needs to be struck between focusing on people's needs and on the God who can meet those needs.

A group that achieves this balance has the energy to help the needy within its ranks as well as the energy to reach out to those outside the home church who are similarly needy or in need of a Savior. In chapter 10 we will look at some of the ways home churches can be agents of transformation in our society.

NOTES

1. In this respect Lawrence O. Richards's words were a great encouragement. See *You the Parent* (Chicago: Moody, 1974).

2. A theory of Christian education along these lines may be found in another book by L. Richards: *A Theology of Children's Ministry* (Grand Rapids: Zondervan, 1983). See especially the section on the importance and character of the modeling process (pp. 78–79).

3. See, for example, R. Trudinger, *Home Groups: God's Strategy for Church Growth* (Plainfield, N.J.: Logos International, 1979) 94–98.

4. See further M. and M. Frances, *A Patchwork Family* (Nashville: Broadman, 1978) 78ff., and M. Zimmerman, *Celebrating the Christian Year* (Minneapolis, Minn.: Bethany, 1993).

5. Vanier, *Community and Growth*, 204–5.

6. J. Kouzes and B. Posner, *Credibility: How Leaders Gain and Lose It, Why People Demand It* (San Francisco: Jossey-Bass, 1995) 96.

7. Joseph Higginbotham, "The Generationally Indigenous Church," *Regeneration Quarterly* 5 (1, 1997) 32–33.

10

AGENTS OF TRANSFORMATION

Reaching Out to the
Community at Large

Throughout this book we have insisted that vision for community and vision for mission are closely connected. We have also described methods of outreach used by home churches and interactive congregations. For example, outsiders can be drawn into an encounter with Christ when baptism is viewed as an opportunity for mission as well as a welcome into the church. The semipublic character of the home in ancient societies opened up possibilities for mission through hospitality, welfare, and open-house meetings for church. Through the centuries various church renewal movements have maintained a consistent relationship between nurture and mission as well as a creative, multifaceted approach to mission.[1] Strategies for developing interactive churches include church planting through home churches and the home church as a pilot mission church in a congregation. We have eavesdropped on discussions about multiplying home churches and interactive congregations as a way of "extending the table" and "broadening the circle" to newcomers from outside the church. In chapter 9 we explored the potential for mission to take place through inreach.

Church and mission are inextricable. They cannot exist apart from each other. Trying to explain the nature of that link by means of simplistic statements such as, "the only purpose of the church is mission," "the chief goal of a home church is to evangelize," or "the church is the only society that exists primarily for its nonmembers" is not helpful here. Such statements may be stirring, but they confuse the issue. In this chapter we want to define more clearly the relationship between nurture and mission and, in particular, identify the various types of mission in which interactive churches can engage. This will lead us to consider the broader significance of home churches and their larger congregations.

THE RELATIONSHIP BETWEEN CHURCH AND MISSION

What is the main purpose of the church? The Westminster Catechism states that the chief purpose of the individual believer is "to glorify God and fully to enjoy him forever." Translated into terms appropriate to the fellowship of believers, our chief end is to glorify God and to honor one another (or glorify God in one another) and to enjoy God and one another forever. That is what gathering for church is all about! It is where we pay attention to God and to one another and where we take pleasure in God and in one another. It is where we serve God and one another and where we delight in God and in one another. It is where we submit to God and to one another, where we love God and one another.

In order to attain this purpose, we must seek to build up one another so that our church life together reflects the same quality of life that characterizes the members of the Godhead. As we do this, we become a signpost, to each other and to our wider circle, of the kingdom of God, a preview of what the kingdom is all about, a visible bridge between the present and the future. The chief end of church is to create an alternative society in the midst of the world, one that reflects within itself and transmits to the culture at large the attitudes, values, and standards of the kingdom. We are, then, a colony of heaven, providing a model of what our corporate citizenship in heaven involves while challenging the earthly societies in which we reside. Only as we develop an alternative model of reality, a foretaste of heavenly community, do we have something to contribute to those around us. Otherwise all we have to offer is promises and words. We look for ways of extending the influence of the kingdom into our homes, neighborhoods, workplaces, and societies. We can do this independently through individual work and witness in the various settings in which we find ourselves each day.

The more we build up one another in church, the more effective we will be in mission, in *being* it and *living* it as well as *doing* it. The more mission focussed we are as people, the more we deepen our fellowship in the church. Part of our responsibility in church is helping one another identify what mission entails for each of us—what our personal mission statement looks like. We should encourage, pray for, and support every member to fulfill that mission.

In summary, we cannot simply define the church as existing primarily for others and for mission. It exists primarily for God and for community. It is not just a *means* to some missionary end. It is an *end* itself, not an end only *for itself*.[2] In other words, it is not an end purely *for itself* so much as *for others*. If this sounds somewhat paradoxical, it is no more so than the language of certain other Christian convictions. What it means is that church society is open, not closed; inclusive, not exclusive.

The church is a gathered, as well as a scattered, society that is present wherever Christians happen to be. It is the regular gathering of believers to sing, pray, eat, learn, and share; it is the cluster of organizations around them (many of which are designed to reach the outsider); and it is also the scattered members of the community as they go about their daily activities during the week. When we are scattered, we can view ourselves as members of the all-encompassing heavenly church. Viewing ourselves this way allows us to link up with any other believers who are at hand, wherever we happen to be. We can associate with people outside of our congregation. Regardless of other believers' church connections, we are all co-members of the heavenly church.

This means that our congregations and home churches do not have to be heavily involved in all kinds of evangelism or social action for their members to take part. Mission does not always have to take place through church organizations and programs. Members of home churches do not have to share the same vision for mission but may be led in different ways, among different people, within different contexts. We can engage in mission on our own, wherever we are, even when we are without the company of any other Christians.

THE DIMENSIONS OF MISSION

Nearly thirty years ago a World Council of Churches report, *The Missionary Nature of the Congregation,* identified smaller family-type churches as one of four structures that are suited to vital mission in a pluralistic society. The description of these churches, which are made up of not more than one hundred people, perfectly matches what we have called home-church-based congregations. We often interpret mission too narrowly— as something that happens overseas, as evangelism or social action alone, or as work for which people receive special support rather than a set salary. Only if we understand mission in the broadest sense, as being any and every activity connected with the kingdom of God, will we appreciate the full set of options available to any group of people.

What are the basic dimensions of mission? (1) Mission has a civic and cultural as well as an evangelistic and social dimension. Indeed, the whole of life is to be brought into contact with the transforming power of the gospel. (2) Mission is directed to structures as well as people. If we fail to understand this, we will leave a central and pervasive aspect of our society out of the picture. Individuals exist within structures—family, workplace, society—and we can only minister effectively to them if we minister to institutions as well. To assume that structure is changed when individuals are changed only leaves structures to go their own way, becoming ever more autonomous and intrusive. (3) Mission requires us to be sensitive to all groups in society, especially to those who have the least voice and the greatest need. As David Prior says:

> It is clear, therefore, that after the example of Jesus we should be seeking out the needy and the marginalised, while being sensitive and straight with those who cross our path who are not so clearly in need. Here it is right to say that in Africa and Latin America, the needs of the underprivileged are blatant and overwhelming. . . . But who are the needy and the marginalised in Europe and North America? Whom should the church, and in particular our home churches, be seeking out? Because the majority of people who cross our paths do not have such blatant needs, in what direction should we deliberately move in order "to seek and to save the lost"? Of course, the needy are not exclusively the materially impoverished. The marginalised are not only those in

slums . . . but all whose background or occupation pushes them to the margins of society.[3]

These marginalized groups include single-parent families, the elderly or incapacitated, unmarried mothers, children, the unemployed, immigrants, addicts, and ex-prisoners. Precisely because individual home churches and their congregations provide a closely knit, practically oriented support system, they have something special to offer such people, though that is far from being all they can contribute. At times they also undertake wider action among such groups. Lois Barrett describes Mennonite home churches in North America that have sponsored refugees, supported voluntary service units, developed housing for the poor and elderly, and engaged in peace education and conflict resolution.[4] Such home churches and home-church-based congregations can also complement or link up with various secular and Christian organizations that work among such groups. They have helped people who just cannot cope with the pace of modern life—the isolated and the lonely, those who favor alternative lifestyles, or those who have been wounded by involvement in highly regimented sects.

As Scott Peck points out, communal groups offer a low-capital, high-touch, people-initiated approach, similar to Alcoholics Anonymous and fellowships modeled on it that have brought healing to millions of individuals throughout the United States and the world.[5] All this has been accomplished with virtually no organization, the founders having sensed that excessive organization is antithetical to community. There are no dues, no budgets, no buildings. Yet communal groups have made an enormous impact for good.

Evangelism and Church Planting

Some who become involved in home churches and interactive congregations temporarily shunt evangelism aside.[6] There are two reasons for this. First, they see a need to develop their relationships with one another and establish the foundation of their common life. They know they have a lot to learn about becoming a genuine community and realize that unless they do they will have little to show people about how the gospel brings people into relationship with each other as well as with God. Second, they are unsure that what often passes for evangelism is the best way of sharing the gospel with others. Before they can proceed, they need to find new ways of approaching people, ways that are more attuned to their basic questions and circumstances.

Sooner or later a concern to share the gospel with others will come to the fore. There are two ways to pursue this. First, some people have a greater God-given capacity and boldness to evangelize than do others. The church needs to endorse this gift and encourage its exercise. Second, what happens in church gatherings flows into the daily contacts that church members have with neighbors, colleagues, and relatives. Meeting with people and talking with them about God, personal issues, and relationships in light of the gospel comes naturally to church members because that is what they do regularly in church. They discover relevant ways of linking their convictions and values to issues that everyone is concerned about. Church members also recognize the importance of showing hospitality to others and practice it frequently. Just as eating and drinking together is central to what happens in church, so it is central to what happens in evangelism. Home church members realize that their best opportunities for evangelism lie with people who form part of their everyday contacts, what Tom Wolfe calls the wider "oikos," or network of relationships—the people with whom we live, work, travel, volunteer, and play.

> The basic thrust of New Testament evangelism was not individual evangelism, not mass evangelism, and was definitely not child evangelism. The normative pattern of evangelism in the early church was *oikos* evangelism . . . sharing the astoundingly good news about Jesus in one's sphere of influence, the interlocking social systems composed of family, friends and associates.[7]

Thus evangelism takes place in a range of everyday settings as we encounter others and interact spontaneously with them.

People in home churches have found other creative possibilities for engaging in evangelism. The following paragraphs provide brief descriptions of a few of them.

- Realizing how much a meal and a homely atmosphere reduced the threatening aspects of discussing Christianity, a married couple decided to open up their home on the same Saturday every month. They invited everyone they knew. The occasion began with a meal, included a discussion (introduced by a talk) of some problematic aspect of modern life, and concluded with more homemade refreshments, allowing people to mix and chat late into the evening. This "open night" drew a wide variety of people, among them a number of lapsed Christians and unbelievers.

- Concerned about the importance of developing a sense of neighborhood, a middle-aged woman whose children were in school decided to spend time getting to know the people in her immediate neighborhood. Since she was one of the few people not out in the workforce during the day, she was welcomed by those shut in through age, illness, psychological problems, or physical handicaps. Over the years her genuine interest, ready availability, sympathetic listening, and wise advice led many people to seek her out, particularly in times of crisis. Increasingly, she found opportunity to discuss spiritual matters and to pray with them.

- Several members of another home church established a preschool group in an area where few support facilities or social activities for parents existed. Their willingness to give freely of their time to the preschool group, along with their general concern for the problems of those who brought in their children, led to personal discussions and finally to a weekday Bible study. Eventually, a number of these people joined the home church itself.

- We ourselves were involved in starting a kind of "agnostics anonymous group," which advertised in the local paper and drew a dozen or more people interested in discussing issues of belief and unbelief. What was different about this group was that it focused on experiences and events in people's lives that raised doubts about the Christian faith, not just arguments against it or hesitations about it. This personal focus, which stemmed directly from home-church experience, led to a more effective encounter with various aspects of the gospel.

- Realizing that many nonchurchgoers were nevertheless interested in spiritual matters, a marketing consultant took out an ad in the local paper for a meeting in a restaurant that would explore such issues in a nontraditional church gathering. He was surprised at the number who came and also invited others to attend the next meeting. This church in a restaurant, which includes a meal and revolves around storytelling and songs rather than sermon and hymns or choruses, opens new possibilities for people who are seekers and for disenchanted churchgoers, especially in today's "eating out" culture.

- Holding meetings outdoors, as home churches and inter-active congregations can and frequently do, attracts interest. Whether it be a baptism by the river in a public park or an open-air holiday celebration, it creates an opportunity to invite people who prefer, as they put it, "to worship God in the open air" and to connect with interested passers-by and onlookers. Until recently, Mennonite congregations in Ethiopia were for-bidden to meet in public, except for funerals. The funerals, which were conducted through the city streets, made a great impact on the community people, and the church grew.

- A pastor and his wife went into a new housing development to found a church. They rented a typical home and found part-time work. Without divulging their ordained status, they began to get to know their neighbors and started a regular Sunday morning "drink on the verandah" to which various families came, bringing their children, who played in the yard. After a few months they asked if anyone would be interested in having an informal church gathering in the house. Many of them did and came to faith as a result. In time, other home churches de-veloped, with everyone coming together monthly for home-church-based congregational meetings in a rented hall.

Social and Vocational Responsibility

Members of home churches are encouraged to include all aspects of their lives in their church gatherings.[8] Doing this en-ables them to envision greater ministry possibilities through their workplaces and in their wider communities. As they share some of their work situations and specific social concerns, they start to gain a clearer appreciation of how to think and act in Christian ways. And as they work to create a culture that re-leases people's gifts, that supports people's attempts at service and at caring for others, and that helps people to overcome any disadvantages they may have, they become aware of what can be accomplished in their workplaces. Not that the assistance they get in church is enough; in-depth discussion with col-leagues and coworkers is also necessary in coming to grips with the fundamental challenges and opportunities in these areas. The following paragraphs describe some real-life experiences.

- In one of his first books, *Christianity and Real Life,* well-known lay author William Diehl wrote with passion about how the home church he helped get under way in his local Lutheran church assisted him and others to connect their religious convictions with their workplace dilemmas. Since little attempt was made in congregational meetings to bridge the gap between church and work, the weekly home-church meetings were invaluable in practical terms.[9]

• For years a community church that had reshaped itself into a congregation of home churches tried various ways of developing a ministry to a poor, ethnic neighborhood. These well-intentioned efforts resulted mostly in frustration. A breakthrough occurred when one of the church members, on graduating from medical school, set up a practice in the neighborhood. This practice quickly gained a positive reputation and became a focal point for broader ministry to the community in which some in the church were able to participate.

• After some years of encouraging people to see their work as a form of ministry itself, not just as a context for ministry, members of a cluster of three home churches came to realize the contributions they themselves had made through their service-oriented occupations: directing and assisting in institutions for psychologically disturbed youngsters, high school counseling, administering and teaching in a school for children with intellectual disabilities, chairing a group of L'Arche communities for the handicapped, supervising a federal program for the elderly, working in a resource center for church and society, counseling part time, advising for a government employment scheme. Other members made contributions in the civic and cultural areas.

• A Baptist congregation designed home churches that are equipped to have a special ministry in their immediate vicinity. The people involved in these home churches are encouraged to live on the same or on adjacent streets, often renting accommodations together. Thus the home church is well placed to identify the particular needs of people in the street and to alleviate them. This particular home church model probably works best with predominantly single, younger, and childless married couples.

• A nondenominational congregation that is built on a base of home churches has found that its very structure attracts a wide range of needy people. Inreach is carried on through the home churches and in an ancillary ministry of counseling, and the congregation as a whole is now developing organic ways of reaching out into the wider community. This has come about because the church possesses a particular ethos or culture that is attractive to needy people, not because it is conducting specific outreach programs.

- An independent home church located on the fringe of a large city has achieved considerable outreach into the neighborhood. It has come to exercise influence out of all proportion to its size through personal contacts made by its members and its growing reputation in the community. Financial assistance to needy families, practical help to single parents, emotional support to people who are psychologically or mentally disturbed, long-term accommodations for homeless young people, an "open home" for lonely people wanting a chat—all this was undertaken by a small group of fewer than a dozen committed people.

- A group of Hispanic house churches has been heavily involved for some years in improving the community and working for justice among Latinos in their region. Their efforts have included setting up English-as-a-second-language classes, training young people and women for job possibilities, supporting civic and political initiatives to better the lot of their neighborhood, etc. Others have recognized the function of home churches as playing the role of "good Samaritan," both individually and structurally (in the inner city especially).[10] Many other possibilities exist for home-church-based congregations to pursue social responsibility and justice.

- The diverse ministries of one urban home church that was part of a loose network of similar groups were summarized by one of its members: "The group did not have one major focus for ministry, but we committed to supporting our members in whatever practical ministry they were involved in." A lot of these ministries focused on disadvantaged young people: providing unemployment counseling, lending assistance in finding housing, as well as supplying part-time tutoring. Members of the community either worked with youth or managed youth welfare programs. Others participated in play groups or school-based activities. Some served on advisory bodies to state and federal government on youth and community affairs or taught part- or full-time at a nearby college in the field of welfare. A food cooperative distributed small amounts of groceries to disadvantaged families and to two local projects that provided housing for youth.

It is important to recognize that there are ways in which home churches help alleviate the wide range of social problems that exist in our society. They do this by engaging in what we might call "preventative social medicine," that is, by help-ing members to become whole people so that they do not further drain already overloaded counseling and welfare re-sources. This leads us back to the basic point made earlier, that the most significant contribution the church can make is to ac-tually *be* the church!

When it functions properly, church promotes genuine care by encouraging members to care for one another. This caring involves all aspects of life—physical, material, psychological, relational, social, and vocational. The church cannot meet every need. Sometimes people's difficulties or circumstances are such that professional help is required. But many of the problems that require professional counseling can be avoided or can be sufficiently dealt with in such a community. Just as Paul encouraged the Christians in Corinth to find people in their own group to look into a dispute instead of allowing it to go to court, so interactive churches can address or prevent many disagreements ordinarily requiring skilled help. Mem-bers facing serious situations such as bereavement, unemploy-ment, disability, or divorce can find the support they need without resorting to professional help.

The growth of twelve-step groups in churches is helping many people to do just what is described above. But they have arisen partly because of the lack of comprehensive, intergen-erational communal groups in the church. Although twelve-step programs can be helpful, they tend to provide piecemeal or temporary assistance to people, instead of the more com-prehensive, inclusive, and long-term care that a home church or basic Christian community can provide. The traditional con-gregation that lacks twelve-step or other kinds of support groups is in a precarious position. Overall, the failure of the church to really be the church contributes to the need for social and welfare services. Church life that is particularly legalistic, divisive, or poverty-stricken even generates problems in people who did not previously experience them. We now rec-ognize the harm that "toxic" or "codependent" church life can cause.[11] When the church properly fulfills its role as a caring community, the need for social welfare services will diminish. The healing and wholeness that the church produces naturally overflows through the lives of its members, positively affecting others in the wider community as well.

There is another side to this. The basic principles of Christian community, appropriately modified for a secular framework, can be implemented in the marketplace or, for that matter, everywhere else in society. Although these principles do not translate fully into all contexts, and they never translate without change in any setting, they can make a significant contribution to some businesses such as family businesses, cottage industries, partnerships, or cooperatives. Using cooperatives as an illustration, all members can participate in formulating the association's ground rules and in making decisions that affect important aspects of its operation and the actual running of its day-to-day business. Size should be limited in order to maintain a personal atmosphere. A cooperative should reflect the actual skills and interests of its members, rather than searching for maximum profit on the one hand or competitive glory on the other.

One of us was involved in just such an enterprise, a craft shop numbering some sixty members that was consciously set up on modified "early church" principles. All voluntarily shared in the production and evaluation of items for sale, in making decisions about policy and the association's daily operations, and in staffing the shop they rented and other public exhibitions. The cooperative aimed at providing an outlet for its members' gifts, being a community in which they could develop their craft. Any profit made by the shop was given to charity, and the size of the association was restricted to avoid unnecessary competition or overproduction. The point here is not just that it was successful—itself an achievement in our increasingly large-scale and profit-maximizing world—but that it drew people, particularly housebound suburban or retired women, out of what felt like an aimless existence, provided a place where they felt they counted, utilized and enhanced their skills, and drew some of them away from their reliance on antidepressants and professional help to cope with their loss of identity and their loneliness. They established strong relationships with others, and a network of genuine care developed to support those going through difficult times. Through its vocational contribution and its social consequences the cooperative has made an impact on the lives of its members and on those shoppers who came into the cooperative looking for a link with others in addition to something to buy.[12]

Cultural and Civic Dimensions

According to Jacques Ellul, in his seminal book *The Presence of the Kingdom,* it is not primarily evangelism or social action that should occupy us as believers today but the creation of a distinctively Christian style of life—one that does not so much deny the world as confront and transform it. Out of such a witness may come a basis for the new social order we so desperately need. The ancient world, catalyzed by Christianity, and the medieval world, stimulated by the Reformation, led to the emergence of a new type of culture and a new form of civilization. Something similar is needed today. Ellul contends that the quest for a distinctively Christian way of life, both individual and corporate, would ultimately give a greater impetus to our evangelistic efforts and to our attempts to bring social change than anything else we can do. Arguing that contemporary Christians are more influenced in their style of life by their social environment than their spiritual convictions, Ellul says that the search for a new style of life should embrace every aspect of life, including

> our way of practising hospitality . . . the way we dress and the food we eat . . . the way we manage our financial affairs . . . being accessible to one's neighbour . . . the position one ought to take on current social and political questions . . . the decisions which relate to the personal employment of our time.[13]

These issues are precisely the ones that are best worked through in home church and interactive congregational settings. Here they are not just subjects for study but matters that people must do something about. Here they are not just a matter of individual concern but part of a communal search for a church lifestyle that fully reflects the largely countercultural values of the kingdom. Ellul writes,

> This is necessarily a corporate act. It is impossible for the isolated Christian to follow this path. In order to undertake this search for a "new style of life," every Christian ought to feel that he is supported by others, not only for spiritual . . . but also for purely material reasons.[14]

Ronald Sider picks up a similar thread in *Rich Christians in an Age of Hunger:*

The God of the Bible is calling Christians today to live in fundamental nonconformity to existing society. . . . The overwhelming
majority of churches, however, do not provide the context in
which brothers and sisters can encourage, admonish and disciple each other. We desperately need new settings and structures. . . . What are some of the promising models of Christian
community for our time? House churches within larger congregations, individual house churches and very small traditional
churches. . . . It is in that kind of setting—and perhaps only in that
kind of setting—that the church today will be able to forge a faithful lifestyle for Christians in an Age of Hunger. In small house
church settings brothers and sisters can challenge each other's
affluent lifestyles . . . discuss finances . . . share tips for simple
living.[15]

Naturally, such financial commitment is easier to discuss than
to make. Most of us are defensive about how we spend or give
away our money. But Sider's point holds true: the way we use
our money—as well as the way we use our time—should be a
normal component of church discussion.

Such an approach to church life can make another contribution. It can show how lightly the church can travel through
this expensive, large-scale institutional world. Community-
sized interactive congregations based on a home-church structure do not need large and costly buildings in which to meet.
Nor do they require complex organizational structures staffed
by full-time salaried officers. They are "resident aliens" whose
major denomination, so to speak, is the heavenly church, but
who network and cooperate in mission and training without
costly overhead or superfluous organization. Vernon Eller
writes eloquently of such an approach to church life in his book
The Outward Bound. He suggests that congregations see themselves less as commissaries than as caravans, which travel
light, can change direction easily, and are always moving
forward.[16]

There are many ways in which a more communal approach
to small church and congregational life can help counter tendencies in our society toward greater fragmentation. The redis-
covery of the extended Christian family has brought people
across the generations into touch with one another again. The
support system provided by a home church improves communication between parents and their children, strengthens mar-
riages, provides varied and concrete role models for children,

provides singles with a familial—and families with a less nuclear—environment. Given the increasing incidence of divorce
(among Christians as well as others), this is a major contribution
to the foundation of the whole social fabric. It is becoming increasingly clear that children of single-parent families tend to
run into more problems and generally achieve less than others.
In certain settings, such as the African-American context, restoration of the family is a preeminent concern. An extended Christian family approach to small churches within the congregation
and an understanding of the congregation as primarily a clan
made up of such families could play a significant role in amelio-
rating the problems we have mentioned.

Another problematic aspect of Western society is what
Margaret Mead called the "sexualizing" of all encounters between the genders, even those at the most mundane level.[17]
This sexual dimension intrudes unhelpfully into most encounters that occur between men and women, especially
singles. People either react to this by becoming overly reserved with one another or by becoming overly familiar. A
familial environment in church helps to desexualize relationships, while encouraging appropriate physical expression
through hugs, kisses, and embraces. It also provides a more
secure context for building close friendships across gender
lines and marriage boundaries.

Home churches and interactive congregations are making a
broader social contribution through the creation or renewal of
rituals. We live in a society that is losing the habit and also the art
of using long-standing rituals to celebrate a wide range of major
life stages and experiences. They are fading away and being replaced by programmed events planned by professionals. We
need to find new/old ways of celebrating birthdays, moving into
a new house or moving away from town, graduating from
school, receiving an award, finding a job, marking a friendship,
getting engaged, getting married, having a child, celebrating a
special street or neighborhood occasion, or grieving over a
death. Congregations of home churches have developed more
informal and participatory ways of marrying people in a home or
garden setting, marking the fiftieth birthday of one of their members in an especially convivial and honoring way, and taking responsibility for burying their members. These help to renew
rituals of celebration in a culture where old rituals are fast fading
away. In *Moral Fragments and Moral Community* ethicist Larry

Rasmussen emphasizes the potential that such a renewal of central Christian practices holds for renovation of the wider society.[18]

The following paragraphs describe some specific examples of how some home churches and interactive congregations are making contributions to the broader society.

- On learning that a middle-aged mother and her two school-aged children were deserted, one home church invited her to join, without any obligations, for as long as she wanted. The aim was to give her a place to belong as she began to work through her pain and doubts, and to provide her children with a surrogate family. The family accepted the invitation and became vital members of the group, staying over two years before moving to another city.

- The same group encouraged one of its members to leave the rather menial job with which he was very dissatisfied. They covenanted to support him and his family until he was able to establish a guitar-making business in his backyard shed. They maintained this arrangement for almost two years, paying for most of the utilities, helping out financially in other ways, and making it possible for the family to take holidays.

- A cluster of home churches held an annual fair to which members brought something they had created in the last year. People brought everything from the usual arts and crafts objects to photographs, paintings and films, songs, stories, compositions, even special dishes they had cooked. Each year there was general amazement at the talents possessed by a group of ordinary people. In a small way this event was reclaiming the world of arts and crafts, as well as folk and popular culture, from their expropriation by professionals and the media. This kind of activity could generate a revival of home-made culture and lay the basis for a real contribution to craft and art in general. For, as Jeremy Begbie says, this will not come through the talents of a few highly trained performers in the church but "through the emergence of new forms of ecclesial corporate art, in which the unique relationships generated and sustained by the Holy Spirit are allowed to affect the very character of artistic creativity itself."[19]

- An educator, Bill Andersen, has developed a model for education derived from the early Christian understanding of the church. It has a strong holistic, participatory, and family-type character. In Australia this model has exerted some impact on the Christian Schools movement. It is a radical alternative to the more traditional or packaged approaches to education. The experiences of contemporary home churches and congregations based on them could add something to the provocative and exciting suggestions he makes.[20]

- Members of our previous cluster of home churches in Australia were involved in a working group of senior public servants in the federal capital. Meeting over four years, it gradually developed seminars for other public servants in all major cities and organized the first-ever National Conference of Christian Public Servants in the country. Some of them also contributed to a book arising out of the conference.[21] Three of the five key people came from one home church, and another home church led sessions at the conference. This demonstrates how wide-ranging the influence of a comparatively small group of people can be.

The well-known ethicist Stanley Hauerwas has pointed out that the democratic society in which we live did not begin primarily from abstract doctrines but arose from the living experience of Puritan congregations who regarded themselves as a fellowship of equals under God. We do well to remember how much these fairly small communities of believers, along with Quaker and Anabaptist groups, helped shape the wider civic and political context that we have inherited and that so much of the world has imitated. They teach us that the most lasting contribution the church can make to politics is to "be itself," a genuine community, not to generate statements about particular issues.[22] The church can show us new insights into the nature and structure of a more participatory form of democracy that could help offset the creeping centralization and bureaucratization of modern government. But this will happen only if churches become genuine colonies of heaven that reflect the values and dynamics, economics and politics, of the kingdom of God. Functioning in this capacity could lead to more profound political changes than direct attempts to influence or change the political system. Not that such attempts have no place. They are a vital part of Christian witness. But their place is secondary rather than primary.

We can positively affect people in other countries by developing a style of life that puts as little pressure as possible on their natural and human resources. An ethical country should have economic and political measures that properly reward the countries from which it gets its resources. We could do much by changing our consumer-oriented, resource-wasting individual and corporate way of life, a way of life prevalent even in the church. As Jean Vanier writes,

> Communities which live simply and without waste help people to discover a whole new way of life, which demands fewer financial resources but more commitment to relationships. Is there a better way to bridge the gulf which widens daily between rich and poor countries?[23]

The sociologist Christian Smith has shown the staggering amount of resources that would be freed up in the West if all our churches learned to travel light as do interactive congregations based on home churches.[24] This option is light years ahead of an approach that consists of occasional contributions by churches and appeals to governments to increase financial aid to such countries. Churches in the West that emphasize the quality of relationships, help people integrate their private and public roles, and make technology a servant rather than a master begin to provide a concrete model for Christians and others in developing societies so that they can escape the worst features of Western society even as they incorporate others from which they could benefit.

SOME GENERAL REMARKS

Clearly, church and mission can be correlated without being confused. With respect to sharing the gospel with others and founding communities among them, Hendrik Kraemer, in his prophetic book *A Theology of the Laity,* argues that by developing new forms of fellowship and community in the church:

> a greater act of evangelism would be done than all evangelistic campaigns together. . . . The direct approach has no great promise, because the de-religionising of vast sectors of people in modern society has deep-seated and long-range historical causes. The indirect approach, by really being communities of mutual upbuilding, of witness and service, by building in the desert of modern life genuine Christian cells, is the one indicated. . . . For the

world wants to see redemption. It is not interested in its being talked about.[25]

Regarding ministry in the work-related and social structures of our cities, Art Gish declares in *Living in Christian Community,*

> Our primary work in social change goes beyond changing the hearts of individuals or transforming power structures, for it comes from the understanding that the main social structure through which God's redeeming work is effected in the world is the Christian community. . . . our hope for a new social order is found more in . . . building up the body of Christ, the firstfruits of the new order. The creation of Christian community is the most radical political action one can ever experience, especially if it involves breaking down social barriers, proclaiming liberty to the captives and establishing justice. It is the coming to concrete reality of a new life that will not only show what is wrong with the old, but point so clearly to the new which is possible that the old can no longer command our loyalty and devotion. . . . Our responsibility to the world is always first to be the church: to embody what God wants to say to the whole world, to live and demonstrate what salvation means.[26]

With respect to cultural and political transformation, the well-known historian Herbert Butterfield insists that

> the strongest organisational unit in the world's history would appear to be that which we call a cell; for it is a remorseless self-multiplier; it is exceptionally difficult to destroy; it can preserve its intensity of local life while vast organizations quickly wither when they are weakened at the center; it can defy the power of governments; and it is the appropriate lever for prying open any status quo. Whether we take early Christianity or sixteenth-century Calvinism or modern communism, this seems the appointed way by which a mere handful of people may open up a new chapter in the history of civilisation.[27]

Home churches are not the only cells through which this takes place. Other units such as vocational groups, action-oriented task forces, and residential communities also have a significant role. But home churches are a good example of what the economists Finn and Pemberton call "small disciplined communities," and the theologians Lee and Cowan call "voluntary mediated structures."[28] They do have an irreplaceable and fundamental role to play.

In this book we do not claim that home churches are a panacea for all the challenges and opportunities we face. But we argue that they are foundational to any quest for renewal in church and society. They are critical for any attempt at regrouping the people of God for community and mission. They open up a way of "getting back to basics" and "bringing the church up to date" at the same time. To have their proper effect, however, they must never be regarded as a halfway house, an introductory step to more conventional congregational structures. They must not be seen simply as a means to an end, for example, as a way of meeting members' needs or drawing in new people, and they must be introduced not as an appendix to the lives of individuals or a church but as the basic unit of congregational life.

Only so will home churches and congregations based on them fulfill their potential. Only so will their members truly come to call the church their home. Only so will they become a home for the increasing number of people who are looking for a place to belong. According to Robert Wuthnow, the church of the twenty-first century

> will probably remain vibrant as long as it can provide people with a strong sense of community. . . . For centuries the Christian church has been the mainstay of community life in the West. . . . But now our society seems to be at a loss for community. The question that faces us, then, is whether it too is beginning to succumb to the impersonal answers that fragment our society.[29]

NOTES

1. See further Snyder, *Signs of the Spirit,* 278.
2. On the biblical basis for the distinction between church and mission, as well as their intrinsic connection, see Banks, *Paul's Idea of Community,* ch. 15.
3. Prior, *The Church in the Home,* 117.
4. Barrett, *Building the House Church,* 132.
5. Peck, *The Different Drum.*
6. On home churches and evangelism and church planting, see more generally Smith, *Going to the Root,* chs. 7–8.
7. T. Wolfe, "Oikos Evangelism: Key to the Future," in *Future Church* (ed. R. Neighbour Jr.; Nashville: Broadman, 1980) 166.
8. On home churches and social and vocational responsibility, see more generally Smith, *Going to the Root,* ch. 8.
9. W. Diehl, *Christianity and Real Life* (Philadelphia: Fortress, 1976) 97–104.

10. For more on this see J. Kaufmann, "Structure, Injustice, and Insensitivity: Who Is My Neighbor Anyway?" in *God So Loves the City: Seeking a Theology for Urban Mission* (ed. C. van Engen and J. Tiersma; Monrovia, Calif.: Marc, 1994) 27–52.

11. V. Hoffman, *The Co-Dependent Church* (New York: Crossroad, 1991).

12. R. Banks, "The Early Church as a Caring Community and Its Implications for Social Work Today," *Interchange* 30 (1982) 40–43.

13. J. Ellul, *The Presence of the Kingdom* (London: SCM, 1951) 148.

14. Ibid., 149.

15. R. Sider, *Rich Christians in an Age of Hunger: A Biblical Study* (London: Hodder & Stoughton, 1978) 163–68.

16. V. Eller, *The Outward Bound: Caravaning as the Style of the Church* (Grand Rapids: Eerdmans, 1980).

17. M. Mead, *Culture and Commitment: A Study of the Generation Gap* (New York: Natural History Press, 1970).

18. See especially the concluding chapter of L. Rasmussen, *Moral Fragments and Moral Community: A Proposal for Church in Society* (Minneapolis: Fortress, 1993).

19. J. Begbie, *Voicing Creation's Praise: Towards a Theology of the Arts* (Edinburgh: T. & T. Clark, 1991) 224.

20. W. Andersen, "A Biblical View of Education," *Journal of Christian Education* 77 (1983) 15–30.

21. R. Banks, ed., *Private Values and Public Policy: The Ethics of Decision-Making in Government Administration* (Sydney: Anzea, 1983).

22. S. Hauerwas, "Politics, Vision and the Common Good," in *Vision and Virtue: Essays in Christian Ethical Reflection* (Notre Dame, Ind.: University of Notre Dame Press, 1981) 239–40. See further S. Hauerwas and W. Willimon, *Resident Aliens: A Provocative Christian Assessment of Culture and Ministry for People Who Know That Something Is Wrong* (Nashville: Abingdon, 1989) 43ff.

23. Vanier, *Community and Growth*, 234.

24. Smith, *Going to the Root*.

25. H. Kraemer, *A Theology of the Laity* (London: Lutterworth, 1958).

26. Gish, *Living in Christian Community*, 293.

27. H. Butterfield, "The Role of the Individual in History," in *Herbert Butterfield: Writings on Christianity and History* (ed. C. T. McIntire; New York: Oxford University Press, 1979) 24.

28. D. Finn and P. Pemberton, *Toward a Christian Economic Ethic* (Minneapolis: Winston, 1985) ch. 9; Lee and Cowan, *Dangerous Memories*, 169.

29. R. Wuthnow, *Christianity in the Twenty-First Century: Reflections on the Challenge Ahead* (New York: Oxford University Press, 1993) 33.

APPENDIX

Some Questions about
Home Churches

This appendix answers some of the most commonly asked questions about home churches.

Question: Do people in home churches have a tendency to be inward-looking and cliquish?

Response: In our experience this is a temptation for any group of people. Even a large congregation can be inward-looking and cliquish in relation to other Christian groups or traditions, or to the community and wider society. As J. Oswald Sanders observed, it is people in the larger institutional churches who are most likely to have this problem, for it is very easy to become so involved in church activities that there is no time to be involved with other people. Attitude, not size, is the determining factor here. Members of home churches do tend to devote time to one another, which results in a growing self-confidence and maturity that frees them to give more of themselves to others. They are able to give to people outside their own group precisely because they receive so much from the group itself. Learning to listen to and care for others within the home church equips them to use these skills for the benefit of the wider body of believers of which they are a part. A small group encourages people to become more aware of their own gifts and to employ them for the benefit of others generally, whether the congregation, interdenominational or parachurch groups, or the wider community.

Question: Do home churches breed an atmosphere in which all the members are expected to share their inner selves? Not everyone can cope with this.

Response: Home churches operate in a different way from encounter or therapy groups. People are accepted as they are, whether or not they wish to share their inner selves with others. Inevitably, some are ready to do this from the start, either because their need is great or their temperament inclines them in this direction. Others open up gradually over a period of time as they begin to feel secure. A few may not be ready for this until some crisis hits. So far as this kind of sharing is concerned, everyone is allowed room to proceed at their own pace and to do it in their own way. While some people see intimacy as the core of the home-church experience, even the barometer of the depth of community in the group, this should not be the case. The real core of a home church is the bond that slowly develops as people struggle to become a group with its own identity, personality, and goals, and as they slowly develop a shared history of fellowshiping with God and one another as a group. Within this family some will be more open about their inward journey and others more open about their outward journey. Certain issues may be shared with only one or two other members, not the whole group. A healthy home church contains subcommunities of people who become more intimate with one another or pursue common interests. Not all inner feelings or issues are appropriate to share with a group anyway.

What a home church can do is provide a sympathetic, safe, and compassionate environment for anyone to speak who wishes to do so, and for others to listen, share the concern, and pray with and for the person involved. There is no need for this concern to result in an artificially cultivated "hothouse" atmosphere. Mutual concern can flower in a natural way, just as plants in a garden gradually grow by opening up to the warmth of the sun.

Question: Do home churches only attract suburban middle-class people who like to gather in discussion groups?

Response: In the West the majority of home churches, like the majority of the population, are suburban and middle-class.

In the third world basic Christian communities occur mainly among the poorer groups in the population. In any case, as we have indicated in this book, home churches exist among a wide array of social groupings: poor groups, ethnic groups, blue collar workers, and countercultural groups. Many groups include members who vary from one another educationally, occupationally, and culturally. It is true that the ethos and dynamics of a home church made up primarily of working class people or of immigrant families tends to be different in certain respects from that of a predominantly middle-class home church. In the first instance, the concerns of members tend to be more concrete and their gatherings more informal; in the second instance people often are far less inhibited, and there is a closer connection between their lives inside and outside the meetings. Where a home group has a mixed membership, in time there comes a growing understanding and appreciation of each other's culture and ways of operating. Like most small groups, middle-class home churches initially tend to place too much emphasis on cognitive study of the Bible or therapeutic personal sharing. This works for some of the members but means that those whose minds work differently or who relate in less intimate ways—and are no less the worse for it either—tend to feel excluded. Such groups need to broaden the way they seek to learn about God and bond with one another. They need to include possibilities for more right brain types of learning and for ways of relating that spring more from doing things together. As they pursue this, these groups will also find that they draw in other parts of their own middle-class members' lives, especially their teenagers and children, for we are all made up of more than minds and hearts. We have imaginations and bodies too. For groups that include intellectually or socially challenged people, all this is even more relevant.

Question: How do you help a home church be a place where people engage in serious learning and not a place where they share their ignorance or prejudices?

Response: If it is operating properly, a home church is well suited to in-depth learning and well protected against mere sharing of ignorance and prejudices. First, because a home-church structure encourages the participation of all present, someone who does not understand is free to ask questions. Anyone who feels others are simply airing their prejudices is free to say so. The assumption that ordinary Christians are ignorant and prejudiced is usually held by people who believe that truth can only be communicated and safeguarded by preaching and formal teaching. But if ignorance and prejudice are all that church members raised on teaching and preaching bring to a home church, this is a terrible indictment. Ordinary Christians have learned about God in a variety of ways, including preaching and teaching. They have a powerful new way of learning if they come together earnestly seeking the mind of the God and the help of the Spirit. They have the opportunity to share with one another what they have learned over time about God. They can ask the questions they may have kept hidden for years, questions that open up the possibility of discovering new things about God and more profound ways of living out the gospel.

Second, because what takes place in the home church is regarded as fundamental to members' lives, as crucial to their ability to live out the gospel during the week, members of a group will not be satisfied with airing ignorance or prejudices. People generally come to home church because they are hungry—hungry for a deeper understanding of God and hungry to live an authentic Christian life. They generally come to a home church with an openness to truth and are therefore willing to acknowledge their ignorance and reexamine their prejudices. Mostly they are teachable and responsive to the Spirit.

Third, it is clear from the NT that the Holy Spirit reveals the truth about God primarily in and through a community. The Spirit gives a certain amount of understanding to each person in the group. When people come together and pool their knowledge, checking and evaluating each person's contribution in the process, a fully orbed understanding of God and life begins to appear. There is a special role for those who have a longer experience of God or a deeper understanding of the Bible and Christian teaching, but these people do not have the whole truth either. Where an individual home church cannot fully answer its own questions, it can always invite in someone from another group who knows more about the subject or someone from outside who has wisdom on the matter. And since home churches meet with one another regularly in larger gatherings, and core members from different groups meet together for mutual support, prayer, and counsel, there are wider checks on individual groups moving in undesirable directions.

Question: Are home churches likely to head off on a tangent, especially if there is a dominant person in the group?

Response: Wherever any one person dominates—whether in a small group or a large congregation—there is a danger of all these things happening, even if the person is theologically trained. For example, many pastors pontificate on matters far outside their field of expertise, and many small group leaders assume that they know best how to apply the Bible to complex everyday life issues. In a home-church setting, however, anyone in the group can question the attempt by one person to impose his or her understanding of God on everyone else. Since no one, not even the most learned theologian, has a full understanding of God, this ability to question is most necessary. And since even those who do have a broad and deep understanding of the Bible do not always know how that applies to the specific and highly varied life situations of different church members, the contribution of everyone in the group becomes absolutely essential. Anyone in a group who disagrees with another's interpretation of the truth or senses that the group is opening itself up to some error is free to speak up. It is precisely because a home church is not led or dominated by any one person, and (as with the Constitution) because there are mutual checks and balances through the diverse people making up the group that the home church opens up the possibility of developing a rich, multilayered understanding of God and life. Now and again there is a problem with someone "holding the floor." Sometimes this is a newcomer who has many, many questions. Sometimes it is a person who has never been properly listened to. It doesn't hurt the group to allow these folk to "dominate" for a while because the way to overcome the difficulty is by meeting the need to be heard. In doing so, the group gives value to the person concerned. As the person feels more loved and accepted, there is less need to dominate. The trick, as always, is to balance the needs of the various members of the group.

Riding a hobby horse is a different matter. Only once in our many years of home-church life have we met with someone who was completely unresponsive to the group's concern and patience in this respect. This was a man in his mid-forties for whom setting the world straight on the issue of Sabbath observance was a personal mission in life. Every discussion ended up focusing on this topic. The group invited him to take a series of studies on the issue over several weeks. At the end of that time, since he had not persuaded others to his point of view, he left, presumably in search of another group to propagandize. Such people tend to be more interested in their own ideas than in the people around them.

Question: Do you find that a home church is too small to have an adequate breadth of gifts and resources to draw on and that the few who have outstanding gifts don't have enough scope to practice them?

Response: It is worth reminding ourselves that some things are more easily learned when a group is small than when it is large. First, members can come to understand and appreciate each other more and to recognize each others' weaknesses and strengths. Second, they can clarify what they are looking for in a church and what the Bible has to say about it. Third, they can help each other reorder and consolidate their priorities and responsibilities better. It is much easier to work through these questions in a smaller group. Of course, whether the home church has few members or many is secondary so long as it is desiring to learn and to live in the Spirit. God, who knows what they need and when they need it, can be trusted to provide all that is essential for their welfare. Indeed, people are often surprised by the range of gifts possessed by the most ordinary Christians.

While most groups are tempted to complain at some point that they do not have all the gifts and maturity they would like, gradually they begin to see that if they are thankful for what they have and encourage those through whom they are exercised, more will come their way. Sometimes this takes place through the further development of the giftedness and maturity of the group, sometimes through the addition of new people to it. God can be relied on to provide whatever is necessary for the functioning of the group but will not necessarily do this when we would like.

Also, as has been stated, an individual group is not thrown back purely on its own God-given resources. As there is need, others from the wider congregation or house church cluster can be called in to complement or supplement what we have. In an emergency situation or a situation involving long-term shortage of members, home churches can always help each other out by sharing members with one another for a time or even permanently. As for the opposite situation, when a home church has people within it whose giftedness or maturity should be shared with a larger number of people, opportunities for this exist in ministry to other groups or to the wider congregation. Sometimes a home church might set one of its members free from time to time to give to others what they have benefited from so much themselves. Within a home church such gifts often develop quickly and in a holistic fashion, and there is often stronger support and encouragement for their wider expression.

Question: Since they lack a single appointed leader, how do home churches deal with people who require discipline? Are people likely to get away with things that should be openly challenged?

Response: This is not a problem specific to home churches. Questions on how to handle church discipline exist in the typical local church. How often does discipline in the early Christian sense take place in a local congregation that does have an appointed leader or leaders? All kinds of disobedience toward God go unchallenged. Members harbor private sins like envy, jealousy, or pride, they act unethically in their workplaces, they neglect their spouses and families or even abuse them. Even in the typical small group in a church there is a tendency to tread lightly in regard to people's lives and to avoid questioning their lifestyle choices, especially when it comes to how they spend their money or time. It is precisely in a home-church setting, as people begin to feel secure about opening up to one another and committing themselves to developing a distinctive Christian lifestyle that calls into question many of the wider society's values, that discipline becomes a real possibility.

Initially, discipline happens in a home church in a quiet, unobtrusive, unspoken way—through the words of a hymn, the reading of Scripture, the message of a study, and, most especially, the passing comment, thoughtful action, or example of another. This operates subliminally, often in a profound way, much as the ethos of a family helps shape the character of its members and acts as a natural constraint on their tendency to go in another direction. Sometimes people's non-Christian behaviors have their roots in terrible experiences people have suffered, either in the past or in the present, and the individuals concerned need understanding and counsel rather than criticism and condemnation. Many people in home churches go through a crisis of faith or a crisis in relationships yet, through the patient acceptance and guidance of a group, manage to come through it to a deeper commitment to God or others.

If necessary, when there is evidence of someone's acting in a way that is seriously detrimental to individuals or to the group as a whole, a basis has been established so that the person can lovingly be called to account and encouraged to change. Mostly such situations can be dealt with by one or two people in the group who have a close relationship with the person concerned or are especially respected by all members of the group. Such action should always be preceded by prayer; during prayer we realize the importance first and foremost of speaking to Christ about a brother or sister rather than speaking to a brother or sister about Christ. Sometimes God does what is necessary without our having to say a word to the person in question. Now and again a group has to confront one of its members. This is always difficult but the outcome is generally positive, with all concerned being forced to examine their attitudes and conduct. Sometimes discipline is necessary. Because home churches develop loving relationships between members, this discipline is less painful for everyone involved.

Question: Do home churches encourage people to focus on spiritual and relational concerns at the expense of effective outreach and mission?

Response: This question was partly answered in the discussion about whether home churches are inward looking and cliquish. A good place to start in answering the rest of the question is to consider the well-functioning family. A healthy family is one that spends time together, eats and drinks together, shares stories about what happened during the day or week, and holds family councils to decide important issues or projects. Precisely because they deal with "in-house" matters in an intentional way, such families create people who have the inner resources and energy to give themselves to others. Where parents model this to their children, children in time begin to imitate their behavior. It is the same with a well-functioning home church.

Just as the family ministers to others by opening up their home, so too with a home church. It extends hospitality to strangers who may be lonely and need company, in crisis and need help, at a loss and seek answers, and offers them a place to belong. Here they see and experience for themselves the reality of God in the lives of others. They also receive the love of God in tangible ways. As in the early church (see 1 Cor 14:23–25), this provides a setting in which some people come to faith in Christ. Many people come to home churches looking for more effective ways of making their faith relevant to the people, situations, and structures around them. Life so often gets compartmentalized between private and public, spiritual and everyday, church and work. These people want to reflect Christ in all their activities and relationships in a way that is natural to themselves and relevant to others. In other words, they desire to give their whole lives an outgoing and missionary dimension. In this area a home church can make an important contribution to each of its members. It can help each one see the significance of everything they do during the rest of the week and assist them to define the particular ways in which they can make their most effective contribution to the people and structures around them. Having done this, a home church can then encourage all of its members to regularly "check in" on how they are doing, where they need any particular help, what they can pray for, and whether it can be supportive in any special, even financial, way.

Question: Is there an inherent instability about home churches? Do most of them fold after a while?

Response: The fact is that most of them do not fold. A few disband for understandable reasons, such as members moving. Other groups end because they were built on an inadequate foundation, for example, as an add-on in a congregation's program. Members are thus too busy to give them the priority they deserve. Or the group may be too homogeneous and lack older, mature Christians who could act as a stable pastoral center. Some groups cease to exist due to lack of support from the wider church or other home churches in their cluster. But generally speaking home churches tend to have a long life. Home churches may look more fragile than highly-structured organizations. But because of the strong relationships that develop within them, they can be suprisingly resilient.

In any case, why is a certain amount of instability a bad thing? The family unit, which is the basis of our whole society, is probably the most fragile yet most durable institution we have. Too often we feel secure because we place our trust in the wrong things, such as leaders, programs, resources, and techniques. In a home church, stability—desirable as it is—comes from our degree of trust in God's faithfulness and our growing trust in one another. A small group, aware of its dependence on God's provision, can be remarkably enduring, offering strength and protection to its members, particularly to those in special need.

SUGGESTED READING LIST

Atkerson, Steve, ed. *Toward a House Church Theology*. Atlanta: New Testament Restoration Foundation, 1996.

Banks, Robert. *Going to Church in the First Century: An Eyewitness Account*. Beaumont, Tex.: Christian, 1990.

_____. *Paul's Idea of Community: The Early House Churches in Their Cultural Setting*. Rev. ed. Peabody, Mass.: Hendrickson, 1994.

Baranowski, Arthur. *Creating Small Faith Communities: A Plan for Restructuring the Parish and Renewing Catholic Life*. Rev. ed. Cincinnati: St. Anthony Messenger, 1993.

Barrett, Lois. *Building the House Church*. Scottdale, Pa.: Herald, 1986.

Birkey, Del. *The House Church*. Scottdale, Pa.: Herald, 1988.

Branick, Vincent. *The House Church in the Writings of Paul*. Wilmington, Del.: Michael Glazier, 1989.

Castillo, Metosalem. *The Church in Thy House*. Manila, Philippines: Alliance, 1982.

Cowan, Michael, and Bernard J. Lee. *Conversation, Risk and Conversion: The Inner and Public Life of Small Christian Communities*. Maryknoll, N.Y.: Orbis, 1997.

Doohan, Helen. *Paul's Vision of Church*. Wilmington, Del.: Michael Glazier, 1989.

Edwards, Gene. *How to Meet Under the Headship of Jesus Christ.* Beaumont, Tex.: Message Ministry, 1993.

Finger, Reta Halteman. *Paul and the Roman House Church: A Simulation.* Scottdale, Pa.: Herald, 1993.

Fraser, Ian M. *Living a Countersign.* Glasgow: Iona Community, 1990.

Girard, Robert C. *Brethren, Hang Together: Restructuring the Church for Relationships.* Grand Rapids: Zondervan, 1979.

Hadaway, C. Kirk, Stuart Wright, and Francis DuBose. *Home Cell Groups and House Churches.* Nashville: Broadman, 1987.

Hinton, Jeanne. *Walking in the Same Direction: A New Way of Being Church.* Geneva: World Council of Churches Publications, 1995.

Hoffman, Virginia. *Birthing a Living Church.* New York: Crossroad, 1988.

Krupp, Nate. *God's Simple Plan for His Church—and Your Place in It.* Woodburn, Ore.: Solid Rock, 1993.

Lee, Bernard, and Michael Cowan. *Dangerous Memories: House Churches and Our American Story.* Kansas City, Mo.: Sheed & Ward, 1986.

Lohfink, Gerhard. *Jesus and Community: The Social Dimension of Christian Faith.* Philadelphia: Fortress, 1984.

O'Halloran, James. *Living Cells: Developing Small Christian Community.* Rev. ed. Maryknoll, N.Y.: Orbis, 1984.

Olsen, Charles. *The Base Church: Creating Community through Multiple Forms.* Atlanta: Forum, 1973.

Price, Peter. *The Church as the Kingdom: A New Way of Being the Church.* Basingstoke, U.K.: Marshall Pickering, 1987.

Prior, David. *The Church in the Home.* Basingstoke, U.K.: Marshall, Morgan, & Scott, 1983.

Smith, Christian. *Going to the Root: Nine Proposals for Radical Church Renewal.* Scottdale, Pa.: Herald, 1992.

Snyder, Howard. *Radical Renewal: The Problem of Wineskins Today.* Rev. ed. Houston: Touch, 1996.

Viola, Frank. *Rethinking the Wineskin: The Practice of the New Testament Church.* Brandon, Fla.: Present Testimony Ministry, 1997.

✠   ✠   ✠

For a wonderful resource on the Internet, visit
www.home-church.org.